Political Participation
and Identities of Muslims
in Non-Muslim States

W.A.R. SHADID AND
P.S. VAN KONINGSVELD (EDS.)

POLITICAL PARTICIPATION
AND IDENTITIES OF MUSLIMS
IN NON-MUSLIM STATES

Pharos

KOK PHAROS PUBLISHING HOUSE

© Kok Pharos Publishing House
Kampen, the Netherlands
Cover Design by Rob Lucas
ISBN 90 390 0611 3
NUGI 651/631

Contents

vi

Preface

This book is the second of two volumes in which the edited version is the publication of the proceedings of the congress on Islam, Hinduism, and Politics in Western Europe which was held in Leiden from the 7th through the 9th of September, 1995, under the auspices of the Dutch Organization for Scientific Research (N.W.O.). This congress marked the completion of the national research project "Religion of Ethnic Groups in the Netherlands", sponsored by the Foundation for Research in Philosophy and Theology (S.F.T.), in which scholars and research assistants from the Free University of Amsterdam, the Catholic University of Nijmegen, and Leiden University have participated. The aim of this concluding conference was to create a platform for Dutch researchers to communicate directly with their colleagues active in the same field of research from other Western European countries.

The contributions of the conference have been divided into two volumes, each dealing with distinct issues. In the first volume, entitled *Muslims in the Margin: Political Responses to the Presence of Islam in Western Europe* (Kampen, Kok Pharos, 1996), the subject was investigated from the perspective of the countries of immigration at large. The present volume stresses the political participation and identities of Muslims in non-Muslim societies, in particular their views on the new societies in which they are living.

Apart from an introductory chapter, the present book contains twelve contributions by specialists from various European countries (Germany, Italy, the Netherlands, Spain, and the United Kingdom) in which the following issues are examined: (I) the role of organizations in political participation; (II) attitudes towards political participation, and (III) identities and integration. A general bibliography is provided, in which the materials pertaining to the individual contributions have been integrated.

Leiden, April, 2, 1996
W.A.R. Shadid and P.S. van Koningsveld

PART I

The Role of Organizations in Political Participation

Political Participation:

The Muslim Perspective

Wasif Shadid & Sjoerd van Koningsveld

The successfulness of political participation by Muslim minority groups in non-Muslim societies depends upon a long series of complex factors. One may discern, on the one hand, the prevailing socio-political climate of those societies at large which determines, amongst others, the space available for residents of a different background to emancipate socio-economically and culturally. On the other hand, there are factors which are mainly, though not exclusively, derived from specific characteristics of the minority groups concerned, viz. their skill in building up representative organizations which can defend their interests, the culturally or religiously based attitudes fostered by them towards political participation, as well as the range of various identities they develop vis-à-vis the prevailing political system of the societies in which they are living.

In a previous volume, entitled *Muslims in the Margin: Political Responses to the Presence of Islam in Western Europe* (Kampen: Kok Pharos, 1996) we have already published a collection of articles by various specialists focusing on the first set of factors mentioned in the above paragraph. The present volume aims at completing the previous one. Its twelve contributions study mainly the subject of political participation from the perspective of the Muslim minority groups themselves. They have been arranged in accordance with the previously mentioned three major themes, I: The Role of Organizations in Political Participation; II: Attitudes Towards Political Participation; III: Identities and Political Participation. Their authors represent various specializations within the social and religious sciences, and are attached to institutions of learning in France, Germany, Italy, Morocco, and the Netherlands.

I

The role Muslim organizations may play in the various processes of political participation is studied in four distinct ways in the first section of this
book. First of all, there is a comparative, international case-study by Ali
Kettani on the political impact of Muslim organizations in various Western
countries, including Australia, France, Spain, Germany, the United Kingdom, and Belgium. Secondly, the focus is narrowed towards the national
level of a single country, viz. towards the activities of the three major
Turkish-Muslim organizations in Germany, in the contribution of Valéry
Amiraux. An even more detailed picture is brought out in the third and
fourth articles of this section, first of all, in a study of the role played by a
Pakistani women's organization in Manchester by Pnina Werbner, and,
secondly, in the study of Ottavia di Schmidt Friedberg of the evolving
activities in Italy of a single religiously based organization named the
Senegalese Mouride Brotherhood.

In discussing the subject of political participation, a factor primordial
importance is the process of naturalization which many Muslim immigrants in Western Europe are undergoing at the moment. In his contribution *Ali Kettani* estimates that about 40% of all Muslims of the EEC
countries have acquired European citizenship at this time. This illustrates
that the EEC Muslim Community is becoming increasingly European and
that its problems are becoming an internal European political affair. Its
firm will to take root in Europe is further illustrated by the number of
prayer halls and mosques, estimated for 1995 at 6,000.

From an international, comparative perspective, it appears that, contrary
to the situation in Australia, Muslims of most Western European states
have been thus far unsuccessful in creating representative organizations at
national levels which can function as spokesmen for the Muslim communities with the respective government authorities. In France, they have been
unable to change the prevailing policy which tends to regard Islam as a
foreign religion or as a problem of immigrant workers. Witness, for
example, the willingness of the French Government to cooperate with the
countries of origin in order to control the immigrants religiously. In Spain,
important progress has been made by the new Constitution of 1978 which
guarantees the cultural and religious diversity of the country. However, the

Islamic Commission of Spain, which has the legally established competence of negotiating Islamic religious affairs with the Spanish Government, continues to exclude representatives of the two main native Muslim organizations of Spain, as well as the Muslims of Ceuta and Melilla. Also in Germany Islam continues to be dealt with as a "guest religion" and as subject to foreign affairs. This situation is enhanced by the existing obstacles in acquiring German citizenship and by the fact that religious organizations can only gain access to various kinds of public support after they have been recognized as a "Body of Public Law" - a goal which has been pursued by Germany's Muslims without any success so far. Various forms of inequality in the treatment of Muslim organizations noted in the preceding lines also prevail in the United Kingdom and, more specifically, in Belgium, where twenty years of official recognition of Islam has not lead to an equal distribution of public means between non-Muslims and Muslims.

In discussing the future of Islam in the EEC countries, Kettani distinguishes the "Australian Scenario" and the "Bosnian Scenario". In the first case, the Muslim Community will be encouraged to integrate in the country and its rights will be recognized. While remaining Muslim, the community will assimilate, within a few generations, a large part of the culture of the country. According to the author, some EEC countries are moving slowly in this direction. However, most are not. To avoid the second, frightening scenario, the EEC countries should defend the rights of the Muslim Community, prevent their governments from using the religion of their Muslim subjects in different international political games, and consider "the establishment of Islam in the country as a new national fact to be approached within the great principles of unity in diversity and respect of human rights without hypocrisy".

The obstacles in acquiring German citizenship, the tendency of the German government to deal with Islam as an issue of foreign affairs, and the inability of Germany's Muslim organizations to acquire an equal access to public means for religiously coloured activities are discussed in detail by *Valéry Amiraux*. In her study of the three major Turkish Muslim organizations of Germany, she demonstrates that the German Government continues to work mainly with the organization that is linked to the Turkish Government in Ankara. However, the other two organizations, derived from non-government orientated religious movements in Turkey, are much more successful in adjusting their activities in Germany to the place religion (in general) occupies in non-Muslim Western societies and in catering to the needs of their members as they exist within the German context. The new strategies developed by these non-government oriented organizations imply a widening of the classical proposals of Muslim religious organizations, in particular regarding sports, education, music, and women's groups. Notwithstanding the continuing importance of the political developments in Turkey, these organizations are focusing their attention in a more outspoken manner on the situation within Germany itself. Thus, they are striving for easier access to German citizenship and for the attainment of the same status as the other religions, viz. by being recognized as a Body of Public Law. These options aim, amongst others, at redefining Islam in Germany while giving it a new sense and legitimacy as a religious reference, both on a collective level and a personal one, in order to keep Islam alive as a personal life-option in Germany.

The creative force religion may play in processes of emancipation is brought out further by *Pnina Werbner* in her study of the Al Masoom Trust, a Pakistani women's organization in Manchester, which promotes among other issues, a common-sense feminist understanding of the equality of women and men. Roughly speaking, three historical phases may be identified as markers of Manchester's public diasporic sphere. The first phase, between approximately 1950 and the mid-1980's, was a period of communal reconstruction and consolidation dominated by first gener-ation immigrant Pakistani men. Pakistani women had no representative voice in any of the numerous associations founded during this period. It was only from the mid-1980's onwards that the monopoly of older men came to be increasingly contested by women and, to a lesser extent, by young men. The 1990's witnessed the emergence of a gendered and familial Pakistani public space of voluntary action. The author describes this space as "a space of 'fun', that is, marked by gaiety, transgressive humour, music and dance". During this period the Al Masoom Foundation was formed. The reasons for its emergence at this historical conjuncture are both local and global. As for the latter, the rise of political Islam worldwide has been associated in Britain with the formation of young women's Islamic associations, which have triggered off a debate about the equal treatment and equal rights of women on the basis of the true tenets of Islam. The discourse produced by these organizations tends to distinguish between "custom" and "culture", on the one hand, and Islam, on the other hand, while attributing the main causes of the subordination of women to the former. The case study of a Manchester Muslim women's organization thus appears to fit within the pattern of the three main recent processes in the Islamic politics of identity in Britain in the 1990's: (1) the visibilization of Muslim political activism in the public sphere since the Rushdie affair; (2) the emergence of a *transnational* consciousness among Muslims in Britain in response to human rights violations, for instance, in Bosnia; and (3) the emergence of a *gendered diasporic public sphere* in which the women's independent collective voice has to be taken seriously by men.

The role which religiously based organizations can play in helping its members to adjust to the conditions of a totally new surrounding is illustrated by the study of *Ottavia di Schmidt Friedberg* which focuses on the Senegalese Mouride Brotherhood in Italy. This Sufi organization provided its members with an existing network which only had to be adapted to the new conditions of the Italian surrounding. It represents a very efficient, yet loose and fluid, network. Through its first emigrants, the Mourides were able to organize the departure of emigrants from their home country and to help them by providing jobs and shelter upon arrival in Italy. They also provided information on Italy and the Italian language and developed a step-by-step method for integrating into Italian society, first giving the young immigrant Mouride disciple lodging in a community house and introducing him to the job of peddling, while helping him later to find a job as labourer. Moreover, the Mouride brotherhood works as a network of solidarity and mutual insurance, providing help in case of sickness, legal and judicial problems. However, at the national level Senegalese and Mouride organizations have proven to be far less effective. Consequently, they do not participate in the national Italian debate about the ways to benefit from the law on religious minority rights. No project or statement was developed on the subject by the Mourides, but an agreement between Islamic associations will be necessary to make a concordat with the State and to acquire official status.

II

The culturally and/or religiously based attitudes towards political participation are analyzed in the four contributions of section II of the present volume. Shadid and Van Koningsveld present a critical analysis of Islamic normative discussions on the subject of political participation by Muslims in non-Muslim states. In their analysis, they take into account the views expressed on this subject by various contemporary Islamicists. The discussions which are dealt with continue to take place in various countries of the Muslim and the non-Muslim world. In the second article, written by Ahmed Andrews, the scope is narrowed more specifically towards the various Muslim attitudes towards political participation that can be discerned in the United Kingdom, as illustrated by the case of the City of Leicester. The position and attitudes of the 160 Muslim local councillors of the United Kingdom is dealt with by Kingsley Purdam, while this section is concluded with the contribution of Stacey Burlet and Helen Reid focusing on the attitudes and possible role of young men in Pakistani-heritage Muslim communities, as illustrated by the case of Bradford.

During the last years various scholars have attempted to qualify the position of Muslim minorities in contemporary Western Europe in the terminology of the classical Islamic Law. In doing so, they usually assumed that the classical dichotomy of the world into a "Territory of Islam" and a "Territory of War" has not lost any of its validity in the present time, and that Western Europe should be qualified, within this terminology, as part of the "Territory of War". Six examples of these assertions are dealt with in the article of *Wasif Shadid* and *Sjoerd van Koningsveld*. After discerning four different stages in the development of Islamic thought about the status of Muslims living under non-Muslim rule, the author analyze the numerous contemporary Islamic discussions concerning Europe and the West and the position of Muslims living there. In this way they discern four different kinds of views: (1) a pragmatic view rejecting the classical dichotomy while taking the existing division of the world into nation-states as its point of departure; (2) an idealistic or utopian view which does not discuss the classical dichotomy either, but which introduces the (classical) concept of the Ummah to refer to the ideal of the transnational and universal unity of all Muslims in the world; (3) the view aiming at the reinterpretation of the Islamic tradition in the light of the prevailing conditions of the modern age; (4) the traditionalist view which adheres to the old dichotomy and occupies, within the European context, a marginal position.

These four different views yield various religiously underpinned opinions about a series of subjects related directly or indirectly to the extent to which a Muslim could participate in the political life of a non-Muslim society in which he/she is living. Special attention is given here to the discussions concerning the permissibility to stay in the non-Muslim world, as well as to the subjects of naturalization, political participation, military service, and Islamic family law within a non-Muslim context. The conclusion is that a rich variety of Islamic opinions exists concerning the status of Islam and Muslims in non-Muslim societies. The stereotypes unjustly (re)produced by contemporary Islamicists concerning this subject do not take into account this variety of opinions.

The contribution of *Ahmed Andrews* concerning the Muslim attitudes towards political activity in the United Kingdom yields a similar conclusion. The author stresses, first of all, that the existing Muslim attitudes should not be understood primarily within the framework of the classical Islamic constitutional law. The historical experiences of Islam in India, where religious scholars have found ways of coexistence and even cooperation with non-Muslim, British rule, is a much more relevant background for the prevailing attitudes of British Muslims of Asian origin today. The permissibility of Muslim participation in British politics is clearly stressed by the opinions of most of the interviewed religious leaders of different Islamic religious orientations. The opinion of more fundamentalistic groups who argue that Muslims should not join Western political parties appears to carry little influence with the many Muslims who stand as candidates in the UK's political parties; a group like *Hizb ut-Tahrir*, which appears to have a following among a section of Muslim youth, and which argues for the total non-involvement of Muslims in the Western political process, is rejected by the majority of the Muslim community.

The extent of Muslim political participation in Britain, both in the active and the passive sense, is further illustrated by the study of *Kingsley Purdam* on the over 160 Muslim local councillors in the United Kingdom.

Although little research has been carried out on the political participation of Muslims, the author even stresses that "it is apparent that in comparison with the wider British population they display a high level of activity". To this should be added, however, that most political activities in Britain by Muslims are displayed at the local level. The British electoral system is favourable to this development. However, even though Muslim voters may soon form an important factor in the balance of power at the national level as well, British political parties appear to be very hesitant in admitting Muslim politicians to the national parliament and government. In addition, almost all Muslim councillors state that they have experienced some form of discrimination within their local political parties. Muslim party membership is growing. Muslims seem to constitute a new grass roots Labour movement. Nevertheless, this increased membership is widely viewed by other Labour Party members with suspicion.

A specific form of political participation is discussed by *Stacey Burlet* and *Helen Reid* in their article which focuses on the role of young men in Pakistani-heritage Muslim communities. A series of events which took place in Bradford during the summer of 1995 resulted in various calls for the direct involvement of male youth in the representation of the Pakistani-heritage Muslim community in Bradford. These calls were based on the conviction that this would provide the youth with a public platform for their opinions as well as a means to bring about change. The authors discuss, among other topics, the attitudes towards these calls of different actors within and without the Muslim community. The existing 'community leaders' would have to give up a portion of their own power, which they may or may not be willing to do. Other members of the community's subgroupings, including women, are also unsure about the proposed changes in community representation. Their concern is that the changes may be exclusively directed towards male youth and their interests, and not aimed at increasing democratization within the community. The Bradford case illustrates that the prevailing processes of differentiation in the representation of various groups at the local level will inevitably affect the Muslim communities, as well. This seems to be the natural and logical outcome of their integration in British society.

III

Cécile Nijsten points out that there is a process of secularization taking place under Muslim youngsters which indicates that the observance of Islamic ritual practices and agreement with Islamic cultural norms and values seem to be in decline. This is also in accordance with results of previous research. However, the author emphasizes that these findings have to be interpreted with some precaution, since many of these young-sters say that they intend to start living by Islamic rules when they get older or get married and have children.

The author concludes that religion and ethnic identity are strongly related and that religious commitment and socio-cultural integration are to some degree negatively related. However, a causal relationship cannot be drawn. This means that it is equally plausible to assume that social and identificational integration lowers religious commitment as to say that a lower religious commitment fosters social participation. The results also reveal that when youngsters start feeling more Dutch, a decline in their religious commitment can be expected.

Furthermore, the author points out that structural participation and political participation are not related to religious commitment. Therefore, the policy of the Dutch government can be directed towards a combination of stimulating structural participation with a Muslim identity. However, it cannot be predicted what will happen when these young Moroccans are confronted with, for example, difficulties in finding a job. Therefore, the author observes that the fact that a positive attitude towards Dutch society - affective orientation- and religious commitment can go hand in hand leads to an optimistic view about the possibilities to be a Muslim and feel part of Dutch society.

In relation to the opinion of the youth concerning opportunities avail-able to them as Muslims living in the Netherlands, the author concludes that they are satisfied, but their fears are concentrated on the attitude of the Dutch towards foreigners and the negative image of Islam which is presented in the media. Therefore, they plead for more positive informa-tion and a more balanced view of Islam and its adherents in order to change this image.

Also, the contribution of *Jan van der Lans* and *Margo Rooijackers* provides valuable results on the cultural orientation and identity of Turkish immigrants in the Netherlands. One of these results is the evidence that differences in social-cultural identification are not related to immigration history but depend primarily on the language spoken in the parental home. Based on this result they expect that, with the shift of generations, a dual ethnic identity or a mono-ethnic Dutch identity will become more prevalent.

Furthermore, the authors argue that it is not true that young immigrants who prefer to remain exclusively or dominantly attached to a Turkish ethnic identity participate to a lesser degree in the Dutch society than young Turks who consider themselves as being partly Dutch. The former category also feels at home in Dutch society. Put differently, a monoethnic choice for a Turkish identity does not necessarily mean segregation. The latter category, on the other hand, does not reject the cultural heritage of traditional behaviourial codes, but goes on to conform, except for the rules that are restrictive to women. This means that, contrary to other findings in which a secularization process has been observed, the results of this study indicate that these young people are not less committed to Islam, and, in general, they continue abiding by its rituals and behaviourial rules. However, most of the religiously committed young immigrants think that it is more difficult to be a good Muslim in Holland than in Turkey. Yet, many of them evaluate the societal conditions for Muslims in the Netherlands as satisfactory.

Finally, the authors conclude that there are still many among these young people who opt for a Dutch ethnic identity without giving up their cultural heritage. Therefore, governmental support in maintaining that heritage would prove more helpful to their integration process than a policy which frustrates these cultural needs. This means that whether migrants and their offspring will feel at home and whether they will be incorporated into the society will primarily depend on the degree to which they perceive that they have the same rights and opportunities as the indigenous population, while at the same time not being forced to give up the traditional cultural resources of their self-respect.

In his contribution *Frank Kemper* compares the attitude of older male Moroccans in the Netherlands towards Islamist movements in the country of origin with that of older Moroccan teachers, representing the small intellectual elite in their ethnic group. Also, this contribution concentrates on several aspects of the cultural or religious identity of those immigrants. The results show that while a third of the immigrant workers seem to sympathize with the Islamist movement, the largest group prefers to stay aloof from political matters in the countries of origin. The attitude towards the Islamist movement is closely linked to the religious commitment. Immigrant workers opposing such movements (20%) tend to put less emphasis on moral conduct, have less social attachment to the mosque community, and have a lower overall level of religiousness compared to all other respondents.

By contrast, half of the teachers sympathizes with the Islamist movement. However, their sympathy cannot be interpreted as a matter of religious commitment, since they exhibit a lower level of overall religiousness. The author states that, in this group, sympathizers as well as opponents of Islamism cannot be differentiated from one another or from the neutral group on religious grounds. Therefore, their preference for the Islamist opposition in the Arabic world has to be considered as an expression of a secular political attitude.

On the basis of these results, the author concludes that sympathy for radical Islam cannot be interpreted as a retreat from western society, because among immigrant workers and teachers alike, the sympathizers of Islamism do not significantly differ from the other respondents concerning traditional habits, relations with the Dutch people, or preference for segregated neighbourhoods. This means that, among the first generation Moroccan immigrants in the Netherlands, pious fundamentalism with its emphasis on personal devotion is widespread, while Islamism as an outspoken political ideology has only limited appeal. This phenomenon is particularly remarkable in relation to the more secularized minority of intellectuals. Furthermore, the author concludes that the overall involvement in Dutch politics is generally low, although the anti-Islamist immigrant workers show a greater participation in local elections than the others do.

Seán Mcloughlin discusses in his contribution the homogeneity of Muslim identities. He argues that Muslim unity can only be understood to exist in specific contexts due to the fact that there are multiple identification positions that Muslims -British, Pakistani, Mirpuri, Bradfordians-choose to prioritize in different situations. These constructions are temporary and negotiated. Therefore, any attempt to understand either Muslim unity or disunity as representing an empirical reality of inherent force is surely to miss the point. Furthermore, the author argues that Islam should not be conceived as a timeless and monolithic set of customs and traditions connecting all Muslims for all time. At the other extreme, the notion of a plurality of islams is also misleading. He suggests that Muslims must be seen as being in a debate concerning what speaking in the name of the umma means in different contexts that are always situated in certain power relations. In describing contexts such as the dinner, it is important to talk about the power and significance of connections between Muslims without suggesting that such positionings are indissoluble. Similarly, it is crucial to comprehend the contingency of adopting such a position without interpreting it as an example of "lapsed" religiosity, as Islamists often do. Only cultural-racist stereotypes of the Muslim other and primordialist constructions of Islam feel the need to dichotomize an essential difference between the traditional and the modern; the Islamic and Western; the Muslim and the British; and the namaazi (prayerful) and the Bradford City football supporter.

1

Challenges to the Organization of Muslim Communities in Western Europe

The Political Dimension

M. Ali Kettani

The 15 countries of the European Economic Community (EEC) have a total area of 3,216,795 km2 and a total population in 1991 of 365,943,000 persons. These countries have a long history with Islam and Muslims. However, by the turn of the 20th Century their total Muslim population did not exceed 10,000.

The number of Muslims in the EEC countries could be assessed with reasonable approximation. It jumped from insignificance in 1901 to about 4.5 million in 1971 above 10 million in 1991, and around 11.5 million in 1995. Table 1.1 gives the number of Muslims by state in the EEC in 1991 and their percentages. Muslims formed 2.8% of the total EEC population. France has the largest number of Muslims (4 million), and the largest percentage (7%) of all EEC countries. Table 1.2 shows that the number of Muslims in the EEC countries in the period between 1971 and 1991 tripled and their percentage in the overall population rose from 1.3% to 2.8% (3.1% in 1995).

On the turn of the 20th Century, the change of the demographic pattern of the Muslim World from stagnant to expanding and that of Western Europe from expanding to stagnant was barely noticeable. While the demographic expansion of Europe in the past was a result of scientific and technological preeminence leading to military power and colonial expansion, that of the Muslim World occurs while it is militarily, economically and politically subjugated.

Table 1.1. Muslims in the ECC in 1991*					
State	Area in km2	Total Population X 1000	Muslim Population X 1000	% Muslims	% Muslim citizens
Germany	356,628	79,500	2,500	3.1	4.0
Italy	301,224	58,000	400	0.7	12.5
United Kingdom	245,813	57,700	1,500	2.6	66.7
France	547,026	56,900	4,000	7.0	62.5
Spain	504,750	38,426	350	0.9	22.9
The Netherlands	33,612	15,010	450	3.0	13.3
Portugal	91,530	10,450	20	0.2	50.0
Greece	131,944	10,264	300	2.9	50.0
Belgium	30,000	9,987	450	4.5	6.7
Sweden	449,750	8,591	100	1.2	20.0
Austria	83,849	7,812	120	1.5	25.0
Denmark	43,069	5,146	100	1.9	20.0
Norway	324,219	4,254	50	1.2	10.0
Ireland	70,282	3,523	20	0.6	20.0
Luxembourg	2,586	380	10	2.6	10.0
Total	3,216,795	365,943	10,370	2.8	39.1

Today, the Muslim Community of Western Europe originates from two main sources: 1) the return to the "Metropole" of the indigenous elements who fought with the colonial power against the liberation movements of their own people (Harkis to France from Algeria, Moluccans to the Netherlands from Indonesia, etc..); and 2) workers from former colonies (or otherwise a Muslim country) to supply cheap labour for the expanding economies of Western Europe in the 1960's and 1970's. Once the Muslim Community has been well established in the 1980's, new streams started to add new Muslims to existing ones: brain drain, family reunions, refugees, illegals, and converts.

The fascinating part of the modern establishment of the Muslim community in Western Europe is that it is a result of a miscalculation of all parties concerned. The "collaborator" emigrated to the "Metropole" with the idea that he shall return home as soon as possible when things calm down. The "Government of the Metropole" did not plan to introduce a new "Muslim

Community". They thought that if these people gave their lives for the "Metropole" against their own people, they must be easily assimilable. They would lose their Islamic identity and, at least the second generation, would become undifferentiable from other citizens, even in terms of religion. Things did not work that way, neither the "collaborators" could go home, nor the second generation lost its Islam.

The import of labour from Muslim countries happened as a result of a decision made up by four parties concerned: 1) the Government of the Western European country (receiver); 2) the Government of the Muslim country (sender); 3) the Muslim worker; and 4) the Western European Employer.

None of the four actors above intended to establish a Muslim community in Western Europe. The Receiver Government thought that they would be using a neutral manpower that would work for a given length of time and go back home with no social effect on the Receiver country. The Sender Government thought that they solved an increasing unemployment problem and in the same time established the basis of an infinite source of hard currency. They had interest in keeping control of the emigrants, or better have them rotated. The Muslim worker thought he would make some money to build himself a decent economic base back home. The European employer wanted to solve his labour problems and was not concerned by the rest.

As time went on, Muslim workers started families, while the children born in the land of immigration started feeling at home. As they grew up, even if their parents wanted to go return, they were certainly not interested. As emigration moved from individuals to families it became permanent, and the amount of hard currency sent to the country of origin started to fall. The emigrant worker has also established his niche in the economy of the Receiver country and cannot be sent home without much damage to both the Receiver and the Sender country.

State	*No. of Muslims in 1971 (X 1000)*	*% in 1971*	*% increase 1971-1991*
Germany	1,150	1.5	117
Italy	150	0.1	700
United Kingdom	750	1.3	100
France	2,000	3.9	100
Spain	90	0.3	289
The Netherlands	130	1.0	246
Portugal	1	0.01	1900
Greece	110	1.3	173
Belgium	120	1.2	275
Sweden	17	0.2	488
Austria	35	0.5	243
Denmark	16	0.3	525
Norway	5	0.1	900
Ireland	2	0.07	900
Luxembourg	2	0.6	400
Total	4,478	1.3	132

*Table 1.2. Increase of the Muslim Population in the last two Decades in the EEC**

As Muslim immigrants became settlers, they started to interact with the host society, were influenced by it and certainly influenced a section of it. As many took the local nationality, by keeping it (Harkis), by birth (second generation), by naturalization, or those who became Muslim, by conversion, Islam became more and more nationalized in all the EEC countries. Table 1.1 shows that about 40% of the Muslims of the EEC countries are citizens of these countries. Thus, by 1991, the EEC Muslim Community became European and its problems are not any more problems of emigration, but have become internal European problems indeed.

Islamic revival

Until the late 1960's, the Muslims in the EEC countries did not seem to care to preserve Islam. The majority did not present any sign of religiosity. As the economic growth of the Receiver countries started to slow down, Muslim workers started to think of returning home continuously delayed. However, the savings were never large enough to start a new life back home, and the prospects for the health care and education of the children as well as for their future employment were infinitely better in the Receiver countries.

Table 2.1 shows that in 1961 the number of mosques in the 15 EEC countries was about 380, including 350 mosques in the well established old Muslim communities of West Thrace and Rhodes in Greece; 7 of the 14 remaining countries had not a single mosque, and 3 others had only one prayer hall each. Except for West Thrace, there were no Islamic schools and no Islamic organizations.

By the end of the 1960's, this situation began to change. As the workers started to see that their stay was becoming indefinite, they started families, and Muslim immigration changed from a "bachelor" temporary one to a more "permanent" family establishment. Thus, heads of families started to worry about their own, and their families' spiritual welfare. Consequently, various Islamic institutions, especially prayer halls, started to appear. Factories saw in responding to this demand a cheap way to keep the workers happy. The Receiver governments saw in this phenomenon a good sign of integration, as long as it was limited and discrete.

The demand was responded to by the better educated and the more settled among the workers, as well as by Muslim students in European universities. In fact, almost everywhere the first Islamic organizations were established by university students. By 1971, the number of mosques jumped to 607. In 1981, it reached 2,124, was about 5,000 in 1991, and 6,000 in 1995.

The sudden increase of the number of mosques and prayer halls in the 14 states of the EEC (excluding Greece) from 32 in 1961 to 4445 in 1991, i.e., a 140 times in 30 years, is indeed a clear sign of the establishment of Islam in Western Europe. In the 1980's, quantity has been strengthened by better quality. From rented halls, apartments, garages and stores, the "Prayer halls" became real "Islamic Centers", owned by the Muslim Community, including each a mosque, a school, and social services.

For the last ten years, Islam established itself in Western Europe. New elements are joining in: the second generation and the local converts, the two eventually fusing in new Islamic communities that have roots in the EEC country to which they belong. This new fact created new actors. Of the four original ones, the employer is having a decreasing influence in the events whereas the individual Muslim immigrant's action is becoming more organized.

The most important new actor is the Local Muslim Community (LMC) now having its own individuality; another is the Saudi Government which, although it has no citizens in Western Europe, acts from its position as the Custodian of the Muslim holiest cities, Mecca and Medinah. A third actor is the local citizenry organized in neighbourhood associations, defence of the environment associations, etc... A fourth are political parties; a fifth the Churches (Catholic, Protestant, Orthodox, Jewish).

Table 2.1. Growth of the Number of Mosques in the ECC countries

State	1961	1971	1981	1991
Germany	10	50	600	1000
Italy	1	2	20	100
UK	10	125	230	600
France	4	33	421	1500
Spain	0	5	40	120
The Netherlands	5	20	250	400
Portugal	0	1	5	20
Greece	350	350	380	400
Belgium	0	15	120	300
Sweden	1	1	20	180
Austria	1	2	20	120
Denmark	0	1	10	50
Norway	0	1	4	40
Ireland	0	1	2	5
Luxembourg	0	0	2	10
Total	382	607	2,124	4,845

As a general rule: the LMC seeks to establish itself in the EEC country, defend its existence and guarantee its future by gaining equality with the other religious communities. The Receiver Government, often resists the LMC desire through all kinds of legal impediments. The Sender Government tries to keep control on their citizens without wanting them back home as they want their remittances, but have no jobs to offer on their return. The Local Citizens are aroused by extremists among them to resist the sudden cultural presence of Islam in their midst. The position of the churches is ambiguous: in the beginning, they tried to help Muslims get established, later they became restless in front of their increasing presence. The political parties started to show interest in the Muslim vote as more Muslims became citizens.

Five basic characteristics of Islam form the boundary conditions of any form of organization of a Muslim Community. The first, the absence of a "church", implies that the Muslim individual is the source, the beginning and the aim of any Muslim organization. The second, the universality of Islam, implies that there is no Islamic limitation for a new Muslim community to be established anywhere in the world. The third is the fact all Muslims form part of a universal "Ummah", irrespective of race, social class, national origin, or religious officiation before accepting Islam. The fourth is the principle of Shurah, i.e., decisions are made by consensus of a Muslim assembly made up by all Muslims. The fifth is the fact that there is no "Compulsion in religion". This implies that a Muslim community thrives in a multi-cultural environment if the same rights are guaranteed to all.

In a real situation, other forces are present: within the Muslim community in question; outside the Muslim community but among Muslims in general; and outside the Muslim community but within the country under consideration. The first are a function of the diversity of the Muslim community: national origin; differences of madhhab, degree of commitment to Islam, and of the knowledge of Islamic principles, etc... The second are a function of Muslim countries: governments, political parties, sufi orders, individuals, etc... The third are a function of the country of immigration: Government agencies, churches, political parties, employers, trade unions, etc....

The case of Australia, a successful trial

Australia has the dimensions of a continent with its 7,682,450 km2 and its population of 18 million. Its present Muslim community traces its origin to 1860 when the first camel driver, Dost Mohamed, a Pathan from Kashmir and two other Afghans arrived in Melbourne with a string of 24 camels from

Peshawar (in Pakistan Today). Today, the number of Muslims of Australia could be estimated at about 500,000 persons (about 3% of the total population of Australia), with a diversity of national origins unparalleled by any country of Europe. They numbered around 100,000 Muslims in 1976, and their fast rate of increase goes on unabated.

Since the beginning in 1860, the Ghans tried to organize themselves in Muslim communities, but by 1948 their organization became a shambles, and Muslims appeared to be on the verge of disappearing. About that time, an unexpected Islamic renaissance, initiated by new immigrants from Bosnia, occurred, providing the initial impulse to the present organisational effort. From one Islamic local organization in 1948, the number jumped to 9 in 1960, 13 in 1970, 42 in 1980, 77 in 1990 and about 100 in 1995. In 1954, Imam Ahmed Skaka, the Bosniac religious leader of the Muslim community of Adelaide (South Australia), requested the State of South Australia to grant him the status of marriage celebrant for the Muslims, the way priests and rabbis were. His request was first approved, then withdrawn in 1956. The matter reached the Federal Supreme Court, and in 1961 the then Chief Justice dismissed the case declaring bluntly: "I will never allow any Muslim religious person to marry any one in this country!". This was felt as a terrible blow by the Muslim community. By then, they were about 30,000, organized in 10 Muslim associations in four Australian states (South Australia, New South Wales, Victoria, Queensland). In a general meeting held in April 1963, the "Australian Federation of Islamic Societies" (AFIS) was established with the main purpose of leading a united fight for the right to have Muslim marriage celebrants. United, they succeeded in their aim.

By 1974, the very loose and weak organisation of AFIS became inadequate. The crisis became obvious as the Muslim population increased in numbers and diversity. AFIS could not stop the centrifugal forces within the Muslim Community. The continental dimensions of Australia made it very difficult for a two-level national body to be effective. Things became worse as all multi-national Muslim organizations started to disintegrate into their national components.

This writer arrived in Sydney on 9/11/1974 with the purpose of re-organising the entire Muslim community of Australia. He sat with its leaders in New South Wales in meetings where the rules of organization at the local level were defined as well as the means and ways to form a new organization. It was agreed also that unity could be established only if a minimum of diversity is accepted and even encouraged. This author met with all the six Muslim local associations then in New South Wales and agreed with them on the following principles:

The gradual transformation of Islamic societies based on ethnic, national, racial or sectarian ground into ones based purely on geography. The local society may use the language or the madhhab of the local majority, but the difference should not appear in its name. The local Islamic societies in each state would form an Islamic Council which would represent the entire Muslim Community in that state, and all the Islamic councils in the different states and territories of Australia would form a Federation of Islamic Councils. This author then visited the Muslims of other states of Australia and convinced them of the same.

Intense work during 1975 completely transformed AFIS into the "Australian Federation of Islamic Councils" (AFIC) based on the above-mentioned three-tier system. Thus, were organized all the 16 local Muslim organizations of Australia. After twenty years, AFIC is stronger than ever, encompassing the 100 local Muslim organizations existing today. The local societies, state councils and AFIC National body, all have constitutions delineating the duties of each. All are based on the free election of office bearers, by individual members in local societies, by the local societies in State councils, and by the State councils in the AFIC Executive committee. The elected representatives of all member societies form the Federal Congress which meets once a year to decide on AFIC general policy. The AFIC President and Vice-President are elected every two years by the Federal Congress. They nominate the other members of the Executive Committee for approval by the said Congress. Neither the President nor the Vice-President could hold more than two consecutive offices.

Under this system, AFIC embarked on a gigantic task securing recognition for the Muslims in Australia by the Australian authorities on an equal basis with all other religious bodies; recognition as the representative body of the Australian Muslim Community by the Muslim World; the necessary finances for establishing Islamic institutions such as mosques, schools and Imams, bringing back to the fold of Islam lost communities, and presenting Islam to non-Muslims.

This system succeeded for many reasons. First, the desire of the Australian

Muslim Community to unite as a community by integrating its members in one national organization within the Australian social environment, found support in almost all Australian political parties, at both the state and the national level. Second, the representation of the Muslim states which would be interested in controlling the Muslim community was weak in the beginning. When it became stronger later (Turkey, Saudi Arabia), the Muslim Community was already irreversibly organized. Third, the influence of Muslim ambassadors in trying to control the Muslims was limited, as Canberra was remote from the centers of Muslim concentration. Finally, the system of organization of the Australian Muslims was good enough to absorb the major ethnic, madhhab or political diversities of the Australian Muslim community.

The case of France[1]

The relation of France with Islam was continuous since the Battle of Poitiers in 738 CE, after continuous Muslim incursions from Al-Andalus, starting 716 CE. In fact, Narbonne (Arbunah) remained the capital of a Muslim province for 40 years (719-759). Since the fall of Muslim sovereignty in French territory, the different French regimes never allowed any Muslim presence in France until the mid-18th Century.

After the fall of Algiers in 1830 to French forces, for the first time a large number of Muslims became French subjects against their own will. The relation of France with Islam changed from looking at Muslims as dangerous enemies to seeing them as backward people to be civilized. Napoleon III dreamt of building up a French Muslim Empire by conquering more Muslim territories. For the first time since the 10th Century the establishment of Muslims in France became possible again. Nevertheless, the number of Muslims in France remained very low and did not reach 1,000 before 1900. At the outset of World War I, they were less than 10,000. Most of these were from Algeria and their stay in France was only temporary. After the War, France needed manpower and found it readily available in the colonies, especially Algeria. The number of Muslims jumped to 100,000 in 1920, to reach a peak of 120,000 in 1924, and fall back to 70,000 in 1935. After World War II, France needed more manpower and the North African pool was ready to supply it. The number of Muslims in France reached 240,000 in 1952. But their real growth occurred in the 1960's after the independence of the colonies, especially Algeria in 1962, hitting the million mark in the 1960's and quickly the second million mark in 1975, doubling again in less than 20 years.

During this period, France wanted to use the few underprivileged Muslims it had on its soil and the many Muslim lands under its control to present itself as a Muslim power, with Paris as capital of a "Muslim Empire", deserving a mosque. Thus, the idea of building a large mosque in Paris was promoted by French (non-Muslim) politicians since 1849. But the project was executed only in 1922. The land was granted by the City of Paris and the funds were collected from the Muslim French colonies, especially Morocco. The Mosque was opened officially by Moulay Youssef, the then Sultan of Morocco on 15/9/1926. It remained the cornerstone of French policy towards Islam to this day.

The policy of the French governments since Napoleon III has been consistent in their uneasiness to see Islam established in France. This is the basic reason for the lack of organization of the French Muslim community on a national, representative and autonomous level. The French "leading elite" has a narrow view of the French identity that excludes Islam a priori. As long as Muslims in France were foreigners with a temporary stay there was no problem. When they became French citizens by origin (converts), birth or naturalization they are assumed to assimilate, i.e. forget about Islam and the Arabic language altogether. This, they did until the 1960's.

The first signs of Islamic revival in France started in 1963 with the establishment of the "Muslim Student Association of France" and "The Religious Islamic Association". Three elements helped in the re-Islamization of the Muslims in France: the contact between the Muslim students and workers; the positive response of the French industry to the demand of Muslim workers for places of worship; and the initial support of both the Catholic and the Protestant churches.

In 1976, the President of the French Republic decided to create a Secretariat of State for Immigrant Workers Affairs which was going to work on the four following points: to control the "population movement"; to continuously exchange views with the countries of origin of the immigrants; to give the immigrant worker the right to retain his cultural and religious affiliation; and to look for the necessary conditions for a real equality between immigrants and French citizens. Thus, the French Government insisted on looking at Islam as a problem of the immigrant workers. Moreover, it decided to cooperate with the countries of origin of immigrants to control the immigrants religiously. Since then, the successive French governments rarely looked at Islam as a French religion that has to organize itself outside any interference. They continued in believing in the fallacy that Islam will remain foreign in France, i.e., temporary. As Islam is "scary", it is left to governments of Muslim countries to control it through means that are not necessarily democratic.

As for the Muslim governments, they continue believing in the fallacy that their citizens and their descendants abroad will remain under their control and will not introduce new religious ideas back home. Thus, Algeria was given full control of the Mosque of Paris to try to control the Muslim community. Saudi Arabia and Morocco tried to interfere seeking their own control. So did Turkey through its Diyanet Imams.

However, one increasingly important category of Muslims did not fit in the scheme: the French citizens, including the converts and their children (the largest number in Europe, about 200,000), the Harkis and their children (about 500,000),[2] the Beurs (children of immigrants born in France) and the naturalized. These formed national groupings that tried to be independent of governments, but were met by either official indifference or, worse, interference. With the discredit of the Algerian Government within the Muslim Community of France due to the 1992 military putsch, the French tried to help establish what some officials describe as a "French Islam", i.e. a tamed Islam under the control of the Government. For this purpose, the Ministry of Interior established a "Council for Reflection on Islam" and handpicked some Muslim leaders to form it with the purpose of organizing the Muslim community in an "acceptable way".

While Muslims in France struggle to obtain the rights guaranteed to them by the French Constitution, they continue to be subject to official harassment: non-recognition (including in Alsace which has a special Concordat situation); persecution of girls wearing hijab in public schools; expulsion of Imams and religious leaders; etc...

The case of Spain[3]

The history of Spain with Islam dates from 711 CE. Since then the shrinking Al-Andalus became a centre of civilization not only for the Islamic, but for the entire world. Since the fall of the last Muslim Andalusian city, Granada, in 1492, to the Christians, Muslims entered a tragic era of suppression and forced Christianization. Thousands were burnt at the stakes for their hidden Islamic conviction. All lost their properties and many were enslaved. Thousands of mosques were taken over and converted into churches.

This situation lasted until 1610 when a certain number of Muslims (about 240,000) were expelled from their ancestral homes. Islam appeared to be completely wiped out from Spain until the 20th Century. However, it remained an important substrate in the identity of Andalusians.

As Spain conquered part of Morocco in 1912, foreign Muslim individuals could venture in the country, but no Islamic activity of any sort was tolerated. Spanish Muslims had no choice but to keep their faith secret or move to the Moroccan colony. During the Civil War, as General Franco brought in many Moroccan soldiers, some Muslim presence was tolerated, including the establishment of a mosque in Cordoba. Muslim cemeteries were also established in Granada and other cities. All this presence disappeared soon after the victory of General Franco. The mosque in Cordoba was became a storehouse.

In 1967, a timid law of freedom of religion (No 44/ 1967) was promulgated, allowing Jews, Protestants and Muslims to organize religiously and establish their centres of worship. In 1971, the first Islamic organization was established officially in Granada by foreign Muslim students, and later branches were established all across the country. In 1973, the Mayor of Madrid granted a centrally located piece of land to Muslim embassies to build a mosque.

The situation of Islam in Spain changed altogether with the death of General Franco in 1975. The cultural and religious diversity of the country was genuinely guaranteed in the new Constitution of 1978. Gone the absolute pre-eminence of Castilla and the Catholic Church. Spain became practically a federal state of 17 autonomous regions. One of the largest, Andalucía, established in 8 southern provinces in 1980, was based on an Andalusian nationalism proud of its Islamic past. A new era started not only for the immigrants to live their Islam freely, but also for the Spanish citizens, many of them Andalusians, who wished to return to their Islamic roots.

Since 1980, many started to revert to Islam, in two main foci, one in Granada with a Sufi inclination, the other in Sevilla, then Cordoba, with an Andalusian Nationalist inclination. This resurrection was often supported by local elected authorities and resisted by the Catholic Church. During the 1980's, while the Muslims in Spain, including the reverts, enjoyed full freedom of worship, their position as a community was not recognized. They were allowed to function by registering in the Ministry of Justice as religious organizations, but they were not given the privileges that Catholics, Protestants and Jews had. It was only on July 14, 1989, that the Spanish Commission for Religious Freedom recognized Islam officially, thus closing an ugly chapter of continuous oppression that was opened with the conquest of the first Muslim cities of the Peninsula in the 10th Century. But was it closed really?

The mentioned Law established the possibility that the Spanish State reaches with recognized "Religious Communities" agreements of cooperation. For this to apply to the Muslims, the latter should unite into one representative grouping. Somehow two Muslim federations were formed: the "Spanish Federation of Islamic Religious Entities", headed by a Spanish-naturalized Syrian former employee of the Ministry of Interior, and the "Union of Islamic Communities of Spain", headed by an Andalusian former member of the "Comunidad Islamica de Espana", both constituted by immigrants, mostly from Morocco and Syria, with some native Spanish representing paper organizations. These two federations formed themselves into the "Islamic Commission of Spain". The two main native organizations, each one representing a true federation, the "Yamaa Islamica de Al-Andalus" and the "Comunidad Islamica de Espana", as well as the Muslims of Ceuta and Melilla, were left out. The "Commission", recognized as representative of the Muslims by the Government, illegally kept them out, and the Ministry of Justice did nothing about it. This Commission never negotiated anything with the Spanish Government, and the Muslims of Spain remained a second rate religious community.

Somehow, as in France, some in Spain are happier to treat Islam as a "guest religion" and would not like to see it established in the country. This control could not occur if the "Commission" were really representative, as almost half the Muslims of Spain are citizens, many of them natives. The odd group in the Muslim Community is that formed by the native reverts, who are increasing in numbers and influence within the Muslim Community.

In spite of this situation, Islam keeps growing. From nil in 1980, the number of mosques grew to 200 in 1995 in Spain, and to 40 in Andalucía alone. The first Islamic University (Ibn Rushd University of which this author is the Rector) was established in 1994 in Cordoba by one of the major Spanish Muslim communities (The Yamaa Islamica de Al-Andalus), denied membership in the Commission.

The case of Germany and the UK[4]

The first Muslim Community in Germany was made up of members of the Ottoman Embassy who settled in Berlin, then the capital of Prussia, in the 18th Century. After World War I, some Muslim soldiers in the armies of the Allies, caught as prisoners of war by the Germans, chose after their liberation to settle in Germany. They were joined by a few Muslim tradesmen and a trickle of German converts. Hamburg and Berlin were their main centres.

After World War II, many Muslim soldiers deserted the Soviet Army and settled in Bavaria. In 1961, Germany reached an agreement with Turkey for the transfer of Turkish manpower.[5] Since then, the story of Islam in Germany became parallel to that in other EEC countries. The number of Muslims in Germany was about be 1,000 in 1920, 20,000 in 1951, 1,150,000 in 1971 and 2,500,000 in 1991. About 75% of the Muslims of Germany were Turkish in 1991, several thousands native Germans, and about 100,000 were German citizens. The number of Muslims keeps increasing through the arrival of refugees, especially from Bosnia in latter years.

The first Muslim organizations were established in Germany after World War I, but many more were started after World War II. Few Muslims are German citizens as the right of citizenship in Germany is not due to birth, but to blood. Those who are German among Muslims are converts or those who have one German parent (often the mother). Only a small trickle of those who sought German nationality received it. Thus, the greatest majority of the children of Muslims born in Germany remains foreign.

Freedom of religion is guaranteed by the German Constitution where religious organizations are dealt with as Bodies of Public Law. They can deal with the Länder and the Central State on the basis of that law, which necessitates among other things, a representative organizational structure. The Body of Public Law receives much support from the State, such as contribution for the cost of pastoral activities, tax exemption, subsidies, etc... For a religious group to enjoy these privileges, it has to be recognized by the State as a Body of Public Law. Protestants, Catholics, Jews (30,000 people) and others are recognized. Muslims are not, in spite of their efforts to fulfil the conditions required. Thus, Islam is not taught in school to Muslim children, as other religions are to their adherents. German authorities (State and Länder) seem more interested in pleasing foreign Muslim governments (e.g. Turkey) to control religiously their citizens, rather than integrate Islam in German society.

As in France, the Muslim Community of the UK has its roots in the colonial past. The first Muslim migrants to Britain were Yemenis from Aden, who established themselves in Cardiff where they built in 1870 one of the first mosques in the country. By the 20th Century, Muslims from India settled near London. During the first half of this century, Muslims arrived from Cyprus, Egypt and Iraq. On the eve of World War II, the Muslim population of the UK numbered about 50,000 people. It picked up momentum after World War II, reaching 100,000 in 1951, 750,000 in 1971, and 1,500,000 in 1991. About two-third of all UK Muslims are UK citizens. They are also well organized at a local level.

To the contrary of France, there is no separation between Church and State in the UK. The official religion of England is the Anglican Church. To the contrary of Sweden, which has an official Church, the UK has no specific system by which the state may "recognize" a given religious community. This means that the official Church has preeminence over others, especially in education. However, the UK State guarantees freedom of religion and makes financial contributions to pastoral activities, exemption of taxes, etc... To be able to enjoy these privileges, the religious body must be recognized by the State as a Charity Organization.

One example where Muslims in UK feel particularly mistreated is the continuous denial to accept their schools on equal footing for support as the Christian and the Jewish ones. Yusuf Islam (the former Cat Stevens) struggled towards this end to no avail. The second is the Rushdie Affair. While obviously the UK, as well as other Western governments, wanted to use this affair in their war with the Iranians, for the British Muslims the whole affair is a clear case of discrimination against them as they discovered that the Laws of Blasphemy apply only to Jews and Christians. Thus, in the UK also, Islam is considered as a foreign religion.

The case of Belgium[6]

Until World War II, there was practically no Islam in Belgium. The first Muslims were refugees from Albania just after the War. In the 1960's, the number of Muslims increased quickly through the introduction of labour first from Morocco, then from Turkey. The number of Muslims in Belgium reached about 120,000 in 1971, 350,000 in 1981 and 450,000 in 1991.

The first effort at organising the Muslim Community occurred in 1961, when a group of young Muslims from Brussels started to gather for Friday prayers and on the occasion of the two Eids. They were helped in finding halls by the embassies of Senegal and Pakistan. In 1963, the Muslim ambassadors formed a "General Islamic Council" (GIC) with the main purpose of establishing the first mosque in Brussels.

In 1967, the late King Faisal of Saudi Arabia visited Belgium and the then Belgian Prime Minister offered him a building in the Place du Cinquantenaire to be converted into a mosque. The latter, in the form of a mosque, was built in 1883 in the Fatimid style by Belgian tradesmen who lived in Egypt. The occasion was the 50th anniversary of the establishment of the State of Belgium. It remained empty until it was offered officially in a public ceremony to King Faisal on 28/5/1967. The mosque was put under the management of the GIC who established in it the "Cultural Islamic Centre" (CIC), recognized by the authorities on 26/4/1968. The Cinquantenaire Mosque was remodelled through funds from Saudi Arabia and opened to worshippers in 1977. Since then, it played in Belgium the role played by the Mosque of Paris in France. But while the Mosque of Paris was controlled by the Algerian Government, that of Brussels is controlled by the Saudi Government.

Most Islamic associations are established as "Associations Sans But Lucratif" (ASBL) as per the law of 1921. However, as the law necessitates 3/5 of the members of an ASBL to be Belgian for the association to be a legal entity, most Islamic associations ended functioning without this quorum, i.e. without the status of a legal entity.

Article 14 of the Belgian Constitution guarantees freedom of public worship, freedom of thought and freedom of organizing religious public ceremonies. Article 16 guarantees the freedom and independence of ministers of religion. Article 17 assures that the ministers shall receive a salary from the State. The law of 4/3/1870 stipulates the recognition of four cults in Belgium: Roman Catholic, Protestant, Anglican and Jewish. Only to these four cults the above laws are applicable. This law regulates not only the salaries of priest and rabbis, but also their right to dispose of places of cult as well as the teaching of their religious believes in the public schools of Belgium.

It was in March 1971 that the first project of law to recognise Islam as the fifth recognized cult in Belgium was deposited in Parliament, which adopted it after lengthy discussions on 19/7/1974. For this law to be effectively implemented the following legal complements were necessary: royal decrees defining the organization of committees in charge of the temporal aspects of the Muslim communities; a law defining the salary scales of the Imams and other ministers of the Islamic cult; royal decrees recognizing the administrations of the Islamic cult that would be established within a geographical area of its responsibility; and a law modifying the "School Pact" (Article 8 of the law of 29/5/1959) concerning the teaching of religion in primary and secondary schools.

Then a Royal Decree was issued on 3/5/1978 for the organization of committees for the temporal organization of the Muslim Community in Belgium. A law of 21/1/1981 fixed the Imam salaries. These laws show a genuine desire of Belgium to integrate Islam in the country. However, this theoretical recognition of Islam is not yet translated fully into reality.

First, if one looks at the salaries decided by the law of 23/1/1981 for the ministers of different cults, one realizes that there is a hierarchy among equals. If the salary of the Chief Imam is 1, that of the Chief Rabbi is 1.143, that of the Pasteur Président of the Protestants is 2.01, and that of the Archbishop is 3.22. Furthermore, unilaterally, the Belgian Government recognized the Director of CIC in Brussels as the Chief Imam. The latter is nominated by the Muslim World League (Mecca), a Saudi Organization. CIC itself is run by GIC, made up of Muslim ambassadors in Brussels. Consequently, the Belgian authorities put Islam and Muslims in Belgium in the hands of foreign governments for obvious political reasons.

Thus, the contradiction (some say hypocrisy): The authorities claim that the laws of recognition cannot be implemented fully because the Muslim Community failed to organize representative elections in the mosques, in each province, as required by the recognition laws. In the same time, the same authorities recognized CIC as the representative of the Muslims and put it in charge of carrying out the elections. Obviously, CIC has a vested interest never to carry the elections. This situation created a blocking of any effort to enable the Muslim Community to enjoy the rights granted to it by the 1974 laws.

Even when later, the Belgian Government withdrew their recognition of CIC as representing the Muslims, it continued to refuse recognizing the elected representatives of the Muslims, and put conditions that in fact undermine the democratic process they pretend to demand.

The impact of the Bosnian tragedy

The Bosnian tragedy will have a lasting effect on the psyche of the Muslims of the EEC countries for two main reasons: it supports the conceived idea that Muslims have of Christians and reinforces the fears that Muslims have of Western Europe concerning their future.

Muslims in general believe that Christians do not like them, consider them non-believers and are out to destroy them whenever they get a chance. History proved them right until the freeing of the colonies starting with the 1940's. The development of secular ideas, that made room for Muslims in Europe, gave the impression that religious antipathies are a matter of the past. For the first time, Muslims, Christians, Jews and atheists could cooperate fully and sincerely on such matters as human rights, democracy and the protection of minorities.

The tragedy of Bosnia proved to the silent majority of the Muslims of Western Europe the contrary. The Bosnians are Nordic-looking Slavic Europeans, different from the other Europeans only by their Islamic religion and their Islamically influenced culture. The war of the Serbs against them is not a political war in which one group wants to implement its hegemony on another group, it is a war where Muslim Bosnians falling in the hands of the Serbs are being killed, expelled, annihilated, their mosques destroyed, their books burnt. It is a physical and cultural genocide against a European Muslim nation. It is reminiscent of what happened centuries ago to Muslims in Spain, Portugal, Italy, Hungary, and most other European countries, to Jews as late as World War II, to the Albigenses and the Huguenots in France, and many others. It is the negation of all the principles on which the Modern World claims to be established.

The way the United Nations (controlled by the West) and the EEC are treating the matter is seen by most Muslims in Western Europe (and elsewhere) as support to the aggressor against the aggressed. On what moral ground the Bosnians are prevented from arming themselves to defend their lives? What credibility the United Nations have when they claim a territory protected, disarm its people, and then shamelessly deliver it to butchers? What credibility is left for an EEC that sympathizes publicly with the aggressor, forces the legal democratically elected, internationally recognized government to sit on a equal footing with thugs, declared by the World Court of Justice as war criminals, and present plan after plan that would lead to the destruction of a state?

The EEC Muslims draw their conclusions: If the EEC governments accept genocide against a European Muslim nation, they may be able to implement the same genocide one day against their own Muslim communities. This is indeed a source of fear that would shape the relationship of Muslims with non-Muslims in the EEC countries in the 21th Century.

Furthermore, the de facto behaviour of most West European establishments concerning matters of democracy and human rights is seen by the mass of Western European Muslims as contradicting the principles declared when Muslims are concerned. This is seen as a disastrous sign of hypocrisy, making most Western European establishments morally unfit to give the example.

Conclusions

Several conclusions could be drawn from the above: (1) Islam has become well-established in the EEC countries. The number of Muslims reached in 1995 about 11.5 million and their percentage in the population reached 3.1%; (2) The number of Muslims in EEC and their percentage in the population will increase in the future. By the year 2015, it is expected to double to 23 million reaching 7% of the total; (3) In the next 20 years, the majority of the Muslims of EEC countries will be citizens of these countries: as more local citizens will convert to Islam, and the greatest majority of the new born to Muslim families will opt for the citizenship of the country of their birth, and more first generation immigrants will seek naturalization. Thus, Islam will become more settled and integrated in the EEC countries; (4) The demand for Islam and Islamic services among Muslims in the EEC countries is increasing and, therefore, the chances that these Muslims will be assimilated in other religious groups are small.

Facing these facts, most EEC establishments, including governments and political parties, are still entertaining the hope that somehow Islam will disappear, through assimilation or emigration. They use the Muslim population in their external political plans, use Muslim governments to negate the recognition they publicly give to their Muslims, and otherwise prevent the Muslim Community from enjoying its rights.

Furthermore, the established laws in the EEC countries promote an exclusive Judeo-Christian environment. They are often insensitive to the feelings of Muslims and encourage Muslim-bashing in the press, the schools and other public places with impunity. On top of this, the Bosnian tragedy promotes a feeling of insecurity in the Muslim community of EEC countries.

What gives hope to the Muslim Community of Western Europe is the true dedication of an important minority which defends the lofty principles claimed but continuously betrayed by most establishments. In this respect, some EEC countries have reached an advanced stage in integrating their Muslim Community in their social fabric. Netherlands and Sweden are certainly more advanced than others. Outside the EEC, one must mention Finland and Austria.

What future Islam has in the EEC countries? Two scenarios are possible. The "Australian Scenario" or the "Bosnian Scenario". In the first case, the Muslim Community will be encouraged to integrate in the country and its rights will be recognized. The community will stay Muslim but will assimilate a good part of the culture of the country within two generations. Some EEC countries are moving slowly and timidly in that direction. Most are not.

The second scenario is frightening as one would expect more hypocrisy, more denial of the rights of the Muslim Community as a community, more diabolization of Islam as a religion, etc... Eventually, if this is not checked, expulsions of Muslim citizens and genocides on the Bosnian-scale are possible in some EEC countries.

To avoid the second scenario, the living forces of the EEC countries should cooperate with enlightened Muslims among them to defend the rights of the Muslim Community, prevent their governments from using Islam in different international political games, and consider the establishment of Islam in the country as a new national fact to be approached within the great principles of unity in diversity and respect of human rights without hypocrisy.

Notes

[*]   Muslim population figures and percentage of citizens are assessed from many sources, especially estimates of Muslim communities themselves. The official values are usually lower.

[1]   See Kepel, 1987.
[2]   See Gilleband, 1973.
[3]   See Kettani, 1992.
[4]   See Detaille, 1993 and Joly, 1993.
[5]   See Bhatti, 1980.
[6]   See Dassetto & Bastenier, 1984.

2

Turkish Islam in Germany

Between Political Overdetermination and Cultural Affirmation

Valérie Amiraux

At first glance, nothing seems to distinguish Germany from other European countries such as Great Britain or France. In these three countries, the national labour market, characterised by full employment and increasing demand for labour in the early 60's, led to the same process of recruitment of foreign workers. Indeed Germany presents the classic chronological profile of a host country, with a recruitment of foreign workers beginning in the 60's (in 1961 the first Turks arrived in Germany as a consequence of a treaty between the two countries)[1] and ending in the 70's (1973 is the year immigration ended in Germany, 1971 is the year of the Immigration Act in Great Britain, and 1974 the year an end was imposed in France).[2]

Nevertheless, Germany has always been treated as a separate "model" in Europe which differs from British communautarism and French so-called "jacobinism" where there is no intermediary between the citizen and the state. This German particularity refers to the very strict definition of German nationality dating back to 1913 and based on blood (*jus sanguinis*) so that becoming a German citizen is still today easier said than done, even with the recent reforms (in 1990 and 1993).[3] But the *jus sanguinis* process is only one of a wide range of variables (Todd, 1994). As far as history is concerned, a nation-building Germany is still perceived as a "differentialist assimilator", as a nation desperately looking for unity. Since 1989-1990 and Germany's unification, the country has been trying to create a real and stronger national unity while at the same time still maintaining and even reinforcing a differentialist segregation towards foreigners which,however, does not lead to group separation as in the United Kingdom.

For a long time, dealing with the reality of migration in Germany meant a big political contradiction, so that we can say that the German political agenda was largely concerned with economic topics while it was admitted and recognised by politicians that Germany was still not a place of immigration. This contradiction between reality (guest-workers filled a gap) and political discourses (Germany is not a migration country) continued until the creation of the *Ausländerbeauftragte* in Bonn in 1978. The 1979 report by Heinz Kühn, the first person in this office, finally clarified the idea that Germany was *de facto* a place of immigration and that the German government had to work on the integration of second generation immigrants. Islam is one part of the ensuring debate and it became a public issue on two occasions. The first took place at the end of the seventies in certain *Länder* debating the question of education: Germany then discovered the reality of a network of Koran schools existing in the country, particularly in Schlesswig-Holstein. The second one is more recent, and concerns the "Islamic activists": a list of "Islamist groups" in Germany was published in the 1994 report of the *Bundesverfassungschutz*, which included several Turkish and Kurdish cultural and religious associations.

Two problems arise concerning Islam in Germany. *Firstly*, the "German" Islam is mainly a Turkish Islam. 28,6% of the foreign population are Turks, that is to say 1,854,900 Turks are living in Germany, of whom 1,324,875 were said Muslims in 1987.[4] Islam is therefore certainly ethnically clearly defined, but there are a great variety of trends in Turkish Islam, so we cannot speak of a homogeneous religion. *Secondly*, it is very difficult to find statistical research on Islamic matters in general, as we had in France since 1989 (large scale national surveys haing been realised there in 1989, 1990 and 1994 on topics like Muslims in France and the Gulf War, Muslims in France and the "veil affair"). It is generally admitted that statistical information like official census data only partially answers the questions of social scientists. For example, the German census data do not include precise information on religious affiliations.[5] M.S. Abdullah, referring to data from 1987, speaks of 1,7 million Muslims living in Germany, 75% of whom are Turks. According to his report, 30% of the Muslims in Germany regularly attend religious services ("*regular observers*"). Only 10% are members of religious organizations; 22% only occasionally visit a mosque (Abdullah, 1989: 440).[6]

We have chosen to focus in our work on three major Turkish-Islamic movements[7] which we have selected because of their quantitative importance and the fact that they represent the range of trends in the Turkish Islam of Germany. These groups only concern Sunni Muslims.[8] The first is the *Avrupa Milli Görüs Teskilatlari* (AMGT), which considers itself (in the words of its General Secretary, Hassan Özdogan[9]) as the "*biggest non-governmental Islamic association*" in Germany. The other two are the *Islamische Kulturzentren* (IKZ) connected to the Süleymanci order and the *Turkisch-Islamische Union der Anstalt fur Religion* (DITIB), which conducts religious affairs in the name of the Turkish government.

While studying Islam in Germany, we are not trying to describe the situation of a network of groups,[10] nor are we studying the religious behaviour of the Turkish population in general. We have attempted to analyze the way in which the presence of Islam has been redefined since the middle of the eighties, paying particular attention to the strategies directed towards Muslims and other strategies addressed to the German society. With this in mind, we have combined an institutional approach with biographies, and chosen four domains (the family, school, place of work and sports clubs) to observe how Islamic values on the individual level are confronted by German social constraints on a daily basis. That is why we have chosen to work in particular on these three organised groups (AMGT, DITIB and IKZ), which differ in their conceptions of power, politics, and religion, but are presented as "institutionalised" simply because they are official organizations. We were also able to work on an organisational level and approach the individual persons through members of these associations. This combination of two different methodologies allowed us to derive three theses which we will develop here.

First of all, the reorientation of the strategies of behaviour of the main Islamic associations dates back to 1985-1990, which is not specific to Germany and corresponds more generally to the coming of age of the second generation. The same process emerged in Great Britain with the "Rushdie Affair" (Lewis 1994) and in France with the "veil affair" (Kepel

1994). *Secondly*, our study shows *the increasing importance of transnational issues*, that is to say, of the interaction of two models (German/Turkish) concerning the development of an autonomous Islamic identity. *Thirdly*, at the same time, *a growing individuation process* appears more and more clearly among the members of the associations we have studied, revealing an arguably definitive *rupture between the political and cultural/social identification of Islam, as well as between the collective and the individual interests*.

The historical evolution of Islam in Germany

In order too understand the stakes of the Turkish Islamic organizations in Germany, it is necessary to get a view of both the historical evolution of religion in Germany and of Islam in Turkey. Since the Turkish Constitution came into effects on 5th April 1928,[11] Islam is no longer the official state religion of Turkey. Atatürk needed four years (1924-1928) to gradually modify all important religious expressions in order to create a secular state: forbidding religious education, adopting European civil and penal codes, weakening the power of the ulemas and changing such social and cultural symbols as the alphabet and the calendar. These statements essentially concerned the so-called dogmatic orthodoxy of Islam, which Bernard Lewis distinguishes from the popular and mystical brotherhoods (*tarikat*). Concerning the *tarikat*, Atatürk reacted later (1925) to their latent and still important influence, confiscating their properties and closing the monasteries (Lewis 1988).

Generally, we can summarize Atatürk's goal of secularity as an attempt to make religion disappear from state life, without aiming at a non-religious society in Turkey. Two administrative offices had been established by 1924. One was the *Diyanet Isleri Resisligi* (Directorate for Religious Affairs), whose president is directly appointed by the Prime Minister. Islam thus became a department of State, but religion no longer had a political stance in Turkey. If religion regained its political influence and power, immigration would profit by it. With the Turkish political repression (particularly after 1970 and 1980), Germany appeared for some representatives of the Islamic community in Turkey as a refuge. AMGT and the IKZ immediatly moved "officially" to Germany: the IKZ in 1973, and the AMGT in 1976. And this exactly at the time of the 1973 end of immigration which ultimately changed the connection between labour market needs and foreign workers, thus destroying the legitimacy of their presence in Germany.

The German Basic Law clearly explains in its article 4[12] that there is no Church connected to the State, but in social life, State and Church are partners in several domains.[13] The special position of religion in Germany stems from the status of the *Körperschaft des öffentlichen Rechts*, given to the churches which rule and administrate their business autonomously. They have for example the right to levy taxes (*Kirchensteuer*). In the case of Islam, religion was seen on a pragmatical level by the German authorities: Islam as a factor of social regulation should not have been criticized in a country where 8 to 9% of the taxes are given to the churches.[14] Especially because immigrants take over all responsibilities for their religious affairs, and particularly the financial ones.

All political organizations that had difficulties in Turkey moved to Germany. This is not only true for Islamic groups, but also for the left-wing and right-wing organizations (Özcan 1989). The host-country gave them a legal opportunity to continue, to ameliorate and to redeploy their activities. The Turkish population in Germany has since inherited a variety of social, political and religious trends reflecting Islam in Turkey itself. This network is bringing about a synthesis of Turkish and Islamic elements. It corresponds to the legal restoration of the traditional religious tendencies which exist in Turkey. We can divide this reconstitution into three periods. Between '61 and '73, Turkish guest-workers needed the right to live out their religious codes (the demand was very basic and mainly concerned prayer-rooms and halal food). From '73 to '85 Islam was transplanted to Germany for political reasons and the host-country became a place of political-religious activity impossible to conduct in Turkey, then from '85 to '95, we can speak of a differentiation process with the reassignment of roles.

AMGT's origins for the most part lay in Turkish political parties. For reasons of non-conformity with the national requirements of secularism, the National Order Party (*Milli Nizam Partisi*[15]), originally created on

26.01.70 by lawyers, engineers and theologians, was prohibited in 1980. Since 1976, the AMGT has been established in Cologne, where for a variety of reasons it was easier to develop political activities (nonetheless directed toward Turkey). AMGT may be seen as a subsidiary of the Turkish Welfare Party (Refah Pertisi), the Islamic Party which had considerable electoral success in March 1994, winning more than twenty towns and cities including Ankara and Istanbul.[16] While the RP is generally known in Turkey for campaigning for the rehabilitation of the Islamic identity of the Turkish State, in Germany the leaders of the AMGT, comprising 30 branches and 200 sister organizations,[17] aim to secure the status of a *Körperschaft des öffentlichen Rechts* for Islam.

Since they represent a mystical rather than political tendency, the branches of the Süleymanci are usually referred to in Germany as *Islamische Kultur Zentren* (IKZ). From 1925 onwards, they have organized their main activities in Turkey around the education and religious training of young people.[18] This specialisation still has the support of the IKZ's considerable network of Koran schools throughout Germany: IKZ offered some 1,500 courses for 50,000 Muslim pupils (Özcan 1989). They are portrayed as professional religious educators.

DITIB is the "official" Islamic organization in Germany. In Turkey it manages the religious affairs in the name of the State. Therefore, DITIB officials are state employees. In Germany, where DITIB first appeared in Berlin in 1982 (in Cologne in 1985), its representatives are controlled by the Turkish Consulates. Today it is responsible for 16 cultural associations, and officially claims to have almost 100,000 registered members. One of its primary roles is to control what it considers "Islamic deviance" (IKZ and AMGT essentially), especially in Germany since the 80's, on behalf of the Turkish secular state.[19]

All these associations moved to Germany with collective purposes: they address themselves to a community of believers, to a group of migrants. The first period of urgency (building mosques, opening prayer-rooms, creating *halal*-businesses) helped to create a collective space with an initial effective communitarian basis. The network of associations which emerged during the seventies worked as an intermediary in setting up a logical strategy for re-establishing the collective identity which was not recognized as legitimate in Turkey. It survived until the early 1980's, more precisely until the transplantation of representatives for the DITIB in Germany which corresponds to the first real intervention of the Turkish State in the field of migration. Since 1982, when DITIB installed itself in Berlin, each of the associations has begun broadening its strategies.

Choosing new strategies

If we try to describe the three orientations those associations are representing from the point of their creation until the middle of the eighties, we may use the Weberian classification. In Weber's view, domination refers to a way of commanding and obeying and to the belief of those who believe in the validity and legitimacy of this system. AMGT uses a legitimacy derived from a traditional-legal domination based on the popular belief that the Turkish Islamic tradition has been illegally pursued in Turkey in the name of the secular republican ideal. For IKZ, however their way of action is much being determined by a legitimacy based on charismatic domination. Moving to Germany, DITIB clearly benefits from a legitimacy derived from legal domination. Its power derives from law, obedience to rules and submissions to the Republican order. At the same time, DITIB tends to become the victim of its own legalism and loyal obligation towards the Turkish state, especially as regards the question of German's naturalisation process: DITIB, official representative of the Turkish government, does not have the possibility, for instance, to encourage its sympathizers to take German citizenship such as AMGT does.

Distinguishing those three categories of legitimacy helps to put limits on the discourses and actions every protagonist uses. In DITIB's case, the confusion between legal order and legitimacy (attributing some form of inherent characteristics to laws) is the *sine qua non* condition of its range of possibilities (bureaucracy, civil servants and education of religious personnel). Actually, in aiming at achieving political power, AMGT is moving to this type of submission to rules which are capable of immediate legitimation.[20]

Transplanting these different interpretations of Islam from Turkey to Germany meant, as we have said, reproducing in a certain way the political and religious situation in Turkey. While satisfying the first migrant generations, the coming of age of the second generation (which was socialised in German schools, for instance[21]) changed the situation considerably so that progressively all groups had to respond to a lack of legitimacy unknown until then. "*How to translate a residual Muslim identity into a self-consciously Islamic identity is the challenge facing the Islamic thinkers and leaders in the 1990's.*" (Lewis 1994: 178) While mosques represent the largest investment by Muslim communities to preserve religious and cultural specificity, there has also been a proliferation of often complementary and overlapping associations and organizations reflecting diverse political allegiances, especially from 1985-89 onwards. These new strategies mainly imply a widening of the classical proposals, in particular regarding sports, education, music and women's groups.

What do we observe since 1989?[22] In his book on Great Britain, Philip Lewis particularly insists on the language issue, explaining that the English language is becoming more and more the vernacular language among the religious groups of "British Muslims". This is not so relevant in the case of second generation migrants in Germany, where Turkish is still the major language of those associations. A representative member of a mosque in Wedding (Berlin), looking for a new Koran teacher, explained how difficult it is to find a *hoca* who is able to combine an Islamic knowledge with the ability to speak German. They recently found somebody meeting these criteria....but because he was German, he did not speak Turkish and unfortunately could not take part in the administrative meetings of the main organization.

The big change derived from the extent to which associations began to address the youth in new ways: a) changing the nature of their proposals and b) addressing the youth in the sense of a stricter and far reaching social control, leaving the strict communitarian basis of its origins. As Abdullah says: "*Since 1989 the German Islamic movement has unexpectedly become more active.*" (Abdullah 1993: 23) showing that the reality of the settling down process has been understood and that the aim of social control is becoming efficient. Several examples illustrate this action of the Islamic network of associations involved in education or sport.

In 1989, the Islamic Federation of Berlin *Islamische Föderation Berlin*, very similar to AMGT opened the *Islam Kolleg*. This is the only Islamic primary school in Germany and it has been officially recognized by the Berlin Senate in November 1995. Surviving by means of self-support in the beginning, the Islam Kolleg offers a classic program similar to German schools but also includes religious education, and the teaching of Turkish and Arabic. The teachers are from different backgrounds (German, Arabic, Turkish) and are not always Muslims. All courses are taught in German. In addition to this *Islam Kolleg*, two (and very soon three) Islamic kindergartens are now working under the direction of the Islamic Federation of Berlin. Education has always been a great source of friction between Germans and Muslims, and the case of Berlin is very particular due to the Clauses of Bremen (pertaining to Berlin and Bremen), which deny religion the status of a "*Lehrfach*" (compulsory subjects) in public schools, although this is not the case in other *Länder*.[23] On another level, the IKZ centre for the education of *hocas* in Cologne opened a women's section in 1992, completing the existing boarding-school for male students and offering a three year study course. The institute gives IKZ the possibility to recruit adequate persons (particularly with experience of living in Germany and proficiency in German, which is not the case of the Ditib's imams) to teach in their mosques.

Concerning sports, we wish to mention here only two initiatives. The first is a women's initiative: in 1985, M.A. and her sister founded a sports association reserved for Muslim women who wanted to play sports. This association offered ball games and self-defence; the women also went together to swimming-pools where they could swim in specific clothes respecting their religious beliefs. A second initiative, *Hilal Spor*, was founded in 1987 as a football club which today participates with more and more success in the local league (there are 300 members in the 12 to 40 age group). Islam is not presented as the main reason for the foundation of the club. In both cases, the aims were only to fill a gap, mainly because Germany did not offer Muslims the opportunity to practice sport with respect for Islamic traditions. So we cannot assess that religion is the motivation for creating such sports associations, but in the end Islam benefits from it.

Providing adequate personnel (IKZ's initiative), developing appropriate organizations (youth and women in several domains), meeting the needs of the faithful (education, language)... we have of course not given a complete list of all the new organizations founded since 1989. The main stake is, then, to connect the Islamic proposals to a cultural and linguistic world which is today different from that of the parents. The inheritance of the first initiatives in the religious field were clearly not to manage in the long-term. At the same time, the main demands stay generally the same: easier access to German citizenship (which is no longer the first priority, particularly because of the two new laws passed in 1990 and 1993), getting the same status as the other religions, that is to say, becoming a *Körperschaft des öffentlichen Rechts* (priority number one). But the stability of the discourse depends on an adaptation to the new "clientèle", at least for the most independent groups, such as AMGT and IKZ. Even our incomplete description shows how Ditib is increasingly becoming the victim of its own ambiguous status. On the one hand, it is responsible for religion in the name of the Turkish State and the official partner of the German State in many cases. On the other hand, it is, in fact, the less active of the three groups we mentioned, always trying to imitate the others' initiatives. After the creation of the Islamic primary school in Berlin, *Diyanet* suddenly offered to have a similar initiative. To date, we have not seen any other Islamic school in Berlin, despite the fact that, as the main interlocutor for German administration and politicians, *Diyanet* received money from the Berlin Senate to provide religious courses on Islam. Ditib's strategy is mainly a passive one.

All these changes have to be understood not only as the result of a "settling down process" (and as a reaction towards it to maintain a cultural continuity) but also as a conscious response of the associations in order to restore their own credibility by offering a broad range of urban experiences and playing a dynamic role in the urban environment. They aim at redefining Islam in Germany while giving it a new sense and legitimacy as a religious reference, both on a collective level (reaching a real institutionalisation *id est* a legal status) and on a personal one, in order to keep Islam alive as a personal life-option in Germany. At present the Islamic associations work on their political legitimacy in the host-country with the help of a strong cultural religious identity. The collective political project, such as that of the *Refah Partisi*, is still relevant concerning the aims of the associations living in Germany, but with a strong individual basis.

The new basis of Germany's Islam

The transformations we have just described seem clearly to depend on the context: "*The huge investment in a proliferation of mosques is one dramatic indication of both a Muslim commitment to stay in Britain and a determination to pass on to their children their religious and cultural values*" (Lewis 1994: 19). Muslims do not feel secure in their self-made world of pseudo-institutions they have exported to Germany to serve their interests. This shows that, although it has always been described as institutionalised (in the sense of organised), the network does not work perfectly as an institution in Durkeim's sense of the word as "*socially efficient constraint*".

Two paths of thought underlie the redefinition of the Islamic presence in Germany; several loyalties are mobilised through the reorientation of the Islamic proposals: loyalties to parents, to Germany, to Turkey, religious practices and religious feelings. The first is a *transnational* issue, resulting from the historical construction of the Islamic network in Germany and from the German attitude towards the presence of Islam on its territory. The second concerns the undeniable *process of individuation* amongst the young generation socialised in Germany. These two points lead us to a further interpretation of the strategical reorientation we have observed among the associations.

What we call a "transnational" influence characterises a space without national, territorial or political limits, and which is not controlled by a state (whether German or Turkish) and is ultimately defined by its autonomy. Two levels can be distinguished. On the one hand, Germany treats the presence of Islam on its territory as a Foreign Affairs issue, even after more than thirty years of co-existence. The change came recently from the publication by the *Bundesverfassungschutz* of a list giving the name of the principal so-called "extremist Islamic groups" in Germany. Among them appeared the AMGT. On the other hand, the Turkish Islamic network of associations in Germany obviously suffers from its own political overdetermination resulting from historically strong ties with Turkey.

Tolerated by Germany's laws, Islam is therefore not recognised as a part of society. Furthermore, the political aspect and the lack of a consensually representative Islamic institution does not allow Germany to find a partner in Islamic matters. So the stake of judicial identification as *Körperschaft des öffentlichen Rechts* is intended to let Islam become a part of the public identity. In this case, the representatives of Islam could have cultural and legal independence. The result would be a kind of political neutralisation of Islam in Germany and a rupture in the perception of Islam as a transnationally determined issue.

To the present day, Germany has chosen DITIB as a partner for questions dealing with religion, reinforcing the extra-territorial character of Islam in Germany. For example, DITIB received 173,800 DM from the *Senatsverwaltung für Schulen* in Berlin (Berlin Senate education department) to give courses to Muslim children after school.[24] Apart from the will to see Islam remain a Turkish issue (administered by Ankara's government), it is clear that the secular implication represented by the DITIB guarantees Germany that Islam will be contained within the private sphere. For instance, AMGT and IKZ are also working in a "transnational" perspective via their internal organizations. This mainly concerns the circulation of personnel (imams, educators) and money. The political opposition between the different tendencies does not make any sense outside of Turkey, yet still survives both because of the German attitude and of Turkish influence. Furthermore, today this transnational determination is no longer the only privilege of the Islamic organizations. Recently an *Ausländer* party was set up for Germany (*Demokratische Partei Deutschlands*) which had its first informal meeting in Dortmund last May. This *"fifth column of Ankara"*, according to a journalist in *Der Wochenpost*, has been founded officially last autumn on the basis of 500 members. At the same time, a new constitutional agreement gave people the right to vote and to be elected whilst living abroad. This new Turkish political party is presented as the consequence of the unsatisfactory attitude of German political parties towards the Turkish position vis-à-vis the Kurds in Turkey.

So the political aspect of Islam addressed to the community of the believers in Germany survives in this trans-national dimension, directed towards Turkey but organised in Germany. At the same time, the coming of age of the second generation and the reopening of the political possibilities for Islamic tendencies in Turkey changed the relation between the associations and the young Muslims living in Germany. The result is that this political orientation of the Islamic groups is no longer satisfying people whose lives no longer revolve around Turkey.

An obvious individuation process: dealing with the German reality

The goal of an association is mainly to integrate individuals. On the other hand, it is the identification of the members, with the institution which legitimates its unity. The dichotomy between the collective (primo-migrants network) and the individual projects (individual persons growing up between the strict German citizenship laws and the Turkish influence) arises precisely in this dimension. This phenomenon appearing nowadays corresponds to the distinction between demands for power (political issue in Turkey) and the wish for identification (cultural issue in Germany), as far as we consider religion as a cultural phenomenon and the individuals as "lieu de leur culture". "*The modern Western notion is that religion is voluntary or affiliational, an act of faith. As a delayed result of the Reformation and a direct result of the Enlightenment and the French Revolution, the right to choose one's religion was recognized. Religion passed into the realm of affiliation one could enter or leave at will. Even when most people identified with the religion given them at birth. Outside the West, religion remained an ascriptive affiliation. For many groups, religion is not a matter of faith but a given and integral part of their identity and for some an inextricable component of their sense of peoplehood.*" (Horowitz 1985: 50)

The new orientations of the strategies we have quoted above responds to this logic, using the individuals for the interests of the community. Individuation is no longer detrimental to the interests of Islam in Germany. On the contrary, it can be regarded as its starting-point and as a direct consequence of the German so-called "politics of integration". This individuation (or way of dealing with surroundings) has been helped by two new laws in Germany (1990, 1993). Naturalisation is still a restrictive practice, but Germany was not the only country that creates obstacles: Turkey had always been restrictive in terms of dual-nationality. Before 1995 it was necessary for young Turks to complete 15 months of military service in order to be able to apply for German citizenship. At the same time, Turkey confirmed that these "new Germans" do not lose any rights such as hereditary succession. Most of the members of the associations we interviewed are German Muslims today. This demand for German citizenship is particularly important to AMGT's sympathizers. The last Congress of the AMGT (3 June 1995) showed the realist attitude of the leaders regarding the situation in the host-country. "*We are proud of our deputies from Turkish origins[25].....we support them as much as possible....Even if a return to Turkey seems feasible to the first generation, the second and the third generation will decide to stay here. Following facts will clarify this.... the second generation is actively engaged in the political life*" said Osman Yumakogullari, President of the AMGT in Germany.

Looking at the Islamic issue as a Foreign Affairs issue on the one hand and considering the strict citizenship laws on the other, it can always be regarded as an identity link for the Turkish population. Firstly, it is a means of linking between two national spheres (Germany and Turkey) and secondly, it is an area for managing the survival of a religious specificity within the host country itself. At the same time, this approach should not cause any obstacles to a dynamic participation in Germany (on either economical, intellectual or political level[26]). I consider Islam in host countries to be the most relevant model of a transnational dimension that automatically leads to a definitive separation between culture (individual recomposition) and politics (the building of collective aims).

Conclusions

A new type of social and cultural activity has been created by the Islamic associations in the mid-eighties coinciding with the awakening of the objective differences between the second generation and the host society, and with the beginning of racist violence against Turkish people (Mölln in

December 1992, Solingen in May 1993). Today Islam is relatively stabilised demographically and is the third religion in Germany, but the coming of age of the younger generation of Turks is not the only explanation concerning the redefinition of Islam. Moreover, the political overdetermination of the associative network prevented the emergence of a representative for Islam in Germany.

A very strong distinction arises within the Islamic groups between the collective goals relating to Islamic identity and the individual wish of staying and living as a Muslim in Germany. The interests of the Islamic population as a whole are connected to a legal order (obtaining the same status as other religions in Germany, coming to power in Turkey) while the individual goals are much more concerned with social legitimatization (getting citizenship in the host country). In the strategies developed by AMGT and IKZ, the individuals are clearly the starting-point for every new project. It is interesting to note that this orientation corresponds to the construction of a cultural border, and not of a more religious or ethnic one. And the demand for German nationality does not contradict this tendency.

This schism between the individual and the collective level is certainly the main condition of a positive integration of Islam in Germany today. Under this condition, Islam is no longer seen by the host country as a cultural threat to its national identity, since Turkish Muslims ask for German citizenship while retaining their cultural particularities without Islamic political demands. But we may ask to what extent the choices of individuals, or at least the strict separation of political stakes (definitely directed at Turkey) from cultural issues, implies a kind of renouncement of the traditional role of religion which, in turn, refers to a universalist goal.

Notes

[1] Germany has signed labor treaties with the following countries: Italy (1955), Spain and Greece (1960), Portugal (1964), Yugoslavia (1968). The number of foreign workers then amounts to 2, 595000 in 1973 (they were 548,000 in 1961), representing 10% of the working population.

[2] The first consequence of the 1973 Law was a growth in population due to family reunification, coupled with a reduction of the Turkish working population: For the Turks, from 76,2% in 1967 to 38,5% in 1987.

1961: 67,000 Turks (60% are men, 20-40 years old)   1982: 1,580,700
1967: 172,400   1985: 1,401,900
1972: 712,300 (1970: 50% are men, 20-40 years old)   1989: 1,612,600
1974:> million

[3] Several judicial reforms were initiated concerning nationality. The most important are the one of 1973, 1990 and 1993. 1990 was indeed a facilitation of the long administrative procedure which migrants had to follow in order to become German (erleichterte Einbürgerung). The idea of a dual-nationality is also very new in the German debate on nationality and appeared for the first time in 1993.

[4] *Statistisches Jahrbuch 1994*, statistics from 31.12.92.

[5] The *Statistisches Jahrbuch 1994*, under the category "*die islamische Religionsgemeinschaft*", gives 1,422,732 Turks of whom 1,324,875 are Muslims (25.5.1987). In the *Statistisches Jahrbuch Berlin 1994*, under the title "*Religionsgemeinschaften*" there are: the Protestant Church, the Roman-Catholic Church, the Jewish Community, and the "*sonstige Religionsgemeinschaften*" containing the "*islamische Gemeinde zu Berlin*".

[6] On the 16th of June 1993, Helmut Kohl declared to the Bundestag: "*We suppose that among the more than 1,8 million Turks living in Germany (that is to say, 28% of the 6,5 millions foreigners living in Germany),... 4.000 (are) adherents of revolutionary Marxist groups, nearly 18,000 (are) extremist integrationists and more than 7,000 (are) Turkish nationalists and extremists*" (translated by the author).

[7] This article is based on a study carried out over three years concerning the three major movements of Turkish Islam in Germany, more specifically in Berlin. Several reasons justify the choice of Berlin as the place our work. The first reason is the particular East/West configuration of the city directly confronted with the problems derived from the fall of the wall: The main problem is the arrival of migrants from the Eastern countries. Another explanation lies in the notion of capital. Furthermore, most of the "German" Turks live in Berlin (138,457 in December 1993). And, last but not least, every fourth naturalization process in Germany takes place in Berlin. Here follows the number of Turks who took the German nationality in Berlin between 1986 and 1993, in number of persons compared with the total number of naturalizations in Berlin:

	1987	1988	1989	1990	1991	1992	1993
Turks	307	323	-	-	1,331	3,331	4,130
Total	2,742	3,308	-	-	7,515	9,743	9,548

[8] The Alevi movement is something very specific which we have not studied.

[9] Interview with the author, 9.04.92.

[10] Several books present such analyses (Gür 1993, Özcan 1989, Abdullah 1989 and 1993, Binswanger and Sipahoglu 1988).

[11] The previous Constitution (article 2, 1924) still recognized Islam as the official religion of Turkey.

[12] Article 4 (§1) of the German Basic Law (*Grundgesetz*) protects freedom of belief.

[13] "*The agencies divided the six main ethnic groups along religion lines. The Catholic organization (Caritas) takes care of the Catholic groups: Spanish, Italians, Portugese and some Yugoslavs. The Protestant organization (Diakonisches Werk) is in charge of the Greeks. And the union organization (Arbeiterwohlfahrt) is responsible for working with Turks and some Yugoslavs.*" (Katzenstein, 1987: p.225)

[14] That is to say 8,7 billion DM for the Catholic church and 8,6 billion DM for the Protestant church in 1992.

[15] 11,8% at the legislative elections (October 1973).

[16] Evolution of the vote benefiting the Refah Partisi (official party since 1983):

1984: 44% (local elections)   1991: 17% (legislatives)
1987: 7,2% (legislatives)   1994: (local elections)
1989: 8,9% (local elections)   1995: (legislatives)

[17] M.S. Abdullah estimates they have 25,000 members and 85,000 sympathizers.

[18] In October 1983, 909 associations belonging to the Süleymanci helped pupils with their homeworks in Turkey.

[19] Concerning Ditib, M.S. Abdullah lists 90,000 members and 300/400,000 sympathizers.

[20] Actually AMGT in Germany deliberatly chose to develop this legal option: last year M.S. Abdullah produced a Gutachten (expert opinion) for Stuttgart's mayor (he was asking some informations concerning the real activities of AMGT in Stuttgart) which was in reality a plaidoyer defending the organization.

[21] On 30 September 1990, the Turkish population living in Germany was described as follows:

0-17 years old: 35,7%   50-54 years old: 6,0%
18-20 years old: 7,6%   55-59 years old: 3,0%
21-29 years old: 19,9%   60-64 years old: 1,1%
30-39 years old: 11,5%   65-... years old: 0,5%
40-49 years old: 14,9%

Source: Federal Office for Statistics, (SEN F., 1994: 276).

[22] 1989 is evidently a major year in German history. In the immigration field, it is also the beginning of an increase of the flow from the East. In 1989-90, Germany accepted more refugees than any other European country (1991: 256,112, in France in 1991: 47,000).

[23] The court of Karlsruhe passed the Law, that the 35,000 crucifixes in Bavarian class rooms contravene the Basic Law (August 1995).

[24] As other example, the Land of North Rhine-Westfalia chose to let the State Ministry for religious affairs organize Islamic courses.

[25] Leyla Onur and Cem Ozdemir.

[26] As an example, we may evoke the growing importance of Islamic Union candidates in the elections for the councils of foreigners (*Ausländerbeiräte*), such as in Cologne or Hannover. It is now possible to conceive of a political role for Islamic movements in Germany.

3

Public Spaces, Political Voices:

Gender, Feminism and Aspects
of British Muslim Participation in the Public Sphere

Pnina Werbner[1]

During the first week of February, 1994, members of the Al Masoom Trust, a Pakistani women's organization in Manchester, met with three British Members of Parliament in quick succession.[2] The meeting, it has to be stressed, was unprecedented, it was a first for members of the Al Masoom Foundation and a first official meeting between British MP's in Manchester and representatives of a women's organization in the city.

To understand the significance of these meetings and of the narratives articulated in them requires an understanding of past political struggles in the Manchester Pakistani communal diasporic arena. We need from the start to recognise, however, that we are dealing with a moment of transition, a moment in which, in Ricoeur's terms, a new 'text' is performed, a moment of history in the making.

By the time of the meeting with the third MP the story of Al Masoom, the moral narrative of its collective identity, its representational reality, had been established. Mrs. Khan the president and leader of the association, rehearsed and perfected her tale from one encounter to the next. The centrepiece of the narrative was a heroic tale of courage and sacrifice. The women had twice undertaken the arduous and risky journey overland from England through Europe to the border of Bosnia, bringing medical supplies, food, clothing, bedding, toys and even an ambulance to the refugee camps on the outskirts of Zagreb. This heroic narrative which was retold anew in every encounter with each new MP, was not simply verbal - it was an embodied narrative. It was objectified by the women themselves who gathered around the MP in Mrs. Khan's living room, all of them elegantly dressed in splendid shalwar qamiz outfits, the founding members of the older generation seated along with the 'youth wing', all glowing with health and enthusiasm, and wreathed in welcoming smiles for the distinguished visitors. It was objectified by the large room packed with goods ready to be sent on the next trip to Bosnia: crates of clothing, sacks of rice, large tins of gee piled high, individually wrapped and sealed parcels of clothing and toys, each to be given away as a gift parcel for aid to a refugee child. The parcels had been prepared by the women with loving care. Embodying the heroic tale was also the picture album which proved the reality of earlier trips to Bosnia. There were pictures of the refugee camps, of the children and women crowded around the Al Masoom workers who had braved the cold weather and risked their lives for the sake of their beleaguered Muslim sisters and children. There were additional pictures of Al Masoom's other activities - the ceremonial laying of the cornerstone for a children's hospital on the outskirts of Islambad, fund raising concerts held in Manchester, and so forth.

The women had prepared certain demands to make to the MPs: they wanted the issue of Kashmir raised in Parliament, and they wanted if possible permission to send a delegation from their organization to Kashmir. They wanted the local council to allocate them premises from which to work. Mrs. Khan's house is their current base - the front room stacked high with the contributions to Bosnia or Pakistan, the cupboards bursting with electrical goods given as part of dowries to poor young Pakistani brides. Every few months the organization sends a container to Pakistan packed with dowries. Each dowry includes a jewellery set, an electrical good, several outfits, shoes and a bag. These are distributed in Pakistan. All this activity is objectified in the two dimensional photographs which the MP's are asked to gaze at as Mrs. Khan tells the tale of Al Masoom from its foundation in 1990 to the present. She focuses on positive achievements, glossing silently over the internal political challenges and obstacles the organization has faced since its inception.

To the critical anthropologist, certain dimensions of this encounter are evident: the women are relatively affluent and the meeting is a symbolic one: the three MPs, official representatives of the Her Majesty the Queen, are legitimising by the very presence the right of Al Masoom to exist. But whereas the first observation, in recognising the class origins of the women, seems to deny their representativeness, the second observation problemitises that sociological evaluation by raising the possibility that the women are, in fact, representative in a critically important sense: they are agents of change in a gendered war of positions. The women have been accused by members of the Pakistani community in Manchester of all manner of cheating and chicanery. It has been said that they confiscate funds supposedly raised for charity, that despite their claims, they never did go to Bosnia, that Mrs. Khan, their leader, is a corrupt embezzler, masquerading as a philanthropist working for the common good.

At stake, in other words, is an ontological, existential battle. Put very crudely, the issue is one of diasporic Pakistani women's right to act and speak in the public domain in Britain, in what I want to call here the diasporic public sphere. Before going on with my narrative, let me pause to reflect a little on the kind of theoretical framework implicit in my analysis.

Migration and settlement entail more than mere cultural displacement or reproduction. They entail acts of cultural and material creativity. Pakistani public social spaces and symbolic discourses, like their material and organizational embodiments, have all had to be created from scratch. Given that the community is not a single unity, these symbolic creations are often contested, as various factions within the community compete for hegemony or resist the emergence of new groups which threaten establish hierarchies, of authority and subordination. The foundation of Al Masoom represented a challenge of this type to the established symbolic contours of the Pakistani immigrant diasporic public sphere and its various public arenas and official discourses. The challenge was to the dominance of male ethnic leaders in the community and their monopoly over fund raising and charitable work, as well as over the right to meet British and Pakistani dignitaries.

The clash has to be understood as a clash of discourses, of legitimised ideologies and of cultural worlds. We may think of Pakistani postcolonial identities both in Britain and in Pakistan as having been forged by the intersection of several discrete and quite unlike transnational, lived-in cultural worlds, each cultural world with its associated discourses and modes of practice. Most intractable has been the clash between the world of puritanical Islam and a Westernised modernity with its stress on individualism and hedonistic consumerism. But a further clash is equally significant for Pakistanis: this is the clash between puritanical Islam and what is often dubbed 'Hindu' aesthetics (but which in reality is shared throughout North India across Islam, Sikhism and Hinduism) of popular culture, music and celebration, much of it controlled by women in domestic spaces (Werbner

1990: Chapter 9). These ideological clashes have spawned a semiotic field of struggle around the central issue of the position of women in Islam. As Badran argues in her discussion of the history of Egyptian feminism, the struggle has been for the legitimacy of differing and opposed:

'Definitions of culture, authenticity, identity and modernity - and their implications for women's roles' (1991: 207).

Muslim women in the colonial and postcolonial era have been caught in a structural contradiction. The contradiction is between their perceived role as living embodiments of a threatened Islamic authenticity - of traditional values under attack from external colonial and postcolonial forces and ideas - and their conflicting role as participants in the national struggle for independence or economic development. In this latter struggle they deploy precisely the modernist ideas and modes of action which their role as symbolic embodiers of 'tradition' denies. The result of this aporia has been the discursive production by women in the Muslim world of a wide range of intersecting and often inconsistent discourses. These range from an Islamist feminism which advocates strict veiling and separation, and yet at the same time espouses feminist public activism against the secular state, on the one hand, to a strong secular women's anti-fundamentalist movement, on the other. In between these extremes is a liberal modernist Islamic discourse, represented, for example, by the work of Fatima Mernissi, who, like the Islamists, goes back to the early Islamic sources but does so in order to prove the liberal message of Islam which is denied by the Islamists.

One very familiar narrative in this array of discourses is a syncretic Muslim feminism which does not deny Islam or Islamic values but nevertheless demands the safeguarding of women's rights along with a demand for equal rights of participation in the national arena and the public sphere. This particular discursive strand has, both in South Asia and in the Middle East, been the platform of primarily urban middle class women who enjoy all the privileges of their class. Their positioning in the elite has led one critic, Ayesha Jalal, to attack their lack of radicalism, and to argue that they collude de facto in their own disempowerment, even though, as she also recognises, these elite urban women have been in the forefront of struggles for women's familial rights and for the right to greater participation in the public sphere (Jalal 1991).

I want to suggest that running like a threat through all these different, contradictory and cross-cutting discursive formations is a singular slogan and (in the Sunni world) a single exemplary figure. The slogan is that Islam accords equal (if according to some, complementary) rights to men and women. The exemplary figure is that of A'isha, the Prophet's young wife who outlived him by some 40-50 years and was, at one time, the commander of an Islamic army in its battle with a dissenting Islamic faction. A'isha is known for her boldness and her wisdom - she is a source of many of the authentic traditions (hadith) about the Prophet's life and his sayings - and also for her courage and independence. She never remarried and hence lived her whole adult life as an authoritative actor in her own right.

The women members of Al Masoom are mostly devout Muslims who pray five times a day and fast on Ramzan. The majority speak better Urdu than English. Only the younger generation of women born and bred in Britain speak fluent English and even they speak Urdu and continue to wear traditional shalwar qamiz, and to follow traditional urban life styles. But although Mrs. Khan, the founding member and president of the organization, has taught Koran and Urdu in afternoon madrassas, there is, on the whole, little interest among the women in returning to the foundations and sources of Islam. They are not fundamentalists. The light chiffon scarves they drape elegantly around their necks and use to cover their heads only when praying, signify their place in the South Asian Islamic religious spectrum. Nor are the women real experts on the Shari'a, Islamic jurisprudence, the Koran or the Hadith. Their knowledge of the early days of Islam is gleaned as much from popular magazines or the press, and from discussions among themselves, as it is from the classical texts. So when the women evoke the idea of the equality of women in Islam and their equal right to participate in the public sphere; or when they invoke the figure of A'isha, the first woman of Islam - they are invoking commonsensical embodied truths, truths which, although they seem axiomatic to them, are denied by some of the community's menfolk, though not usually their husbands, whether (as they see it) out of ignorance, provincialism or (more likely) self interest, rather than out of any privileged knowledge of Islam.

But this commonsense feminist understanding of their equality with men is relatively new in Manchester. The Pakistani ethnic public arena has in fact gone through a radical transformation in the 1990s during which the authority of Pakistani male elders and their monopoly of communal public space has been openly contested. Very roughly, three historical phases mark the transformation of the diasporic public sphere. The first phase, between about 1950 and the mid-1980s, was a period of communal reconstruction and consolidation dominated by first generation immigrant Pakistani men. This was the period in which the central mosque was built through communal fund-raising and donations, and in which alternative public arenas such as the Pakistani community centre and the municipal council's race unit were founded. It was also a period in which nationalist parties and Islamic sectarian groups were forming in the city, leading to a proliferation of male dominated associations and ultimately, to the purchase of dozens of small sectarian-based mosques in the city. During the whole of this period, Pakistani welfare associations dominated by men liaised with the British state and its representatives, including British MPs. As an aside it needs to be pointed here that the British constituency system means that local MPs created surgeries, that is, office hours, for immigrants to consult them about individual problems, and many of these MPs were also involved personally in specific immigrant deportation campaigns, lending their authoritative voices to the pressure on the British Home Office to grant specific immigrants citizenship where anomalies in the law had surfaced.

Pakistani women had no representative voice in any of these associations (although throughout this time a left wing radical Labour councillor from Gujerat in India sat on the City Council). It was only from the mid-1980s onwards that the monopoly of older men came to be increasingly contested by women and, to a lesser extent, by young men. The 1990s has witnessed the partial capitulation of exclusive control by men, and with it the emergence of a gendered and familial Pakistani public space of voluntary action. This space, I have argued elsewhere, is also a space of 'fun', that is, marked by gaity, transgressive humour, music and dance. In this paper, however, I want to concentrate on the wider political dimensions associated with the emergence of a more gendered diasporic public space.

The early 90s appears to have been a critical historical moment of transition. Among some of the older women there was concern to create ways of incorporating the younger generation, growing up in Britain, into Pakistani activities, for fear of losing them to the wider society. This is the context in which Al Masoom was formed. The *Al Masoom* Foundation ('Of the Innocent' - a term often used to describe young children) was formed in

Manchester in response to this challenge by a Mrs. Kaifat Khan and her husband. Mrs. Khan had moved to Manchester from Oxford where she had been involved for many years in voluntary activities, serving as the Vice Chairperson of the Oxford CRC and chairperson of APWA, the All Pakistan Women's Association, which she had co-founded with the Pakistani ambassador's wife. During these years she was involved in various campaigns, first to set up Koran schools and mother-tongue classes in Oxford, then to bring pressure to bear on a local Girls' Grammar school to accept Pakistani pupils, and later to collect clothing and fund raise for disasters in Pakistan and Bangladesh. Her voluntary activities came up against political opposition both within the community and from the wider society.

By the time she arrived in Manchester Mrs. Khan was a seasoned campaigner with a good deal of voluntary work experience. She established the *Al Masoom* Foundation Trust to raise money to build a cancer hospital for children in Rawalpindi, the first of its kind in Pakistan. The Foundation is motivated by the Islamic notion of *khidmas* and *sadaqa* - selfless communal work and charitable giving. As part of its activities it collects clothing to be distributed to the poor in Pakistan. These are sent in containers and distributed there personally by Mrs. Khan or the voluntary workers of the Burni Trust in Rawalpindi. She explains: 'Our ambition is to help the truly poor, the street boys and girls left behind, abandoned. We collect money and clothes to give to people who have never been given anything, dowries for girls whom no-one knows are there. We have an organization in Rawalpindi. I myself go there - I sit in villages with the very poor, I live with them. We collect clothing from various parts of Britain through our networks of friends.'

Mrs. Khan's home is virtually a warehouse for all the clothing that streams in. The corridors and garage are piled high with bags of clothing. Her cupboards are bursting with tea sets, kettles and irons donated to the Foundation for distribution in Pakistan. She told me: 'We are sending a container to Pakistan in the next fortnight. I have put together dowries for twenty girls. Each receives 15 suits, 2 sets of bedding, 3 pieces of small jewellery (earrings, a ring and a necklace) and £400 in cash (collected as a donation). One suit is a wedding outfit in red. We also give a watch, a small clock, a dinner set, a tea set and an electrical appliance. We send a container

every six months, and each container holds goods worth £600,000. I myself
have given away almost all my jewellery.'

Mrs. Khan has built up a circle of devoted women voluntary workers.
Most of them come from urban middle class professional or small business
backgrounds in Britain or Pakistan, in which *noblesse oblige* (that is, *khidmat*
in Urdu) and its associated philanthropic work for the poor, is an established
tradition (see Caplan 1978). The style of funding through bazaars and shows
is itself, arguably, the product of the colonial encounter and English modes
of voluntary charitable fund raising. In 1992 the Charity mounted a mercy
appeal in a bid to raise cash to save an eight-year-old Pakistani boy suffering
from a fatal blood disease, aplastic anaemia. The boy, who had arrived in
England from Jhelum, had only a few months to live unless £37,000 could
be raised to pay for a life-saving bone marrow transplant. His sister, who
lives in Manchester, was willing to donate her own bone marrow which was
compatible with his, in order to save her brother's life.

The voluntary workers set about raising the sizeable sum of money
through a series of amateur shows and *mina bazaars* (fairs), held in school
halls in the various neighbourhoods where Pakistanis are residentially
concentrated. The very first event they held raised £3000. Mrs. Khan is a
very religious Muslim who has worked as a volunteer Urdu and Koran
teacher. All the shows held by the group at this stage were exclusively for
women and their children. Men did not attend, except as technical assistants
and cameramen. The women are careful not to be accused of un-Islamic
conduct. Nevertheless, the shows are focused around South Asian music,
dance and performance. Mrs. Khan explains: 'I believe that music is not
religiously acceptable in front of men, but it is fine when only women are
present. It is for happiness and our religion does not prohibit us from being
happy. Otherwise the events would be far too boring. Some [religious] people
are', she added, 'too extreme.' To get a flavour of the cultural events staged
by the women, let me describe one of the events I attended, which took place
in a school hall on a Sunday afternoon.

We arrive to find the school hall filling with women and children. Samusa,
rice, curry and drinks are on sale. There are stores for toys, crafts, jewellery
and clothes at the back of the hall, but the highlight of the charity event is
undoubtedly the drama put on by the women volunteer workers of *Al
Masoom*. All the parts, both male and female, are acted by young women and

teenage girls from the local high schools, who dress up as men for the male roles. This in itself creates a sense of fun and humour, reminiscent of the transvestite masquerading and joking at the *mhendi* celebrations at Pakistani weddings which I have described elsewhere (see Werbner 1990, Chapter 9). The drama this time enacts a morality tale of a young Muslim Raja seeking a bride. He wants, he says, an *intelligent* woman, but where can such a woman be found? He seeks the advice of his *wazir* (advisor). The *wazir*'s wife suggests a test: the bride will be the woman who can answer the riddle - how can a live chick be born of a cooked egg? It is rumoured that the daughter of a *pir*, a saint living in a remote area is very intelligent, and the *wazir* is sent to speak to her father. The riddle is put to him and he turns in despair to his daughter.

His daughter, however, who is indeed extremely intelligent, is not phased by the riddle. She tells her father: 'Take me to a place where the Raja goes every day.' The father takes her to the Shalimar Gardens in Lahore. She sits on the ground with a bowl of cooked rice in her hand. When the Raja passes by with his entourage of courtiers she pretends to sow the rice in the ground. The Raja is puzzled by her behaviour and asks: 'What are you doing?' The girl replies: 'I am sowing cooked rice.' 'But how can rice grow from cooked rice?' the Raja asks. 'The same way a live chicken can be born out of a cooked egg' is the triumphant answer. The Raja recognises that his riddle has been answered and asks the girl's father for her hand in marriage. There is a traditional *mhendi* ceremony. The girl is brought into the midst of the celebrating women and this is an excuse for a large number of dancing, singing and musical acts, with the girls around the bride forming an audience within an audience. The drama ends, of course, with a wedding.

The drama is followed by a fashion show of very expensive *shalwar qamiz* outfits, lent by a local sari shop, 'Eastern Collection' advertised in the programme as 'featuring the latest designs from Asia.' Young girls, the daughters and sisters of the *Al Masoom* volunteers, display the clothes in a delightful parade, imitating professional fashion models. The cost of the outfits varies from £150 to £300 and there are, apparently, no buyers. But the women in the audience are invited to come and inspect the clothes backstage and many of the outfits are sold later. After the fashion show is an auction of gold jewellery donated by women from the community. At this point Mrs.

Khan presents a giant cheque for £20,000 to the hospital surgeon who is to treat the boy. The surgeon has agreed to start treatment once the women have raised this initial sum of £20,000. Finally, there is a raffle. I win a clock. The event has raised several thousand pounds and has provided entertainment for women and children.

Mrs. Khan writes all the dramas herself, in Urdu, and her daughter directs them. She is guided, she explains, by several simple considerations: 'When I write the plays I keep in mind that they should have culture and art, but also everyday life. They should also be a little bit funny. And they should have some kind of a message, a moral message. In this play, for example, the question was: who is more intelligent? The king or the poor man's daughter? Because the play should have some music and dancing, I usually include in it a ceremony such as a *mhendi* to provide an excuse for celebration. The women dress up as men so of course, we do make the men look slightly ridiculous.'

In another drama staged by the women at another of the charity shows the plot surrounds the marriage negotiations between an English Pakistani family and a Pakistani-based family living in Pakistan. The dramas are thus based on well-known Islamic fables but also on the everyday, quotidian experiences of the audience. They interrogate on one of the most important social transitions for Pakistanis - marriage - a transitional moment which catches up a family's status and honour, reflects on power relations between men and women, between parents and children, and between different classes and castes. The moral message of the dramas is an Islamic message and the entertainment is at once Muslim *and* South Asian. The two are inseparable for the audience, and this is reflected in the popular culture objectified on the stage. Mrs. Khan explains:

'We always start with a Koran portion and then a *nat* for the Prophet. Then we have a little speech. We make sure there is a little play with music and dance for entertainment. We use 'playback' (in which the singers mime the words of popular songs played on tape and pretend to sing them).'

This is only one event of many the women have staged over a period of several weeks. During this period they have raised £27,700, virtually all of it from ordinary members of the community. Their appeal is directed at the less affluent Pakistani families in Manchester and they themselves are astonished at the fund of good will they have uncovered. When they first tried to approach the business community, the wholesalers and manufacturers, the big retailers and restaurant owners, but they have, with one exception, failed. Their appeal has been greeted with the words: 'Have all the men died in the community?' (i.e. why are women fund raising?).

There have been attempts to discredit the organisers and to demand that they hold public elections for office, a thing most male-dominated associations assiduously avoid doing themselves.

On the face of it, one would expect the women's efforts for such an obviously worthy humanitarian cause to be greeted with praise by community leaders, and to be supported by the Pakistan High Commission. But instead of support, established community leaders and organizations have actively boycotted the events held by the women and harassed them severely, in an attempt to sabotage their association. The High Commission told the women that the High Commissioner could appear at such events only if half the money was donated to Embassy-supported charities. Mrs. Khan herself has received a number of threatening phone calls. One caller threatened that if she involved herself in this bloody show, they would kidnap her son from school. It was a man pretending to be an Englishman but she could tell he had an Asian accent. Before one of the shows, she told me, 'Somebody rang up and said: "We are sick of you, we are going to kill you." I said: "Go ahead and do it! You are a chicken! How can you kill me when you have no guts to come forward and sit in front of me? You are just a coward (*buzdil*)."' Mrs. Khan has not bothered to call the police. These people, she says, are 'just crackers.'

Quite recently, in April 1995, Mrs. Khan was approached by a large man and threatened with a knife to cease her activities. She responded by reporting the incident at a public meeting in front of a local Member of Parliament and representatives of the Pakistani Embassy.

She and her workers are determined to go on despite the attempts at intimidation. Most of the women have their husbands' full backing for their work. Mrs. Khan is a battle-hardened soldier in the field of ethnic politics and is not to be easily discouraged. Moreover, the group succeeded from the start in enlisting the support of the local press. A picture of the workers handing over the giant cheque to the surgeon treating the young boy appeared in one of the free weeklies, along with two articles about the women's appeal. The other women of the community are clearly behind them. At Burnage High School, which had suffered from a terrible racial murder some years before, the school raised £7,700 for the benefit appeal in a day of sports activities and fairs. This was the highest sum ever raised by the school.

Mrs. Khan told me: 'I will not go after the businessmen. I am not interested in them. We are succeeding without them. When our success is clear, they will come to us.'

Al Masoom has long-term plans to build a children's hospital in Rawalpindi. They already have a plot of land set aside for the hospital and have, as mentioned, held the ceremonial laying of the cornerstone in the presence of Pakistan TV and a range of Pakistani government dignitaries and members of the national assembly.

Why has *Al Masoom* emerged at this historical conjuncture? The reasons for this, I want to propose, are both local and global. The rise of political Islam worldwide has been associated in Britain with the formation of young women's associations. Of these the most significant are young women's Islamic 'fundamentalist' associations. In Britain, one unexpected attraction of such groups appears to be that they support legitimised resistance to parental authority (see Lyon, in press). In their discourses, members of women's Islamist groups reconstruct 'custom', and particularly arranged marriages, as the ignorant practice of uneducated and uninformed immigrants from South Asia, including their own parents. The Islamist rhetoric thus recognises a disjunction between the 'true Islam' and *bida*, illicit customary accretions. It is a disjunction long familiar in fundamentalist discourses elsewhere in the Muslim world as well (see Badran ibidem). This rejection of a parental doxa because it allegedly merges custom and religion is a discourse which has now, in effect, 'travelled', to use Edward Said's apt term (Said 1983). The discourse has been appropriated by other, more liberal, women's groups. In effect, the desacralization of 'custom' and 'culture' has opened up a whole new discursive space for women to define their rights vis-a-vis men as well as their parents. Within this new discourse, the subordination of women is merely a further instantiation of male ignorance of the real and true tenets of Islam. The struggle is around the meaning of Islam and of what constitutes religious authenticity. Such a struggle can be conceived of as a struggle for the control of symbolic space, voice and identity. In Bourdieu's terms:

'What is at stake is the very representation of the social world and, in particular, the hierarchy within each of the fields and among the different fields.' (1985: 723)

In this battle of positions it is not merely objective inequalities which have to be dealt with. The argument is one about the very construction of reality, the ability to set agendas for public debate, to decide what are the issues which legitimately need to be tackled. From this perspective, the fact that members of Al Masoom are primarily from privileged backgrounds is not the key issue; the point is that women as a social category require representative actors powerful enough to articulate their very presence, as agents in their own right, and to problematize their current predicaments. The women of Al Masoom, relatively well off as, indeed, most Pakistani women in Britain are compared to their sisters on the subcontinent, have the backing of their husbands and the resources of time and money to articulate this symbolic feminine public space and bring it into existence. The same may be said of the women's movement in Pakistan itself which, although small and urban based, has played a major role in the constitution and defence of women's rights, even during the Zia Islamic regime.

The need to legitimise their activities and hence their very presence in the diasporic public sphere has pushed Al Masoom to perform increasingly spectacular acts of mobilization and to reach out beyond the community to the legitimate representatives of the British state - not only Members of Parliament but local councillors and the Lord Mayor of Manchester. These representatives, wearied of the apparently interminable internecine conflicts between Pakistani male organizations in the city, caught up in inextricable and sometimes violent factional conflicts (on these see Werbner 1991), have enthusiastically welcomed the women with their positive agendas, apparent unity, ready smile, independence and commitment to philanthropic activities which strike a familiar chord in English culture. The women themselves highlight this opposition to the men in the community, and indeed to all men, by stressing that unlike men - who rape and torture women - they abhor politics, by which they mean dirty politics and factional struggles. Women, unlike men, they claim, can unite and transcend politics.

Hence we find a situation which might at first sight appear paradoxical - the ability of a marginal group (women) within a marginal group (Muslim immigrants) to reach out with relative ease to members of parliament or of the city executive. This is, in fact, however, a general feature of British political culture, related to the constituency system as a form of electoral politics which encourages contact between Members of Parliament and their constituents.

In reaching out beyond the confines of the domestic space, Pakistani women have been forced to reach out beyond the confines of their community as well, in order to seek outside recognition and legitimacy in an internal battle for collective public identity. Perhaps the most spectacular capturing of public space so far has been the coordination by Al Masoom of a 'women in black' march through the city streets to protest against the continuing violence in Kashmir and Bosnia. The women who participated came from several different women's organizations in the city. Dressed in black, their heads covered with thick black scarves, the women marched through the streets of Manchester, from its immigrant commercial centre some 3 miles to the Town Hall, shouting slogans such as 'STOP THE RAPE IN KASHMIR' and 'STOP THE TORTURING OF WOMEN IN BOSNIA', their banners in Urdu and English advertising their organizations and the reason for the procession. At the Town Hall the women were welcomed by the Lord Mayor of Manchester. Gerald Kaufman, MP, joined them midway through the march and addressed them outside the Town Hall.

This march, like the trip to Bosnia, points to another kind of reaching out - the reaching out beyond the specifically national diaspora of Pakistanis, to beleaguered Muslims everywhere. This transnational consciousness, the very real and immediate awareness of the global predicaments of Muslims, is also a feature of Pakistani male politics and the politics of the mosque. In their gatherings, the men constantly evoke the predicaments of Muslims in Palestine, Bosnia, Kashmir and most recently, Chechenia. The Muslim media, both in English and Urdu, underlines this concern. Long articles on the situation in Bosnia or Kashmir, on racism in Europe, on Palestine or Chechenia fill a good deal of space. It is significant, I think, that Pakistani women share in this transnational consciousness, and that it is an important part of the socialization of the next generation of British Muslim Asians, both boys and girls. Arguably what is happening through this evident concern with Muslims elsewhere and through the philanthropic donations for them is an ideological and symbolic recentring - from being positioned as a marginal Muslim group in the Islamic world, doubly marginalised because of the racist rejection of the Muslim community in Britain, to being at the hub of a global Muslim universe. By giving to global Muslim causes - new charities for Bosnia, Chechenia, Palestine and Kashmir mushroom daily, and especially so during the month of Ramadan which is a month of fasting and giving - British Pakistanis underline their privileged, elite status. Al Masoom has been in the forefront of this shift in diasporic consciousness, the reconstruction of identity and space which has followed the settlement in Britain.

What has been striking about the transformation in the status of Al Masoom is the naturalness with which the community has shifted from a male dominated diasporic public sphere to a *gendered* public sphere. While some leaders and groups were still questioning the legitimacy of the organization, most others were already allocating space for women's organizations in their communal ceremonies and celebrations as a matter of course. No longer rejected by the business community, the diasporic public space is now being reconstructed *by homology to the private, familial space*, as a gendered space. During ceremonials and public meetings, the women sit in groups and have their own spokespersons.

To sum up, then, I have argued in this paper that critical to the empowerment of Pakistan women in Britain has been the creation of autonomous public arenas. The voices of Pakistani women are not new. Indeed, the struggle for women's rights has been a feature of Pakistani politics in the subcontinent since independence, while the question of the 'position of women in Islam' has been hotly debated in the Muslim world since the 19th century. It is important to distinguish theoretically between the novelty of voices engaged in collective representations and the novelty of the spaces into which these voices have penetrated, and hence also the broader audiences the narratives of activists now reach. This capturing of new spaces is, necessarily, a feature of historically changing constellations of power relations. In the process of capturing a new space, Pakistani women have had to renegotiate the representations of femininity and of the legitimate forms of entertainment acceptable to Pakistanis as Muslims in the diasporic public sphere.

Yet notions of private and public, of sacred and profane, of what is permissable in one space but forbidden in another, continue to dominate the Pakistani diasporic public sphere. This was evident in the problem of representation which arose in relation to an ethnographic film made by an anthropologist, Sylvia Caiuby, of the University of Sao Paulo, about the organization. The women of Al Masoom were very pleased with the first half of the film which depicted them as political activists. They were, however, very upset by the video-representation of the party they held to celebrate the end of eid, '*chandrat*', the night of the moon, in which women paint themselves with mhendi, henna, exchange bangles and sing traditional folk songs mocking men, satirising sexuality and invoking heterosexual love. The party was an all-women party, and only the video camera intruded to record the events for a broader public. The showing of this video, including the translation of the mildly bawdy songs and erotic dances, to a wider audience, caused some distress. As a socialising agent, Al Masoom has to protect its reputation in the community, otherwise, as Mrs. Khan commented, parents will stop sending their daughters to us. The balancing act between what is legitimate and non-acceptable, between the public and the private as symbolic worlds, between male and female, is a difficult one. Male leaders are posed like wolves on the borders waiting to pounce at any unacceptable transgression.

Conclusions

The present paper has disclosed the role of Muslim Pakistani women in communal diasporic politics in Britain. Broadly speaking, it reflects upon three recent processes evident in the Islamic politics of identity in Britain in the 1990s: (i) the *visibilization* of Muslim political activism in the public sphere since the Rushdie affair; (ii) the emergence of a *transnational* consciousness and political activism among Pakistani settlers in Britain in response to human rights violations in Bosnia and Kashmir; (iii) the emergence of a *gendered diasporic public sphere* in which women's independent collective voice has to be taken seriously by men; a sphere in which women have the right to participate and speak out.

My paper interrogates the enabling processes through which a single Pakistani women's organization in Manchester succeeded in opening up a legitimate public space for Pakistani Muslim women through popular cultural activities and humanitarian aid.

I argued that in order to mobilise support, women draw on their multiple identities - as Punjabis, with a tradition of dance, music, laughter and popular drama; as Pakistani nationalists, raising funds for welfare projects and good works in Pakistan; as Muslims who identify with the plight of fellow Muslims in Bosnia or Kashmir, mobilise substantial donations for refugees and demonstrate against the atrocities suffered by women and children; and finally, as women citizens who demand equality and reject the aggressive male Pakistani style of politics of the diasporic public sphere.

The independent activism of the women, has, we have seen, met with serious opposition from some Muslim male local leaders. The male challenge has pushed the women to seek recognition and legitimacy by moving beyond the confines of their community. They have reached out, first, to the British press: their spectacular charitable works have publicised their organization and its activities, their pictures appear regularly in local neighbourhood and city newspapers. Second, they have reached out to British members of Parliament and have gained considerable support from at least one local MP, Gerald Kaufman, an important elder-statesman in the British Labour Party.

This ability of ordinary citizens in Britain to make contact with the top echelons of the political leadership is a feature of the British constituency system which expects MPs to bear personal responsibility for the welfare of their constituents. Arguably, the success of Al Masoom reveals the way Muslim feminist emancipatory politics are facilitated in Britain by the relative openness and pluralism of civil society. In this context, there is no closure of ethnic minority communities. They cannot speak with a single monolithic voice. Their subjectivities - and hence subject positions - are multiple: Pakistani women can align with other women, they can appeal to liberal journalists, to humanitarian activists, to people concerned about human rights. So too Muslim socialists reach out to other socialists, Muslim democrats to other democrats. The political imaginaries of diaspora are thus multiple and the aspirations of diaspora Muslims diverse and often conflictual.

The women of Al Massom have not asked for money from the British state. On the contrary, they demand that fellow Pakistanis donate money to Islamic transnational causes. By avoiding the kind of dependency politics in which many ethnic organizations are enmeshed, they have succeeded in capturing the moral highground and have thus opened up a space for women as equal actors in the public domain. Nevertheless, their public status remains precarious. They occupy the boundary zone where Islam, nationalism, feminist activism and popular culture meet; but whereas their political voice

rings out loud and clear, their sociality must currently remain hidden from
the prying eye of male publicity. Hence the party held by the organization
to mark the end of Ramadan, the 'Night of the Moon', *chandrat*, was closed
to Muslim men because it licensed women to dance sensuously, to express
their sexuality and to joke in a manner which might be construed as
'unIslamic'. Yet it is precisely this conjuncture of the popular and the
religious, the patriotic, feminist and humanitarian, the civic and the private,
which has enabled the women to forge their own distinctive political
imaginary of a tolerant, open and egalitarian Islam.

Notes

1   This paper is based on ongoing research funded by the ESRC, UK, in part within the
    context of a project on South Asian Popular Culture: Gender, Generation and Identity'.
    I wish to thank the Council for its generous support. A version of this paper was
    presented at the Departments of Ethnology and Folk Studies of the Universities of
    Heidelberg and Cologne, and I am grateful to the participants at these two seminars for
    their very helpful comments. Special thanks is due to Aparna Rao for her insightful
    remarks from which I have benefitted greatly.
2   All three were members of the British Labour Party and all were representatives of
    constituencies with relatively large Asian populations.

4

West-African Islam in Italy:

The Senegalese Mouride Brotherhood
as an Economic and Cultural Network

Ottavia Schmidt di Friedberg

The settlement in Italy of immigrant minority groups of Islamic faith and culture must be understood within its social and historical context. This can be summarized as follows: (1) A country of emigrants until the mid-seventies, Italy is new to immigration. Government institutions were not prepared for dealing with it: no legislation on the subject was passed until 1986;[1] (2) Until now, immigrants and natives have not yet fully developed a way of dealing with each other. They were not previously acquainted through the colonialism that brought other European countries into contact with non-European populations.[2] In other West-European nations, relations with their "colonies" have acted, for better or for worse, as a means of learning about each other. This is not the case (with few exceptions) with Italy. The absence of previous relations may be advantageous, on the one hand, because no special stereotypes or prejudices have had time to take root; on the other hand, it may be disadvantageous since a total lack of information is not a good starting point for interaction; (3) While fairly homogeneous from a linguistic, cultural and religious point of view, Italy is a country of considerable regional differences, in climate and socio-economic conditions. Founded as a centralized state, Italy is now moving towards regional autonomy.[3] In practice, many decisions are handled at a local level with the participation of local society. These local differences greatly influence the conditions of settlement of immigrants; (4) Finally, in 1984 Italy fully acknowledged religious pluralism with its revision of the Concordat of 1929 with the Catholic Church.[4]

The following points may be drawn from the above: (a) Italy has not yet planned or put into action any clear state policy on integration. Integration is left to the initiative of the individual immigrant and to immigrant groups, for whom the establishment of social networks is therefore indispensable. The absence of know-how and of a well-defined policy towards immigration puts immigrants in a very difficult situation with regard to life's practical needs (no housing facilities, exhausting bureaucratic delays in obtaining papers, etc.). On the other hand, immigrants are not faced with a predetermined mode of integration. They can struggle to participate in negotiating and creating a way of life suitable to them;[5] (b) Rather than the law in itself, it is its local application that counts. Even more important is the impact of the local economy (with its labour shortage or surplus) on local decision-making. Questions relating to the settlement of immigrants and every-day Islamic practice are handled not so much at the central government level as at the local level; (c) Owing to the recent arrival of Muslim immigrants, the question of Islam cannot at present be separated from the question of immigration. The number of native or naturalized Muslims and of second-generation Muslims is for the moment very small.

The above-mentioned considerations will be further discussed using the Senegalese Mourides as an example.[6]

In Italy, the Senegalese are the most significant immigrant group from Sub-Saharan Africa, numbering about 25,000 "regulars" and an undetermined number of "irregular" and "clandestine" immigrants.[7] The Senegalese make up about 50% of West-African immigrants and about 10% of the Islamic presence in Italy. Emigration started in the eighties, and today Italy harbours the second largest Senegalese settlement in Europe, after France (A.M. Diop 1993). In France, Senegalese belong to different ethnic groups and different Islamic brotherhoods, but in Italy we find a much more homogeneous group. The great majority, at least 70%, belongs to the Wolof ethnic group and to the Mouride Islamic brotherhood.[8]

Confronted, on one hand, with a total lack of facilities for immigrants and, on the other, with relative freedom, the Senegalese quickly realized the importance of self-organization, both for survival and for dealing with Italian institutions and society. Those belonging to the Mouride brotherhood already had their own network: it was just a question of adapting it to new conditions. Some were able to join Italian networks, establishing a link with trade-unions, while others, stressing their ethnic origin, organized *fulbe* networks.[9]

The Mouride brotherhood, a local, end-of-nineteenth-century offspring of a widely known Sufi brotherhood, the *Qadiriya*, is one of the most important contemporary expressions of Senegalese Islam.[10]

From the beginning of this research it was realized that the brotherhood is not unconnected to the management of Senegalese emigration. The *Muridiya* represents a very efficient, yet loose and fluid, network. Through its first emigrants, pioneers of a sort,[11] the Mourides were able to organize the departure of migrants from their home country and to help in providing jobs and shelter upon arrival in Italy. More important, they provided knowledge of Italy and Italians. A sort of step-by-step method of integrating into Italian society has thus been established. Upon arrival in Italy, the young Mouride disciple is given lodging in a community house and introduced to the job of peddling. Peddling can be practised by anybody, regular or clandestine, skilled seller or non Italian-speaking new-comer, with a relatively small amount of risk. Later, when he is better acquainted with the new environment, he may find a job as a labourer.[12]

The Mouride brotherhood works as a network of solidarity (mutual aid association) and mutual insurance (Salem 1981), providing help in case of sickness, legal and judicial problems, etc. The brotherhood, first of all, fills the void left by Italian institutions in dealing with the practical needs of immigrants. As the contrasting case of Moroccans shows,[13] immigrants lacking organization and choosing individual integration may experience severe difficulties. But assistance to newcomers is only the more obvious aspect of the Mouride network, which endeavours also to preserve Senegalese Islamic culture and values, while adapting their practices to new conditions. Young and newly-arrived Mourides do not experience a severe cultural shock: a sort of intermediate society has been created for them in Italy, where Senegalese customs, such as eating together from the same dish or relations of respect between age groups, are observed. The newcomer lives in the community for the first part of his stay or, if he wishes to, for the whole of it. Another important aspect of the Mouride network in Italy is the social control it imposes on the disciples. Not only Italian law but also the brotherhood operates sanctions against departures from acceptable behaviour: the brotherhood will withdraw its assistance from drug-dealers, etc. To be abandoned by their own group is a severe penalty which is strongly avoided by the Senegalese.

In leaving each individual free to choose his own way in life, and while not underestimating personal improvement and success, the network never forgets to stress the link with the society of origin, constantly reminding the disciple of his duty to his relatives in Senegal and to the brotherhood. Money is regularly collected from the disciples and sent to Senegal to aid the brotherhood, for example to pay for religious ceremonies or for new buildings in the Mouride capital, Tuba. The link with the society of origin is maintained and reinforced through weekly gatherings for prayer or chanting and the periodic visits of Mouride sheikhs, who come from Senegal for this purpose. Through their sermons, the sheikhs keep disciples in touch with their home culture and values. These sermons also stress the need to avoid clashes with Italian law and society.

While they make efforts to keep emigration temporary and foster the turn-over of disciples abroad (family reunion has the lowest rate among Senegalese), the Mouride leadership is well aware that some of them will not return. Lack of jobs in Senegal and marriage with Italian women can make it difficult to return home.

The Mouride leadership, in the meantime, faces the following new dilemmas: 1) How to maintain the personal link between sheikh and disciple if the latter stays away many years or, worse, is Italian born? How to deal with the second generation, educated in Italy and non-Wolof speaking? 2) How to succeed in converting non-Senegalese, considering that Mouride Islam is deeply rooted in Wolof culture? 3) How to keep up the flow of money to Senegal? As we can see, economic and religious issues are closely linked. Since its beginning, Mouride Islam has stressed the importance of work as a path to salvation and as a substitute for prayer for those disciples who are less cultivated and less mystically inclined. In Mouride Islam, work and prayer are two sides of the same coin.

In the short run, how do the Senegalese and Mourides manage to organize themselves in Italy?

Overall, they maintain their ethnic and Wolof-tinted brand of Islam. In Italy, "Mouride" is still synonymous with "young Senegalese Wolof male immigrant", despite firm denials by some leaders. During their weekly and annual gatherings, prayers, chants and speeches are held in Wolof and the few Italian or non Wolof-speaking converts present just have to put up with it. The fact that no Mouride books are available in Italian is not considered a crucial problem. Mouridism is still heavily ethnically bound and linked to oral tradition. *Griots*[14] play an important role as the "voices" of the sheikhs.

Official discourses assert the link with the wider Islamic world. No disagreements with, or official positions towards major inter-ethnic Italian Islamic organizations (mostly headed by Arabs or Italian converts) are known to be held, but interaction is kept to a minimum. Sunni Muslims and especially Arabs do not usually approve of many aspects of Mouride Islam, while the Mouride leadership finds it difficult to give way to a more *umma*-oriented and less home-oriented Islam. The number of Senegalese Mourides attending prayer in inter-ethnic prayer-rooms or mosques is small, whereas Mouride gatherings easily number several hundred people.

In Italy, the Mourides have all the characteristics of a community. A leadership is known to exist, even if it keeps aloof. Experienced individuals with a good knowledge of the Italian language and Italian customs are promptly singled out as middlemen between Italian society and the brotherhood. To Italians, the Senegalese Muslims give the impression of being very different, though not in a threatening way: their brand of Islam is considered by many "reassuring" and "non-fanatic".[15] People appreciate their sense of solidarity and their group cohesion and they often value the Senegalese happy-go-lucky view of life. These elements help to establish local relations, and Italians generally like the Senegalese. They are skilful in face-to-face relations, and therefore fit quite well in local Italian society, where this is also important. While few Italians are interested in helping an immigrant with his papers or in renting him a flat, many are ready to do so for friend Modou or Ibra, locally known as a "correct" and reliable person. In this way, if rules and laws fail or are wanting, local relations can help to fill the gap.

A strong feeling of temporariness pervades Mouride organizations. Mourides have their own patchwork geography of Italy. They concentrate in the areas where the first peddlers or labourers found good living conditions, while in other areas they are absent. Often small centres are more important to them than big cities. They adopt the town where they live, and it is not unusual to meet a Senegalese presenting himself as Oumar of Pisa or Abdou of Brescia. Local dialects and accents are learned. They cultivate relationships with local authorities, trade unions, and even the Church. They negotiate with the local society through their middlemen. Police and social workers ask these middlemen for advice every time a problem involving the Senegalese arises. Local associations with cultural and/or social purposes are founded with Italian help and participation. When a sheikh comes, the local town or village Council will often help find a conference room where a large number of people can gather, and local newspapers and television will report the gathering.[16]

Besides Mouride circles (*da'ira*), local "lay" Senegalese associations have been founded, often with the help of CGIL, one of the major Italian trade unions, strongly linked to the former Italian Communist Party. People belonging to the *Fulbe* ethnic group and language have founded their own associations, putting together people from different West-African countries, though the majority are of Senegalese nationality - *Fulbe* are Muslims but rarely Mourides.[17] Mouride circles and local *Fulbe* associations prove to be more vital, if not always more efficient, than their corresponding lay associations. With the passing of time, the know-how acquired by "lay" associations (within which are many Mourides) has slowly been transferred to Mouride associations. Moreover, while a distinction between national and religious or ethnic associations is clearly drawn, the network can be one and the same. The same individual may belong to two or more associations, while belonging to the same network. The same middlemen can act and speak sometimes as a Senegalese and sometimes as a Mouride.

At the national level Senegalese and Mouride organizations have proven less effective. In this broader context, person-to-person and day-to-day relations do not suffice. Continuity is required as well as long-term projects and knowledge of Italian law and politics. Furthermore, the aims of national associations are much less obvious to the average disciple than those of local associations, and thus the level of participation is lower. The wide-spread idea that the Mouride's stay in Italy is temporary also plays a role in the lesser interest in national associations.

In 1989 a Senegalese national association, the CASI (Coordination of Senegalese Associations in Italy), was founded, uniting all Senegalese individuals and associations despite ethnic and religious differences. The CASI is a "lay" association for purposes of mutual aid, of spreading Senegalese culture and folklore and of improving the position of Senegalese in Italy. It was supposed to coordinate the existing regional associations and to help in founding new ones, but after a period of popularity, the CASI is now struggling for survival.[18] Its initial success must be ascribed to the promulgation of the law on immigration (the Martelli law, no.39 of 1990), which made it possible to regularize the position of the Senegalese already staying in Italy; once this need was accomplished, people lost interest in the CASI. A link with Italian organizations was established through relations with the CGIL trade union. According to some observers, the necessity of national coordination was felt more by Italian institutions and by some westernized Senegalese middlemen than by the majority of Senegalese immigrants. According to others, the bond with CGIL was not welcomed by many. Thus, a lay association on a national scale proved less efficient than ethnic or religious networks with a strong local base.

Relations with other West-African groups and associations are not particularly developed. Burkina-Faso and Ivory-Cost immigrants say that the Senegalese are aloof. While it is not unusual to find Burkina-Faso, Ivory-Coast and Guinea immigrants sharing the same shanty-town and establishing a common prayer-room, this is never the case with Senegalese.[19]

In the national arena Mouride organizations have not emerged formally: they are unknown to Italian institutions and have not acquired legal status. Local Mouride circles (*da'ira*) are linked together and keep constantly in touch with one another, but no national coordination of *da'iras* is known to exist. Important Mouride gatherings are sponsored by a long list of local organizations, while no national-level organization is mentioned.

In the nineties a debate arose among Italian Islamic associations as to how to benefit from the law on religious minority rights:[20] no project or statement was developed on the subject by the Mourides, but an agreement between Islamic associations will be necessary to make a concordat with the State and to acquire official status.

While Mouride organizations seem to fail in acting on a national level and while the Senegalese lay national association suffers for lack of participation, transnational relations are well developed. Besides the obvious link with the country of origin, relations exist with Mouride or *Fulbe* settlements in Europe, both for economic and religious or cultural reasons. Mouride middlemen and leaders travel continually throughout Italy, Europe and Senegal. This helps build family or brotherhood networks which overlap two or more European countries (Salem 1981). For example, a *Fulbe* having legal problems in Italy may have money collected for him in Belgium. Regional transnational networks are known to exist and require further research: Sardinia and coastal Spain; northern Italy, French-speaking Switzerland and southern Germany; Piedmont and southern France, etc. Internal Western-European borders are not considered a hindrance. When a religious or an ethnic meeting is organized in an Italian town, intellectuals may be invited from Switzerland, France, the Netherlands and even the United States. There is a constant flow of money, goods, persons and ideas. Finally, Mouride sheikhs seldom organize a visiting tour in a single European country, but more often slowly move from one Mouride centre to another through Spain, France and Italy. The transnational character of the network makes it more resilient and flexible, more apt to survive the failure of one local settlement or drastic changes in local economic or social conditions. Problems arising in one area can be overcome or compensated for by success in another area: for example, if working or living conditions deteriorated in France, disciples can move to Italy or Spain.

The likely performance and the survival of the Mouride network in Italy over the long run is less clear. Should Senegalese and Mouride immigration prove permanent, the leadership will face many challenges: (1) First of all, they will have to deal with the competition of inter-ethnic Islamic organizations. To presume that Italian-born or Italian-educated Senegalese will abandon Islam seems improbable, while the preservation of their fidelity to Senegalese sheikhs and to the Mouride brand of Islam is less obvious. Contact with other Muslims, distance from Senegalese Wolof values and acquisition of Western life-styles might undermine loyalty. One can already observe a loosening of the bond with the original culture among the disciples who are more integrated into Italian society. Some of them are already neglecting many aspects of Mouride community life; (2) Becoming open to converts will also mean a "desenegalization" of Mouride Islam. The religious elements that characterize sheikh Ahmadu's message and its universality will have to be emphasised and teased out from its ethnic specificity. The spread of his message[21] outside West Africa will also cast doubt on the legitimacy of the claim to hereditary leadership by his sons and descendents. On the other hand, community organization and economic success may help the spread of Mouridism.

While to other Africans (Muslim or non-Muslim) and to Black Americans,[22] sheikh Ahmadu's message has an appeal as the message of a Black African "saint" (Carter 1991), to Europeans the appeal of Mouride Islam owes more to the Wolof culture of solidarity and easy-going life-style than to its Islamic principles.

Mouride intellectuals, and some leaders, are fully aware of the challenges westernization, modernization and emigration are posing to their brotherhood.

Conclusions

In Italy, the political activity of Muslim organizations is just beginning. In practice, it is much less important - and much more difficult to organize - than economic and cultural activity. Furthermore, an economically well-off and culturally strong group or association can achieve results without pursuing any official political activity. Like many other immigrant associations, at the moment Mouride associations are more interested in day-to-day concerns than in long-term policy. This may prove a handicap in the long run. But considering its regional structure and the local differences within Italy, local initiatives and local integration can have an indirect impact at the national level. Some immigrant groups seem to understand this quite well and work hard for local integration. Quite different solutions to the question of integration might therefore be adopted by different groups, or by the same group in different Italian regions, in one area inclining towards community integration and in another towards individual integration.

The Mourides seem to understand the above-mentioned points and the need to develop an efficient network at the local and transnational levels, ignoring for the moment the national level. In Italy more than elsewhere the Senegalese Mourides have been driven by the lack of facilities for immigrants to rely on their own form of organization, while in France the Mouride network has lost some of its importance and its efficacy over time with the increasing integration of individual immigrants. Right now this is not the case in Italy. Growing uncertainty in the European context may make the Mouride network and other similar networks stronger, steering them towards community organizations, where religious as well as cultural values and practices are fostered. On the other hand, institutional facilities that promote integration may loosen the ties of the brotherhood, while favouring less ethnically-specific brands of Islam.

Notes

[1]   Two laws regulating immigration have since been issued, no.943 of 1986 and no.39 of 1990.

[2]   Italy's colonial experience was too short and too limited (with the exception of Eritrea) to have had a widespread impact on Italian social and cultural values.

[3]   Today, regional autonomy is acquiring an ever increasing importance.

[4]   Freedom of religion is granted by the Constitution. The law no.121 of 1985 fully regulates the relations between state and non-Catholic religions. See my article with R. Leveau, 1994.

[5]   See my articles 1993a, 1993c.

[6]   Information on Senegalese networks in Italy, France and Senegal was gathered during three years of fieldwork for my Ph.D. Dissertation (Schmidt di Friedberg 1994).

[7]   "Irregulars" are immigrants who transgress Italian laws on immigration, residence and work permits; "clandestines" are immigrants who have no documents whatsoever. See my article, 1995.

[8]   See my Ph.D. Dissertation, 1994.

[9]   Ethnic networks can be observed also among other West-African immigrants, such as Bissa of Burkina-Faso. See my article, 1995.

[10]   The Mouride brotherhood (*tariqa*) stems from the preaching of sheikh Ahmadu Bamba Mbackè (1850-1927), a learned, ascetic and peace-seeking scholar of Islam, at a time when the Senegalese society was facing severe disruption of traditional values and leadership and was confronted with colonial domination. His preaching provided Wolof (Baol) society with new moral and social values while fostering the survival of peasant society through the organization of agricultural labour. While stressing the importance of asceticism and Islamic learning, sheikh Ahmadu acknowledged the fact that these were not within reach of the average disciple. The majority of Baol society, still deeply rooted in traditional, non-Islamic values, was constrained by the practical exigencies of daily life. A compromise was thus arranged. Stressing the fact that work is a substitute for prayer, the common disciple was invited to practice total obedience to the sheikhs and to work for him and for God, while the sheikh dealt with prayer, fasting and the management of Baol peasant society.

[11]   Many of the Senegalese interviewed have stressed the fact that Italy and Italian society were unknown to them. Italy was compared to the American West, an unknown country where fortune could be found, but at some personal risk and

appealing only to the young and the adventurous.

[12] About 60% of the Senegalese regular immigrants in Italy today are labourers.

[13] See my article, 1992.

[14] The repositories of oral history and the orators of Wolof traditional society.

[15] See my Ph.D. Dissertation, 1994.

[16] This was the case, for example, during the Mouride Islamic Week in Brescia in may 1993.

[17] They often belong to the *Tijaniya* brotherhood.

[18] Lack of participation can be seen, for similar reasons, in other immigrant associations.

[19] See my article, 1995.

[20] See my article with R. Leveau, 1994.

[21] Sheikh Ahamdu is reported to have said that his message is for all human beings and to have invited his disciples to spread it "over the seas" (A.M. Diop 1985).

[22] Today the U.S.A. is becoming the stronghold of the Mouride emigration movement (Carter 1991; Ebin-Lake 1992; Ebin 1993). Apart from immigrants, the brotherhood is spreading among black Americans. A Mouride Islamic center is known to exist in New York.

PART II

Attitudes Towards Political Participation

5

Loyalty to a non-Muslim Government:

An Analysis of Islamic Normative Discussions and of the Views of some Contemporary Islamicists

Wasif Shadid and Sjoerd van Koningsveld

During the last years several scholars have attempted to qualify the position of Muslim minorities in contemporary Western Europe and their institutions in the terminology of the classical Islamic Law. In doing so, these scholars claim to give expert interpretations of the norms and values of Islam which have direct relevance for the social, juridical, and political position of Muslims in non-Muslim secular societies. Because of their political nature these interpretations may, in the end, exercise great influence on the daily life of the groups concerned in all the societies of Western Europe. The opinions to be discussed refer, by way of example, to Belgium, Great Britain, Germany, France, Europe in general, and North America.

Our first example is related to the role of the mosque in a non-Muslim, West-European society. The Belgian anthropologist of law, Foblets, attributed to the mosques in Belgium "a role in the preservation of identity in front of the non-Islamic space of the host-country (*Dâr al-Harb*)".[1] *Dâr al-Harb* ("the Territory of War") is a concept derived from the classical Islamic dichotomy of the world into *Dâr al-Islâm* (the "Territory of Islam"), on the one hand, and *Dâr al-Harb* ("the Territory of War") or *Dâr al-Kufr* ("the Territory of Unbelief"), on the other. In the section on *Siyar* or international law of classical Islamic jurisprudence, the quoted dichotomy plays an important role, especially in relation to war and peace. This dichotomy is also significant in terms of the position of Muslims who, for one reason or another, happen to live outside the "Territory of Islam". The image of the mosque in Belgium which is portrayed by

Foblets by qualifying Belgium as part of the so-called "Territory of War" is that of a safe haven in the midst of an ocean of enemies. This image tends to legitimize the negative view of the mosque which exists among many members of the non-Muslim majorities, because it tells us that the surrounding society is perceived, from within the mosque, in a hostile manner, as well. Foblets does not base her interpretation on references to any Islamic sources or to any other kind of information obtained directly from Muslims in Belgium.

The second example is related to the efforts of British Muslims to have Rushdie's book banned on the basis of the existing laws on blasphemy in Great Britain. According to Ruthven, it was "somewhat ironic that Muslim activists have tried, so far unsuccessfully, to have *The Satanic Verses* banned under Britain's arcane blasphemy laws, laws that would originally have condemned them as heretics. Under Islamic law they do not have a leg to stand on: the classical jurists would tell them that they were living in *Dar al Harb*. Their duty is not to uphold the honour of Islam in secular infidel courts, but to migrate to a country where the writ of the Divine Law still runs".[2] This view not only fails to notice the element of a struggle for equal rights in having the Christian-rooted British laws of blasphemy applied to Islam as well, but states plainly, in the name of Islam itself, that Muslims should stop their campaign to uphold the honour of Islam in the West and emigrate right away to the Muslim world. It should be noticed that Ruthven bases her view exclusively on Majid Khaddouri's study on *War and Peace in the Law of Islam*, which deals mainly with Islamic law during the medieval period, and on one medieval polemical pamphlet about the punishment of blasphemy. There is no reference whatsoever to any modern discussion of the issue. The author apparently assumes that no relevant changes concerning the issue have taken place in Islamic thought since the Middle Ages.

The third example is the advice drafted by the German orientalist Nagel about the status of Muslims in Germany, within the context of the German "Quranschuledebatte". The central issues of this debate concerned whether the teachings of Islam are compatible with the German Constitution and whether Muslims in Germany could be obliged to respect the German Constitution if Islamic religious education were to be introduced in German schools. According to Nagel, a Muslim living abroad, for instance in Germany, is seen [in Islam] as a *Musta'min*, which means that they are living in an area qualified by the classical tradition of Islamic Law as *Dâr al-Amân* ("the Territory of Security") or *Dâr al-ᶜAhd* ("the Territory of a Treaty"). Muslims living in such an area enjoy the protection of the State concerned. This protection is interpreted by Islam as the mutual relation resulting from a treaty. In their capacity as proteges (*Musta'minîn*), Muslims in Germany are bound by German law. "As long as the host country does not tolerate attacks on the life and property of the *Musta'-min*, the latter is obliged to respect the totality of the legal order of the non-Islamic host state, even if it would decree something which is inadmissible in the legal world of Islam".[3]

Our fourth example is related to pleas in France, directed to the French Government and the French public opinion, for the creation of a state-founded Faculty of Islamic Theology for the formation of imams and religious scholars. This Faculty should develop and teach a theology of Islam in accordance with the demands of modernity and with the norms and values of the French Republic in which Muslims are living as a minority. One of the spokesman in this discussion was Soheib Bencheikh, a Muslim modernist theologian of Algerian background living in France.[4] In a recent article on *The Theological Formation of Muslims*, he stressed that the situation of Muslims living as a minority in a multiconfessional and secular state with strong Christian influences was without historical precedent. No Sunnite or Shiᶜite legal-religious school had ever foreseen it: "How can one teach in France a theology which is derived from a division of the world into a 'House of Islam' and a 'House of War', as is affirmed by all legal schools of Islam? These are archaistic and dangerous views, elaborated during the age of the great military-imperialist conflict which used to oppose Christianity against Islam and to reduce the history of these two worlds to episodes of conquests and reconquests".[5] Elsewhere, Bencheikh repeated exactly the same argument and concluded: "Therefore, a new theology has to be elaborated; our patrimony has to be desacralized in order to discover the authentic divine message. The one that can match no matter what custom, including the French custom. It is up to us to demonstrate in France of today that Islam is really a universal religion".[6] What Bencheikh is really doing here is projecting an image of

Islamic normative thought as being hostile and dangerous to French society. His major argument is the classical dichotomy of *Dâr al-Islâm* and *Dâr al-Harb*. The French State should create a Faculty to develop and teach a completely different kind of Islamic theology.

The fifth example is the view expressed by the report published in 1987 entitled *Islamic Law and its Significance for the Situation of Muslim Minorities in Europe*. It stated that "the classical Islamic tradition had no substantial experience of Muslims living in a minority situation, since the elaboration of the mainstream of classical shariah law assumed that the normal state of affairs was one whereby a Muslim lived in a society whose structure and fundamental concepts were islamically based".[7] At the same time the report mentioned that most Muslim leaders *in Europe* today regard the old concepts of *Dâr al-Harb* and *Dâr al-Islâm* as outmoded and irrelevant.[8] In the vein of this report it is stressed by many scholars today that it is very difficult or even impossible to know the teachings of Islam regarding the position of Muslims within a non-Muslim state. The "simple reason" for this, says for instance Christie, is that, while much is said [by Islamic Law] on the treatment of non-Muslim minorities within an Islamic state, there are no specific reciprocal guidelines for the behaviour of Muslim minorities within a non-Muslim state".[9]

Our sixth and last example is related to North America, whereto Muslims started to migrate in significant numbers in the late 19th century. In a recent study of Islamic proselytism in the West, Poston explains that Muslim theology "divides the world into two spheres of influence: the Dar al-Islam ('The Abode of Islam') and the Dar al-Harb, or Dar al-Kufr ('The Abode of War', or 'Unbelief'). Only under special circumstances is the Muslim allowed to live for any time in a non-Muslim land".[10] "Why then did Muslims choose to immigrate to North America?", asks Poston. The answer he gives is that the closer contacts between the Muslim world and the West during the 19th century brought about a mitigation of the longstanding tradition which forbade permanent residence in Dar al-Kufr. With reference to the admiration of Western civilization by leaders like Al-Afghânî, ʿAbduh, and Ridâ, Poston stipulates that the Dar al-Harb "was no longer a 'dangerous, uncertain and annoying' place but was instead becoming a model for Muslim advance". He concludes that in this manner "the ideological and theological impediments to residence in a non-Muslim country were removed", so that "the nineteenth century Muslim was free to examine the material advantages of emigrating to North America".[11] He does not specify, however, how this removal actually took place, neither on the ideological nor on the theological level. According to Poston the availability of personal rights and freedoms in non-Muslim countries further served to break down the distinction between the Abode of Islam and the Abode of Unbelief.

From the above quoted six examples it becomes clear that there exists a great confusion among many contemporary scholars of various disciplines and backgrounds concerning the normative ideas of Islam about the position of Muslims living as a minority in a non-Muslim society or state, especially in the West. Usually, their understanding of the new and relevant developments within Islamic thought is completely absent or very superficial, at best. The purpose of the present contribution is to clarify these new developments and trends by answering the following central question: What guidelines have been developed in Islamic thought for the behaviour of Muslim minorities in a non-Muslim state?

The main historical phases during which the Islamic views concerning Muslim minorities have been developed are dealt with in the first section (**I**: *Historical Background*). We shall then focus on the contemporary Islamic discussions about the position of Muslim minorities in Western countries. These discussions are a continuation, within a new historical context, of the age-old historical tradition of Islamic jurisprudence. Here we shall first deal with the discussion about the validity, in the present time, of the classical legal-religious qualifications of the different parts of the world, such as Dâr al-Islâm, Dâr al-Harb, etcetera (**II**: *Europe and the West in Islamic Political Thought*). In the following sections we shall pay attention to specific topics figuring prominently in these discussions (**III**: *Staying in the non-Muslim World*, and **IV**: *Naturalization, Political Participation, Military Service, and Family Law*).

Historical background

Through various periods of the history of Islam specific events have provoked a series of discussions among the legal scholars of Islam about the attitude to be adopted by Muslims who were, for one reason or another, living in an area ruled by a non-Muslim government. Should they attempt to leave their dwelling places in order to migrate to a country ruled by a Muslim government or were they allowed to continue to live under non-Muslim rule, and if so, under what conditions? The different answers provoked by various historical circumstances were crystallized as precedents in Islamic jurisprudence. Incidentally, reference is made to these precedents in contemporary Islamic discussions concerning the position of Muslims living in the West.

During the *pre-colonial era* we can distinguish two different types of historical situations. *First of all*, there was the case of *individual Muslims, or of small numbers of Muslims, who were living -temporarily or for an indefinite period of time- in a country ruled by a non-Muslim government.* We are dealing here, among others, with captives of war, merchants, diplomats, and local inhabitants converted to Islam. As for the captives of war, Islamic law developed a set of rules to which they should abide, if possible, before they could safely return to their country of origin.[12] Concerning the other categories of Muslims, the legal scholars discussed, among others, the purposes for which it was allowed to travel to non-Muslim territory and the conditions under which one could stay there. Many different modalities were taken into account. In principle, though, the legal scholars of Islam accepted such a stay on the condition that the Muslims concerned were able to perform overtly the basic religious pre-scriptions of Islam (prayers, fasting, collecting and distributing alms, etcetera)[13] and that their own safety as well as that of their family was not endangered.[14] Moreover, the classical scholars of Islamic legal thought explain that such Muslims are obliged to obey the laws of the land in which they are residing. They also have the duty to respect scrupulously the condition under which the non-Islamic state granted them *amân* (safety) during their stay in its territory.[15] Here lies the historical precedent for modern Islamic discussions on respecting the rules of visa issued by Western states.[16]

The *second type of historical situation* which provoked discussions on the position of Muslims under a non-Muslim government occurred with *the conquest of sections of Muslim territories by non-Muslim rulers, where, as a consequence, the original Muslim population came under non-Muslim rule.* Examples are the Muslim communities of Christian Sicily and Spain from the 11th through the beginning of the 17th centuries.[17] It was also the case of Bosnia when, at the end of the 19th century, it was brought under Austro-Hungarian rule. The legal scholars who discussed the position of these communities, developed different views. Many of them thought that these Muslims, if they could, should leave their dwelling places and emigrate to the "Territory of Islam"; others found ways to permit them to remain, allowing them, in times of oppression and persecution, to practice the principle of religious dissimulation.[18] At the end of the 19th century, for instance, the Bosnian mufti Azapagic was convinced that the "Territory of War" would become the "Territory of Islam" if Islamic religious rites and observances like Friday prayers and feast prayers would be practised there. It would become the "Territory of Islam" even if infidels were to remain in that country and even if it were not linked to other parts of the "Territory of Islam". He therefore resisted the view that Bosnian Muslims were obliged to emigrate to Istanbul.[19] His view was supported by no one less than Rashîd Ridâ, who stressed that the "Hijra is not an individual religious incumbency to be performed by those who are able to carry out their duties in a manner safe from any attempt to compel them to abandon their religion or prevent them from performing and acting in accordance with their religious rites".[20] Such views are tantamount to legitimizing the existence of Muslim communities under non-Muslim rules under certain conditions, and they are directly relevant to the present situation of Muslim minorities in the West.

In the third place there was the historical occurrence of an even more drastic change *when Muslim governments were totally replaced (by force) by a non-Muslim government or subjected to it.* The first precedent of this situation occurred during the early years of the rule of the Mongols in the Near East. Legal scholars in Baghdad, under the pressure of the conquest of the city, confirmed the authority of the non-Muslim conquerors by signing a fatwâ which stated that "a just infidel was, in fact, preferable to an unjust Muslim".[21] On a much wider scale, however, *this was the situation during the Colonial Era.* Almost every country with a Muslim majority was affected by it. This new situation resulted in a stream of discussions concerning the relations between Muslim subjects and their respective non-Muslim governments. Some of these historical events, and especially the fate of the Andalusian Muslims, are reflected in discussions of the Colonial Era and even in contemporary discussions of religious scholars regarding the position of Muslim minorities in Western Europe of today.

First of all, there was the problem, similar to that of the Andalusian and Bosnian Muslims, whether one was allowed to give up fighting and to remain living under non-Muslim rule, or whether one was obliged to continue the armed resistance and/or to emigrate to an area governed by a Muslim ruler. This problem was discussed all over the Muslim world during the late 19th and the early 20th centuries. Ample details concerning Algeria, India, Lybia, Nigeria, and Sudan were provided by Peters.[22] The historiographer Al-Mannûnî mentions no less than five works written by Moroccan scholars on this subject during the first decades of the 20th century.[23] There are also several fatwâs from Indonesia discussing the same complex of problems related to the expansion of Dutch colonial rule.[24] In Egypt, the Malikite scholar of Al-Azhar, ᶜIllaysh -to be quoted below- also wrote an extensive treatise about this problem. He, among others, referred to *fatwâs* of the Moroccan scholar Al-Wansharîsî about the position of Muslims who had remained in Christian Spain after the fall of Granada in 1492. Al-Wansharîsî had urged the Andalusian Muslims under Christian rule to emigrate to the "Territory of Islam".[25]

The close interaction between (non-Muslim) Europeans and the Muslim inhabitants of the colonies induced a long series of discussions among the Islamic religious scholars about the issue of "assimilation to the Infidels".[26] The discussion of this issue appeared for the first time during the second half of the 19th century and still plays a certain role in some contemporary debates about the position of Muslims in the West. In the early sixties of the nineteenth century Muslim students in Paris wondered whether it was acceptable, from a religious point of view, to adopt Western dressing habits. Al-Harâ'irî, a scholar of Tunisian descent who was teaching Arabic in the *Ecole des Langues Orientales Vivantes* in Paris,[27] defended a liberal point of view in several *fatwâs* which he published in printed editions in Paris. His *fatwâ* concerning the French hat of 1862 was entitled 'Answers to the perplexed ones concerning the statute of the hat of the Christians'.[28] It is stated in its preface that the more than 300 Muslim students in Paris had various practical reasons for discussing the permissibility of wearing the French hat. In the streets and during the lectures Frenchmen were gazing at them full of astonishment because of their strange appearance. They pointed out that the wearing of the French hat had several clear advantages, since France was a very cold country and the brim of the French hat gave extra protection to the eyes. However, some of the students had stressed that by wearing this hat one in fact committed apostasy with all its consequences. Wives in the countries of origin would be divorced automatically and, after returning to the Islamic world, one would have to convert to Islam again, and to remarry officially with one's own spouse. The author, on the other hand, saw no objection whatsoever in the wearing of the 'hat of the Christians', because this practice did not imply any form of assimilation in strictly religious matters. It was only the form of religious assimilation which was forbidden by Islam.

Quite a different attitude was reflected, however, in the writings which aimed to preserve unadulterated the traditional norms of Islam. Al-Harâ'irî's *fatwâ* of 1862 was apparently sent to the Near East soon after its publication, and was brought to the attention of the orthodox Malikite scholar of Al-Azhar, Muhammad ꜥIllaysh.[29] In contrast to Al-Harâ'irî, Muhammad ꜥIllaysh defended an outspokenly anti-Western political point of view. He took part in the anti-British Urabi-revolt and died in prison in 1882. His opinion was capsulized in an unpublished *fatwâ* entitled: 'Refutation of the Epistle "Answers to the Perplexed concerning the statute of the Hat of the Christians".'[30] The author states that the "Christian hat" is forbidden for a Muslim for various reasons. First of all, one cannot perform the *salât* while wearing it due to the fact that its brim hinders the worshipper to touch the ground with his forehead during the prostration. Furthermore, as outer apparel it signifies the low position proper to Christians, but not fitting for Muslims. Thirdly, one cannot claim that wearing this hat is a matter of necessity, which could be argued if these students would be obliged to study outside their own countries. This is not the case, however, since the only sciences which are obligatory from a religious point of view are the religious disciplines. Since it is impossible for these disciplines to be studied outside the Muslim world, students should return to their countries of origin as quickly as possible: they must perform the 'emigration' (*hijra*) to the 'territory of Islam' (*Dâr al-Islâm*) and no longer commit the offence of assimilation to the Infidels.

A second problem, closely related to the issue of "assimilation to Infidels", concerned the adoption of citizenship and nationality of the colonizing state. This problem arose in only a few of the colonized countries, especially in countries of the Maghreb colonized by France. The European concept of nationality was alien to the classical Islamic legal tradition. But since the second half of the 19th century, and especially since the Law of Ottoman Nationality of 1869, it was gradually penetrating into the political and legal systems of the Muslim world. Notwithstanding occasional conflicts, this penetration can be seen, initially and to a certain extent at least, as a mere process of translating the existing social and political realities into a new legal terminology[31]. However, a completely new dimension was added in Tunisia and Algeria, when the French authorities introduced Laws of Naturalization in 1923 and 1927. These laws offered French nationality and the full rights of French citizenship to Tunisian and Algerian Muslims who accepted French civil law instead of Islamic law.[32] This measure met with fierce resistance from the side of many Muslim scholars. The scholars of the Zaytouna in Tunis issued a fatwâ which qualified the person who adopted French citizenship under the said law as an apostate. Their view was supported by similar fatwâs issued by scholars of Al-Azhar and other scholars in Egypt, among them Shaykh Shâkir, the former wakîl of Al-Azhar;[33] Rashîd Ridâ, editor of Al-Manâr; Shaykh ᶜAlî Surûr al-Zankalûnî; and Shaykh Yûsuf al-Rajawî. By virtue of this view a Muslim in the town of Binzert who had accepted French nationality was not buried in the graveyard of the Muslims. His apostasy was confirmed by the local mufti, Shaykh ᶜAlî al-Sharîf. Consequently, he was buried by the French in the section, which was reserved in the graveyard of the Muslims for foreigners and unidentified people. Other scholars, however, merely stated that he had committed a grave sin. The French stipulated the adoption of French citizenship as a condition for anyone who wanted to acquire a position of some importance in the colonial society. This was part of the French assimilation policy.[34] The arguments which were forwarded by the scholars who condemned the acquisition of French nationality during the colonial era as an act of apostasy have been repeated in several recent discussions published in France and the Netherlands concerning the subject of naturalization within the wider context of the integration of Muslim immigrants into Western European societies.[35]

All these discussions resulted gradually, to begin with in India, in the reformulation by reformists of Islamic political views. This reformulation involved, among other aspects, the reinterpretation of the jihâd as a strictly defensive institution.[36] Ultimately, such views also implied a crisis of the age-old concepts of the existence of a "Territory of Islam" alongside a "Territory of War" (sometimes also called the "Territory of Unbelief"), etc. The eventual abolishment of such concepts had, of course, major implications for the Islamically underpinned ideas about the status of Muslims living outside the Muslim world in a minority position.[37] At the same time, however, other scholars continued and still continue to formulate their political ideas with these concepts, as, e.g., the well-known scholar Nasîruddîn al-Albânî, who in 1993 urged the Palestinians to perform a *hijra* from Israël (being *Dâr al-Kufr* or "Territory of Unbelief") to the "Territory of Islam" in order to mobilize their resources and return victoriously to their homeland.[38] Other examples include the works of M.G.S. Hodgson and B. Lewis.[39]

The fourth and final stage in the development of Islamic political views concerning the relation between a non-Muslim government and Muslim subjects occurred *mainly during the postcolonial period.* It is related to *the emergence of the phenomenon of Islamism.* Influential thinkers such as Sayyid Qutb developed the idea that countries with a Muslim majority population could no longer be regarded as part of the "Territory of Islam", since their present legal system was mainly derived from non-Islamic, especially Western, sources which to a large extent were contradictory to the values of Islam. These countries had in fact fallen back into a situation of "Heathendom"; their governments lacked legitimacy from a religious point of view. A re-islamization process of society and government was to be broached, principally through various forms of preaching and participation. At the same time, however, some offshoots of the Islamist revival movement defended the use of violence for the same purpose.[40] Similarly, there are examples of groups pleading for the performance of the duty of "Emigration" (*hijra*) from the society which they consider, for various reasons, as having become a "Territory of War" (*Dâr al-Harb*). Other groups propound that *jihâd* should be waged against the offending society until it is restored to *Dâr al-Islâm*.[41] Echos of these arguments may be heard in contemporary discussions concerning the position of Islam in the West, as well.

Europe and the West in Islamic political thought

Contemporary Islamic discussions which focus on the position of Muslim minorities in Western countries are a continuation, within a new historical context, of the above-mentioned age-old tradition of Islamic jurisprudence. These discussions reflect on the validity in the present time of the above-mentioned legal-religious qualifications of the different parts of the world, especially with regard to Europe and the West in general. In this respect four different attitudes can be observed.

First of all, there is the *pragmatic* viewpoint which (implicitly or explicitly) rejects the classical dichotomy while taking the existing division of the world into nation-states as its point of departure. The conviction that Western countries which have made pacts and treaties with Muslim states are no longer (part of the) "Territory of Unbelief" (*Dâr al-Kufr*) was defended and is shared by many distinguished scholars of Islamic law in the Middle East, such as Abû Zahra (1898-1974), ᶜAbd al-Qâdir ᶜAwda (d. 1954), and Wahba al-Zuhaylî.[42] This is also the implicit position of the Egyptian scholar Al-Qardâwî (to be mentioned below) and of the Malaysian scholar Doi. Doi states explicitly that it would be improper to classify a country as *Dâr al-Harb*, when Muslims within that country can uphold the principles of "enjoining good" and "forbidding evil", i.e. when they can publicly defend the moral values of their religion, and when they can perform the obligatory salat, observe the fasting, give alms, go for *hajj*, build mosques, and maintain other religious institutions.[43] On the basis of the same pragmatic position Doi applies the principle of personal investigation (*ijtihâd*) in order to develop a set of rules for the duties and responsibilities of Muslims in non-Muslim states. In doing so he often follows the example of fatwâs from India, where a similar situation applies.

Secondly, there is the *idealistic* or *utopian* viewpoint which also does not discuss the old dichotomy, but which introduces the (classical) concept of the *Ummah* to refer to the ideal of the transnational and universal unity of all Muslims in the world. An example is the position of the director of the Muslim Institute in London, Kalim Siddiqui, who expressed his views in a document entitled *The Muslim Manifesto*.[44] Nielsen explained that the Muslim Institute in London has identified itself increasingly during the eighties with the so-called "Islamic Movement", an informal conglomerate of rather closely cooperating groups who sympathised with the Islamic Revolution in Iran. Siddiqui does not refer to categories like *Dâr al-Islâm* and *Dâr al-Harb* at all. On the contrary, he makes a distinction between actually existing states (Muslim or non-Muslim), on the one hand, and the universal, transnational, "Nation" or "Ummah" of Islam, on the other. He underlines that Islam is a "political religion", which, according to him, implies that Muslims in the West, for instance in Great Britain, should develop their Islamic identity and culture as part of the worldwide *Umma*. The first step towards this goal is to create and institutionalize a unity at the national level, which was attempted by Siddiqui by his creation of a "Muslim Parliament", in 1992.[45] It is also possible, however, to speak of an Islamic *Ummah* in a national sense, viz., as a unified and well-organized community of Muslims living within one non-Muslim state. This notion can, for instance, be observed among British Muslims of South Asian, especially Indo-Pakistani, background, who thereby project their own cultural history onto the situation in British society.[46]

In the *third place*, there is the most widely spread attitude which aims at *reinterpretation of the Islamic tradition* in the light of the prevailing conditions of the modern age. This attitude explicitly rejects the validity in the present time of the ancient dichotomy of the concepts of a "Territory of Islam" (*Dâr al-Islâm*) and a "Territory of War" (*Dâr al-Harb*) or "Territory of Unbelief" (*Dâr al-Kufr*), and tries to replace it with a new terminology. Thus far, however, no consensus has been reached among the adherents of this view about the precise nature of the new terminology. This position is represented by many scholars who explicitly reject the ancient dichotomy and attempt to replace it with new concepts to be derived from the Islamic tradition. An eloquent spokesman of this view is Shaykh Faysal Mawlawî, advisor of the Sunnite High Court in Bayrout. According to him, the principle which really should regulate the relations between Muslims and non-Muslims is not strife, but preaching (*da^cwa*). The application of the classical dichotomy of the "Territory of Islam" and the "Territory of War" is very problematic in the present day. First of all, how should one define which country can be reckoned to belong to the "Territory of Islam"? If the condition would be a complete observance of the religious prescriptions, then most of the "countries of the Muslims" can no longer be considered to be part of the "Territory of Islam". The same holds true for several other countries, like Turkey, if the mere application of Islamic family law would be used as the criterium. Only if one would use as a criterium the freedom for Muslims to practise the religious ceremonies and observances can most "countries of the Muslims" indeed be reckoned to belong to the "Territory of Islam". But how should one judge, if this be the criterium, the many non-Muslim countries where Muslims live safely and practise their religious ceremonies, sometimes with greater freedom than in some "countries of the Muslims"? According to Mawlawî, it is not even possible to define exactly the "Territory of War" in the present age. In line with the terminology designed by Al-Shâfi^cî, any non-Muslim country might belong to the third category of the "Territory of Treaty" (*Dâr al-^cAhd*). In view of the existing network of international treaties, this seems to be the case of most countries. He prefers, however, to coin the new term *Dâr al-Da^cwa* ("Territory of Preaching"), which refers to the position of the Prophet and his followers before their Emigration to Medina in 622. At that time the Muslims only formed a small group which preached Islam, but they had to respect non-Muslim laws at the same time. According to Mawlawî, the whole world can be said to be a "Territory of Preaching" at the present time. If some accept the message of Islam and apply the Islamic laws, then one can speak of a "Territory of Islam"; the rest of the world, however, remains in relation to them a "Territory of Preaching".

The Moroccan scholar ^cAbd al-^cAzîz ibn al-Siddîq[47] adopted an attitude which is similar to that of Mawlawî.[48] Describing the liberties enjoyed and the numerous religious institutions (mosques, institutes, schools, etcetera) created by Muslims in Europe and America, including the preaching of Islam and the conversion of Europeans and Americans to Islam, he concludes that *"Europe and America, by virtue of this fact, have become Islamic countries fulfilling all the Islamic characteristics by which a resident living there becomes the resident of an Islamic country in accordance with the terminology of the legal scholars of Islam"*[49] Ibn al-Siddîq thus revives the old Shâfi°ite doctrine which states that *Dâr al-Islâm* exists wherever a Muslim is able to practise the major religious rites and observances. According to Ibn al-Siddîq, the safety enjoyed by the inhabitants of Europe (including Muslims) can be illustrated further by the fact that Muslims, who are afraid to profess their religious convictions in their own countries, fly to Europe as refugees from those who claim to be Muslims.[50] This vision of Ibn al-Siddîq was also adopted by Rached al-Ghannouchi, the main intellectual leader of the Tunisian Islamist Nahda-movement. In 1989, at the occasion of a congress of the Union of Islamic Organisations in France (UOIF), al-Ghannouchi declared that France had become *Dâr al-Islâm*.[51] The leading circles of the UOIF adopted this view which was to replace the doctrine, previously adhered to, that France was merely part of *Dâr al-°Ahd*.[52] This view was confirmed in 1991 by the Committee for the Reflexion about Islam in France (CORIF), when it proclaimed in a circular letter of February 1991 that France had become *Dâr al-Islâm* due to the fact that deceased Muslims could be buried in its territory in special sections of cemeteries destined for Muslims.[53]

Finally, there is the *traditionalist* view which adheres to the old dichotomy of the world into *Dâr al-Islâm* and *Dâr al-Harb*. Within the European context this attitude occupies a marginal position. A representative of this view is a Moroccan imam in Amsterdam, °Abd Allâh al-Tâ'i° al-Khamlîshî, who recently published a collection of his religious admonitions.[54] His ideas show close resemblance to those of Morocco's strict and puritanical *Sunni* movement, which is described in detail by Munson.[55] In the vein of this traditionalist attitude, Al-Khamlîshî attempts to apply the classical dichotomy to the position of Muslims in the West today, as if they were concepts valid for every time and place. The same holds true for a booklet on naturalization, published in Paris in 1989 by a certain Muhammad ibn °Abd al-Karîm al-Jazâ'irî, entitled "Changing nationality is apostasy and treason".[56]

Staying in the non-Muslim world

The second subject dealt with in contemporary discussions on the position of Islam in the Western world is the problem of the permissibility of *staying, for the purpose of work, study, commerce, etc.,* in a land ruled by non-Muslims. The participants in the discussions who follow the pragmatic viewpoint described above, take this permissibility for granted; it is a well-established fact that about one third of the total number of Muslims in the world today are living in a minority situation. From this perspective, the very discussion of the acceptability of residing in a non-Muslim country is nothing less than an anachronism and an anomaly.

According to Siddiqui Islam permits Muslims to accept protection of their life, property, and freedom by non-Muslim rulers and their political systems. Muslims who are living in that situation are allowed to pay taxes to a non-Islamic State. They are also obliged to abide by the laws of that state as long as such an obedience does not conflict with their loyalty to Islam and the *Ummah*. According to the *Manifesto*, other minorities, such as Jews and Roman-Catholics, are adopting an identical attitude. The *Manifesto* stresses, moreover, that the duty of *jihâd* remains valid, also for Muslims of the British nationality. This duty may result in active service in an armed conflict abroad and/or to the lending of material or moral assistance to those who are engaged in such a struggle for Islam, wherever they may be in the world.

The Moroccan scholar ^cAbd al-^cAzîz ibn al-Siddîq, who possesses direct knowledge of the situation of the Muslims in Belgium, published a study of no less than 66 pages on this subject in Tangier, in 1985. He addressed this subject at the request of Algerian students who had brought up the matter during his stay in Mecca in the same year.[57] They had told him about the numerous disputes on this subject in Algeria and among the Algerians in Europe and brought to his attention that Algerian legal scholars upheld contradictory views concerning it. According to the author, the view that it is forbidden to stay in countries like Europe and America is devoid of any proof derived from the authoritative sources of Islam. The rule of Islam is that it is permissible to stay in a non-Muslim country, if and as long as a Muslim can perform his religious duties overtly and is not exposed to the danger of losing his belief. The most important of these duties is the performance of prayers and fasting, and the same applies to the other obligatory duties.[58] With the conquest of Mecca, the duty of emigrating from non-Muslim territory was abrogated. Ibn al-Siddîq follows the view of the Shafiᶜites which states that a "Territory of Unbelief" becomes a "Territory of Islam" by the mere fact that a Muslim can overtly perform his religious duties in that place. According to this view, it is better for a Muslim to remain there, because, through his presence, others might accept Islam as well. Moreover, the area might lose its Islamic character again, if he leaves. The author quotes a whole series of classical authorities to substantiate this view. He reminds the reader of the early emigration undertaken by several Companions of the Prophet, by his order, to Abyssinia, a Christian land, where they enjoyed greater liberty to profess their faith than in polytheist Mecca. Moreover, while the *jihad* by the sword is no longer valid, the *jihad* by the tongue (i.e., the preaching of Islam to non-Muslims) continues to be. In this case, then, the preaching of Islam (*daᶜwa*) is an additional duty imposed on the Muslims. However, it is only possible to fulfil this duty by staying among them.[59] This was also the view expressed by Syed Abul Hasan Ali Nadwi, a distinguished Indian scholar from Lucknow, in his book *Muslims in the West*.[60] The popular preacher and controversialist Ahmad Deedat from South Africa, who frequently visits Great Britain and other Western European countries, holds a similar opinion. He argues that the only rationale for migration to a non-Muslim state was the desire to invite others to Islam.[61]

The idea of the *daᶜwa*, in fact, occupies a central position in many Islamic writings on the position of Muslims who are living in a minority situation. The Moroccan scholar Al-Kattânî analyses the duty of *daᶜwa* of Muslim minorities as their duty (1) to organize themselves, and (2) to arrange for Islamic education. It is his view that "a Muslim cannot live in the Territory of Infidelity if he fosters no serious hope that Islam will survive among his children and offspring and will be spread to the non-Muslims. If a Muslim is unable to defend and maintain his belief, it becomes his duty to emigrate".[62]

A more hesitant view, however, was published in 1994 by the editors of the Birmingham journal *Al-Sunna*, which, first of all, reproduced the opinion of the famous Hanbalite scholar Ibn Taimiyya (died 1328). According to this article Ibn Taimiyya was of the opinion that Muslims were allowed to stay wherever they wanted, including the "Territory of Unbelief", as long as they remained obedient and pious to God and they and their family enjoyed security. In addition to the opinion of Ibn Taimiyya, the journal published the viewpoints of two contemporary Saudi scholars, Ibn Sâlih al-ʿUthaymîn and Al-Jubrîn.

Ibn Sâlih al-ʿUthaymîn permits a Muslim to stay in the Land of the Infidels on two conditions: (1) the Muslim concerned feels safe in his adherence to the Islamic faith, which implies that he should refrain from creating bonds of friendship and love with infidels, which contradicts faith;[63] (2) he is able to practice openly and without any impediment the essential religious ceremonies of Islam, including the prescribed almsgiving, fasting, performance of the pilgrimage to Mecca, etc.

Shaykh al-ʿUthaymîn further distinguishes six purposes why Muslims are staying in the Territory of Unbelief: (1) to preach Islam (*daʿwa*), which is a collective duty of the Muslims because it is a kind of *jihâd*. (2) To study the circumstances of the Infidels in order to warn the Muslims against the danger of being dazzled by them. This is also a kind of *jihâd*. (3) To serve as a representative of a Muslim nation. The legal status of this stay must be judged in the light of its purpose. (4) For another specific, permissable purpose, as, e.g., commerce and medical treatment. (5) For the purpose of study, which is more risky in that it may have a detrimental impact upon the faith of the person staying there for this purpose. (6) In order to settle there, which is even more dangerous since it implies a complete intermingling with the infidels and an awareness that one is a fellow citizen who is bound by sympathy and friendship and by the obligation to strengthen the ranks of the infidels required by citizenship. Moreover, his family will be raised among the infidels. Consequently, they will adopt their manners and customs. Perhaps they will even imitate them in their belief and worship. No explicit prohibition is formulated, but it is clear that Shaykh ʿUthaymîn does not approve the presence of the last category of Muslims in a non-Muslim country.[64]

Another relevant case published by *Majallat al-Sunna* in Birmingham concerned the answer of Shaykh ʿAbd Allâh ibn ʿAbd al-Rahmân al-Jubrîn to a Palestinian who had asked whether he could stay in the USA or should return to a nation like Jordan "while the attitude of its government does not differ much from that of the governments of the Arab countries".[65] The answer was that there is no objection against staying in these countries if one is able to practice openly the Islamic faith, to earn one's living in a way which is permissable in Islam, and one's life is not endangered.[66]

According to Al-Khamlîshî (1995), the preliminary question to be answered before passing judgment about the permissibility of naturalization is whether or not it is permissible for a Muslim to live outside the Muslim world, in the "Territory of Unbelief".[67] A distinction should be made between the person who cannot partly or completely perform the prescribed rituals of his religion, on the one hand, and he who is able to perform all the rituals of his religion and fulfill all his duties, both in private and public.[68] The first person is not allowed to stay in the "Territory of Infidelity", according to the unanimous opinion of the religious scholars. In doing so, he commits a grave sin. According to the most plausible interpretation, the second person is not permitted to stay in the "Territory of War" either.[69] Apart from the Shafi'ites, the three most widely spread Sunnite madhhabs forbid staying in *Dâr al-Harb* absolutely. The Shafi'ites stipulate, however, that this residence is only permitted if a Muslim can practice his whole religion. How is the position of Muslims in Europe to be judged? Are they able to manifest their religion completely? According to the author, this is not the case. They may, for instance, have acquired permission to establish prayer halls and mosques publicly, but they have not been able to acquire permission to manifest the ritual of the prayer call in accordance with the way prescribed by the Sharî'a. In this case, they perform the prayer call inside the mosques, which is contradictory to the Sharî'a. In addition to this, even the mosques which have been built with the permission of local governments (without the right to perform the public prayer call) are not safe from various expressions of fanaticism and terrorism, let alone what would happen if they would have the right to perform the public prayer call. How many of them (the Europeans) are not warning the Muslims in writing not to adhere to the religion of Islam in these countries? How many of them are not demonstrating against the opening of mosques in their countries? In short, for a Muslim minority there will never be any safety in any place of the world, neither in its religious nor in its non-religious life, from the fanatic Infidels.[70]

Naturalization, political participation, military service and family law

Finally, attention is given in several of these discussions to the issue whether it is permitted to *adopt the nationality of a non-Muslim state, to participate actively in its political life,* to *perform military service in its army,* and to *accept the prevailing (secular) rules of its system of family law.*

Among the defenders of the pragmatic line of thought, the Egyptian scholar Yûsuf al-Qardâwî expressed his opinion on naturalization during a congress on the subject of integration which took place in France in 1992.[71] As a point of departure he stressed that Islam is an international religion, which was revealed for the whole world, as can be clearly derived from many passages of the Quran. The presence of Muslims outside the Muslim world is a matter required by the nature of this religion. The duty to emigrate from an area ruled by a non-Muslim ruler to part of the "territory of Islam" was, moreover, abrogated after the conquest of Mecca, as is clearly demonstrated by the saying of the Prophet: "There is no emigration after the conquest (viz., of Mecca), but [only] jihad and [good] intention". The prophetical saying: "I have no responsibility for any Muslim who is living among the polytheists" cannot be quoted to invalidate this conclusion, since the Prophet was referring here to Muslims among polytheists who were engaged in warfare against Islam. The presence of Muslims outside the Muslim world is a prerequisite for the preaching of Islam and can serve as a form of support for those members of the local population who convert to Islam. Moreover, these Muslims can look after the affairs of the Islamic Community in the West. If they are unified they can exercise considerable political influence. However, Muslims are only permitted to live in the West, if they are able to preserve their identity, uphold their religion, and protect their family.

As for the problem of naturalization, Shaykh al-Qardâwî proposes to weigh its positive implications against its detrimental implications. In doing so, one should take into account the fact that circumstances have changed since the Colonial Era. In the present day the advantages a

Muslim may acquire in adopting the nationality of his guest-country are, in fact, quite considerable, since it opens to him possibilities and opportunities which are equal to those of other citizens (which was not the case during the Colonial Era). In this way, the influence Muslims may exercise will also increase. As for its detrimental implications, one cannot claim, thus al-Qardâwî, that naturalization implies a kind of clientage and loyalty to infidels forbidden by the Quran. The Quran only forbids clientage and loyalty to infidels who fight against Islam.[72] This is no longer the case in the present era, which is "an era of mutual trust and peaceful settlement; [it is] the era of the symbiosis between ideologies".[73] Moreover, the Quran only forbids the creation of bonds of clientage and loyalty with infidels *instead of* with Muslims.[74] This is not the case when a Muslim preserves his original (Islamic) nationality when adopting a second, Western nationality. According to al-Qardâwî, there is also no harm in fulfilling the duty of military service following the adoption of a Western nationality. The risk of being obliged to take up arms against Muslim brethren also exists in the Muslim world itself, as can be demonstrated by recent wars between Muslims, such as the Iraqi-Iranian war or the Gulf War. Integration, involving naturalization (but without loss of religious identity), Al-Qardâwî concludes, is a desirable matter in view of the advantages which result from it for the Muslims. Possible disadvantages should be overstepped and overcome by the Muslims themselves.[75] Al-Qardâwî's view thus sanctions naturalization in Europe, particularly in the case of the acquisition of a European nationality in addition to that of the Muslim country of origin.

A similar view was defended by Dr. Syed Mutawalli Darsh in the British Muslim weekly *Q-News*, of 11-17 August 1995. First of all, he confirmed that Muslims living in Britain can take the Oath of Allegiance to the Queen. According to him, this oath "is simply putting in legal terms the real situation of the Muslims, that is, to be law abiding, peaceful, and to live in a decent respectable manner, since the Queen represents these basic moral qualities which are supposed to be the fabric of the society in which we live. So when people take the Oath of Allegiance to the Queen, they are promising to act according to the laws of the country, as happens when people are granted British nationality. There is no way for a person seeking British citizenship to avoid being loyal to the Crown and the land". When asked whether it is allowable for Muslims in Britain to join the army and even be ready to fight against fellow Muslims if ordered to do so, he first of all stressed that the British army is one of volunteers. As such, Muslims are not under obligation to join it. "But at the same time, being part of the society they live in and a citizen of the state, it is their basic duty, too, to defend the country in which they live. As far as fighting Muslim countries is concerned, supposing there is an aggressive country, as happens from time to time, when we see a Muslim country occupying another Muslim country by force and against the will of the population, and that country appeals to Britain for help, Muslims in the British army are obliged to help in much the same way as any Muslim army has to help in repelling such aggression. In these circumstances there is no difficulty. But when it comes to fighting a Muslim country for no Islamic reason, we then say that, in the light of present circumstances and under the Declaration of Human Rights, in particular the European Convention, Muslims are allowed on conscientious grounds to abstain from that fighting. But remember that once a person is a member of that society here, it is part of their duty to defend that society".[76]

A recent fatwâ of the Shaykh al-Azhar, Jâd al-Haqq ʿAlî Jâdd al-Haqq touched more explicitly upon the political participation by Muslims in Western Europe, both in elections and as members of political parties and councils. The questions posed to him by Muslims from Denmark can be summarized as follows: (1) Is it permitted for a Muslim to become a member of a secular or Christian political party in Denmark in order to become a candidate in the elections of the municipal councils (in which all residents of Denmark have the right to participate regardless of their nationality, while those who possess Danish nationality, including Muslims, can participate as candidates if they attach themselves to one of the political parties)? (2) The same question was posed with regard to the parliamentary elections, in which only Danish nationals can participate. (3) Is it permitted for Muslims to participate in the elections with their votes to the benefit of one of the Danish political parties? (4) Is it permitted to conclude an agreement with one or more political parties to the effect that the party or parties concerned pledge to take certain measures for the benefit of the Muslims if they win the lections, while the Muslims grant them their votes in exchange?

The Shaykh al-Azhar commenced his answers with a quotation from *Sûrat al-Mumtahina* (60: 5-8)of which the last verse was related by him to the situation of the Muslims in Denmark: "Allah forbiddeth you not that he should deal benevolently and equitably with those who fought not against you on account of religion nor drove you out from your homes; verily Allah loveth the equitable". This verse points to the permissibility of all kinds of social cooperation between Muslims and non-Muslims in one state. In addition, verse 5 of *Sûrat al-Mâ'ida* (4) points to the permissibility of a marriage between a Muslim and a Jewish or Christian woman, and to the fact that the food of Jews and Christians is permitted to Muslims, whether they acquire it from them by way of purchase, as a present, or as their guests. The Shaykh al-Azhar further drew the attention to several articles of the *Constitution of Medina*, ratified by the Prophet between his own followers and the tribes of Medina (including Jews), in which Muslims and non-Muslims were mentioned as members forming together one Nation. This Constitution contained 47 articles with various rules and prescriptions which structured the political order. Generally speaking, the political and administrative structures of the countries where Islam has spread in history have been widely diversified. Rules pertaining to these matters do not pertain to the category of prescriptions which have a permanent character; they have not been mentioned in detail in the Quran which means that they may change.

We are presently dealing in most states of the world with political parties who are competing with each other to rule their country. There are also many cooperative foundations and trade unions, whose purpose it is to promote social, class, or political goals connected to the proper and general interests of their members within the general context of the State. Thus, there is no objection whatsoever against the participation of Muslims in these organizations as long as those Muslims who are participating in political life as elected members of councils and parliaments do not endorse measures which are against the faith of Islam or against the interests of the Muslims. They should refrain from sanctioning measures which permit something which is forbidden by Islam or is contradictory to the principles of the Islamic creed.[77]

Doi defines joining the army in a non-Muslim state as a matter of necessity. He considers it unwise to advise Muslims living in a non-

Muslim state not to join the army. Whenever the army is deployed for the purpose of keeping internal peace, a Muslim soldier can prevent atrocities against Muslims at the hand of non-Muslims. Usually, wars are not about religion, but about land disputes, etc. Muslim soldiers will therefore have to show their loyalty to their country even if it is a non-Muslim state fighting against a Muslim state.[78] Doi does not give an explicit view on family law, but merely states that the interference of a number of non-Muslim states with the Personal Law of Muslim minorities is "the most sensitive issue" (of the list of issues mentioned by him).[79]

The *Muslim Manifesto* of Kalim Siddiqui condemned Muslims who stimulated accommodations to and compromises with British society, and who were against the decree of Khomeiny concerning Rushdie.[80] It pleaded for the establishment of a *Muslim Law Commission* which would be given the competence to decide about matters of marriage, divorce, and inheritance on the basis of an Islamic legal system. Its decisions should be recognized under British law. As is pointed out rightly by Nielsen, the *Manifesto* had, above all, a propagandistic nature: it aimed at mobilizing the younger generation into supporting the Islamic Revolution in Iran. They adopted here a claim expressed towards the British Government at the beginning of the eighties by the *Union of Muslim Organisations of the United Kingdom and Eire* (UMO)[81] of which little had since been heard, with the exception of a study in which the British lawyer Sebastian Poulter analyzed both the technical and the fundamental problems of a possible recognition of Islamic family law in Great Britain.[82] In view of the problems discussed by Poulter, the official recognition of Islamic family law in the countries of the European Union is a possibility to be excluded. A feasible possibility, however, is the institutionalization of Islamic councils of religious scholars which can give advice on the basis of Islamic Law or can suggest decisions in conflicts which could be followed and/or accepted by parties on a strictly voluntary basis.[83] This is actually what we see happening. Such Islamic "courts" can be seen as parallels of the existing rabbinical "courts" which have fulfilled the same functions in Western Europe for many years, on the basis of the religious Jewish Law. As is illustrated by a recent enquiry in France, by far the greater majority of inhabitants with an Islamic background rejects the introduction of a separate statute of Islamic family law for Muslim citizens. This idea was only supported by 17% of the people interrogated, while 78% rejected such a separate statute for the arrangement of marriage, divorce, and other aspects of family law.

Muhammad Hamidullah, a religious scholar who has been working for many years in Paris, adopted the more radical view which rejects any form of nationality based on language, common descent, etc. He states that "in Islam, the community of the philosophy of life is the basis of nationality (Islam itself being that philosophy of life)".[84] However, Muslims have insufficiently adopted this supra-regional and supra-racial brotherhood. Also, they have principles of nationality contradictory to Islam. "Naturalization is now in use among all 'nations'. But to be naturalized in a new language, a new colour of skin, a new fatherland, is impossible without a more or less humiliating form of renunciation, and it is not so genuine as adhering to a new ideology. Among others [i.e, non-Muslims], nationality is essentially an unavoidable accident of nature, but "in Islam is a matter that depends exclusively on the will and the choice of the individual [viz., by believing in the Islamic faith]".[85]

In a similar sense Raza states that "every Muslim must have two sets of identity. This first set of identity will be with Allah, His Messenger and Islam. By virtue of this identity the Muslim will belong to the *Ummah* (community), which is the global Islamic community, irrespective of any national and international boundaries. (...) In terms of Islam, the *Ummah* (community of Islam) exists first, which can then lead to the creation of the Islamic state. The second set of identity will be with the state of which they are naturalized citizens. Muslims are expected to become good citizens of the country in which they are resident, and follow its laws".[86] Raza stimulates British Muslims towards political participation in order to improve their circumstances. He also discusses the possibility of being persecuted as a Muslim, in the same way that the Jews were persecuted in Nazi Germany. According to him Muslims have, in this case, three options: to migrate, to fight the state through its political system, or "to wage a political struggle through legal means". However, "in Britain the first and the third option are not applicable because no Muslim is being persecuted as the Nazis persecuted the Jews. Such options are applicable in many Muslim states from which Britain's Muslims may have come".[87]

Finally, according to Al-Khamlîshî, the Muslim who has adopted the nationality of a non-Muslim country deprives his Muslim mother-state of his own qualities and abilities, as well as those of his children, who will end as apostates. He or his children may be forced to perform military service and, in the end, to combat Muslim brethren of other countries. Naturalization further implies accepting the rule of foreign law. However, this law must be identified with the Tyrant mentioned in the Quran to whom Muslims, by order of God, should not give their loyalty.[88] Furthermore, naturalization implies the strengthening of an infidel nation which is forbidden by the Prophet.[89] Therefore, naturalization is to be rejected on religious grounds. This is also the opinion of a fatwâ published in Paris, whose author identified naturalization with apostasy and high treason.[90]

A recently published study of the preaching of Moroccan imams in the Netherlands shows that "naturalization is an important issue in the religious discourse among Moroccan Muslims in the Netherlands".[91] This study refers to the views of four anonymous imams, the first of whom can be identified with the already-mentioned imam Al-Khamlîshî,[92] whose sermons are now available in printed form. The other three imams show various degrees of willingness to accept naturalization.[93] Arguments transpiring in these views include: (1) Naturalization is only permitted for the sake of propagation of the Islamic faith. However, if it takes place for purposes of a more worldly nature, it does not imply apostasy automatically, especially if the person involved is able to preserve his Islamic identity and that of his children (1990). Islam is a universal religion. Naturalization enables Muslims to contribute to the propagation of the Islamic faith outside the Muslim world (1992, 1993). (2) Naturalization is a matter of papers only. It does not actually affect the (inner) Islamic identity of the person involved (1991). It is not forbidden by Quran and Sunna (1992). (3) Naturalization can be accepted as a matter of papers in a situation of necessity. True naturalization, which, among other aspects, implies the abandoning of religion, is forbidden (1992). (4) The positive results of naturalization outweigh its negative effects. Therefore, it is permitted according to one of the basic principles of the Islamic religious Law (1993).

A sociological study of the Moroccans in the Netherlands of 1979 contained a Guttman scale with eight items which not only represent an evaluation of traits of the original culture, but also the degree of desirability of change in the direction of a Dutch cultural pattern. The result of the analysis implied "that the marriage of a Moroccan girl to a Dutch man is the most difficult item to accept. The one that is next on this scale is naturalization. Reasons for rejecting the latter were nationalism and religion; answers such as 'we are Arabs' and 'we are Muslims' were frequently given. On the other hand, those who do not object to naturalization state that such a step should be considered purely instrumental; they emphasize that true feelings and identity stand apart from nationality".[94] The same study demonstrated a close correlation between the disapproval by Moroccans in the Netherlands of naturalization (both for oneself and for others), on the one hand, and of the emancipation of women, the contact between sexes, the marriage with Dutch women, and the evaluation of Western clothing for women, on the other hand.[95]

Notes

[1]   Foblets 1990, 88.
[2]   Ruthven 1991, 52.
[3]   Mahler 1989, 384-5. H.P. Füssel, "Islamischer Religionsunterricht an deutschen Schulen", *Recht der Jugend und des Bildungswesens*, 1985, Heft 1, 74-77.
[4]   Concerning Bencheikh, see Gozlan 1994, passim.
[5]   Bencheikh 1994, 58.
[6]   Apud Gozlan 1994, 177.
[7]   Cf. Z. Badawi, *Islam in Britain*, London 1981, 27: "Muslim theology offers, up to the present, no systematic formulations of the status of being in a minority".
[8]   El-Manssoury 1989, 72.
[9]   Christie 1991. See also Poston 1992, 39, who states that American Muslims received a training in the Islamic religious sciences in Cairo, Mekka, Karachi, or other such cities that "was seldom applicable to the situation of Muslims residing in the Dar al-Harb. Questions concerning how such Muslims should cope with the problems of living in a non-Muslim culture were either poorly answered or unanswered".
[10] Poston 1992, 31-2.
[11] Poston 1992, 33.
[12] Gräf 1963; Sadan 1980, 106-107; cf. Van Koningsveld 1995[2].
[13] The fixed technical expression used in this respect by Islamic jurisprudence is "izhâr mashâ'ir al-islâm", which literally means: "to manifest the signs of Islam". The precise definition and modalities of the manifestation of these signs was a subject of further discussion among the scholars.
[14] Ibn al-Siddîq 1985, passim; Fierro 1991, 13-19; Lewis 1992, 21-26; Masud 1990.
[15] Salem 1984, 150-1.
[16] See below in our discussion of the views of Mawlawî.

[17] On the Islamic statute of the Muslims living under Christian rule in Spain, see Van Koningsveld and Wiegers in *Al-Qantara* (forthcoming).

[18] Mu'nis 1957; Harvey 1975; Fierro 1991, 20-22; Lewis 1992, 28-29; Wiegers 1994, 2-11.

[19] Al-Arnaut 1994, 249-250.

[20] Ibidem, 253. Ridâ made these statements in a pamphlet he published in 1909 in his journal "Al-Manâr" concerning the situation of the Bosnian Muslims, entitled: *Al-Hijra wa-hukm muslimî al-Bûsna fîhâ*.

[21] Sadan 1980, 114, quoting Ibn al-Tiqtaqâ (writing circa 1301 A.D.), *Kitâb al-Fakhrî fî 'l-âdâb al-sultâniyya*, Paris 1895, 21.

[22] Peters 1979, 39-89; see also Masud 1990, 38-52 and Fierro 1991, 23-28.

[23] Mannûnî 1989, 148-151.

[24] Van Koningsveld 1990.

[25] ʿIllaysh 1901-1903 [1319-1321 H.], vol. 1, 313-334. Cf. the printed edition of Al-Wansharîsî's fatwâ in Mu'nis 1957.

[26] The Arabic term used in Islamic religious literature is *"al-tashabbuh bi-'l-kuffâr"*.

[27] He had been appointed *ra'îs al-kuttâb* (approximately secretary-general) of Tunisia by the Bey of Tunis in 1840. He was a specialist in the natural sciences, medicine, and mathematics. In 1857 he was 'notaire et secrétaire arabe au Consulat général de France à Tunis, membre de plusieurs Sociétés savantes de Paris, auteur de plusieurs ouvrages arabes, de traductions du français en arabe, etc.' (cf. al-Harâ'irî 1857, title-page). In the preface to this work, the translator defends, among other points, the legitimacy of social relations with Christians and Jews, including the participation in meals, if they do not wage war against the Muslims for the purpose of making them abandon their religion (al-Harâ'irî 1857, XV). He defends cooperation with the French and praises their wise and just administration and their promotion of culture and science (al-Harâ'irî 1857, XV). He lists the various kinds of French scientific books which he translated into Arabic (al-Harâ'irî 1857, XXV). He is proud of being the first to translate a French grammar into Arabic. In Paris, he edited also the journal entitled *Birjîs Barîs* [The 'Jupiter of Paris'], published by Rushaid Dahdâh, a Lebanese-Christian scholar. This form of interreligious cooperation was characteristic of the budding Arabic nationalism of this period. Apart from these activities, Al-Harâ'irî published several literary texts. He was, however, not a religious scholar. (Some biographical data may be found in Al-Ziriklî's encyclopedia *Al-Aʿlâm*, vol. 3, 131).

[28] The only copy known to me so far is preserved in the Bibliothèque Nationale in Paris.

[29] Muhammad ibn Ahmad ibn Muhammad ʿIllaysh (1802-1882) was of Moroccan descent. For more information on him, see the article in the *Encyclopaedia of Islam* (2nd edition) by F. de Jong (1985).

[30] *Al-Radd ʿalâ Risâlat ajwibat al-hayârâ ʿan hukm qalansuwwat al-nasârâ*, manuscript nr. 236 in the General Library of Tetouan (Morocco), 26 pages. This text does not appear in the collection of *fatwâs* of ʿIllaysh published in 1901-1903.

[31] Löschner 1971, 1-38: "Staatsangehörigkeit und islamisches Recht". An edict of the Ottoman Grand-Vizir of 1894 still stipulated that the mere act of conversion to Islam was a legal ground for the acquisition of Turkish nationality, which demonstrates that the distinction between the concepts of religion and nationality had not yet been fully completed (Löschner, *op. cit.*, p. 36). In 1905, a Muslim from Tunisia who had settled in Morocco claimed the right to be legally recognized as a Moroccan Muslim, stating that the "Muslim empires are only fractions of one and the same society subjected to this single Law; that there is no nationality in the European sense, which belongs especially to each Muslim state; that only Islam constitutes the Muslim nationality and

that the Muslim becomes the subject of the Muslim state he is living in", so that by the mere fact of his residence in Morocco, he had acquired the local nationality "in accordance, both with Islamic law in general and Tunisian Islamic law" (*ibidem*, p. 7).

[32] A similar but more discretely applied policy was followed by the Dutch authorities in the Dutch East Indies where "Natives" could have themselves officially "equalized" (in Dutch: "gelijkgesteld") with "Europeans", which implied the acceptance of European civil law instead of Islamic law, but not the acquisition of Dutch nationality.

[33] The *fatwâ* of Shaykh Shâkir was republished in Al-Jazâ'irî 1989, 193-8.

[34] Al-Khamlîshî 1995, 455-7; Benomar al-Hasanî 1992-1993, 35-37.

[35] See our analysis of the ideas of Al-Jazâ'irî and Al-Khamlîshî below.

[36] Peters 1979, 135ff; Sadan 1980, 103-104 and the extensive literature mentioned there.

[37] See also our discussion below of the views of Ibn al-Siddîq, Mawlawî, and Al-Qardâwî, all of whom stand in this modern reformist tradition of Islamic political thought.

[38] Al-Arnaut 1994, 242.

[39] Marshall G.S. Hodgson, The venture of Islam, vol. 3 (Chicago 1974) and B. Lewis, The Middle East and the West, 2nd printing, New York 1966.

[40] The terms used in these discussions to denote the means by which the goal is to be reached include: (1) *da'wa*, which excludes the use of violence, and (2) *jihâd*, which includes the use of violence for the same purpose.

[41] Recent examples (from Pakistan and Egypt) can be found in Masud 1990, 29. For our further treatment of the subject it is relevant to point out that the Pakistani young men referred to by Masud made their point on the basis of the argument that in Pakistan the Family Laws Ordinance governed the personal lives of the Muslims instead of the *Sharî'a* law.

[42] Cf. Masud 1990, 43.

[43] Doi 1992, 120.

[44] Nielsen 1991.

[45] See also Lewis 1994, 52-3.

[46] See, for instance, Raza 1993, 53, who concludes that British Muslims have not consolidated their community into an *Ummah*.

[47] For more information on his life and works, see Ibn al-Hâjj al-Sulamî (1992, 428-430).

[48] Ibn al-Siddîq 1985.

[49] Ibidem, p.30; see also p.61.

[50] Ibidem, pp. 49-50.

[51] Apud Kepel 1994, 208. See also Ghannouchi 1990, 60: "In fact, when the term Dar al-Islam is used it connotes one nationality for those residing in it, Muslims and non-Muslims".

[52] Kepel 1994, 271ff.

[53] Kepel 1994, 261.

[54] Khamlîshî 1995.

[55] 1993, 153-158; cf. Van Koningsveld 1995.

[56] I have not been able to find any further information about the author. In view of the contents of the book, one cannot exclude that we are dealing with a pseudonym.

[57] Ibn al-Siddîq 1985.

[58] Arabic: "Wa-awwaluhâ bal ahammuhâ al-salât wa-'l-siyâm ma'a 'adam al-tamakkun min izhâr sha'â'ir al-islâm al-ukhrâ kwafan min al-idhâya" (Ibn al-Siddîq 1985, 14). The author aims at the *individual duties* imposed upon every Muslim. See below in

our discussion of the views of Mawlawî.

59 Ibidem, p. 62.
60 In his book *Muslims in the West*, Leicester, The Islamic Foundation, 1983, especially chapter 10 (pp. 125-33): 'Main duty of Muslim immigrants'. Cf. Lewis 1994, pp. 218-9, note 15.
61 Speech delivered at St. George's Hall in Bradford, August 8, 1991 (quoted by Lewis 1994, 52).
62 Al-Kattânî 1988, 25.
63 "Mubta{{c}}idan {{c}}an muwâlâtihim wa-mahabbatihim mimmâ yunâfî al-îmân": 90.
64 Majallat al-Sunna (Birmingham 1994), 90-91.
65 The implication being that the American and Arab governments have more or less the same attitude towards the application of Islamic law; in neither part of the world does a truly Islamic government exist.
66 *Al-Sunna*, Ramadan 1414, 92.
67 Arabic: *"Dâr al-Kufr"*.
68 Arabic: "immâ an yakûna {{c}}âjizan {{c}}an izhâr sha{{c}}â'ir dînihi kullihâ aw ba{{c}}dihâ wa-immâ an yakûna qâdiran {{c}}alâ izhâr sha{{c}}â'ir dînihi kullihâ wa-adâ' wâjibâtihi sirrihâ wa-{{c}}alâniyyatihâ" (???p. 468).
69 The author prefers the rule he attributes to the Hanafites, Malikites, and Hanbalites which forbids the Muslim to stay in the "Territory of Infidelity" even if he can manifest religion over the (pragmatic) view of the Shafi{{c}}ites who state that the territory where a Muslim can manifest his religion becomes ipso facto part of the "Territory of Islam". According to the Shafi{{c}}ites it is even recommendable for a Muslim to stay there, because his presence might stimulate others to convert to Islam. (Khamlîshî 1995, 470-474).
70 *Ibidem*, pp. 474ff.
71 The following summary of Qardâwî's views is based on the extracts provided by Benomar al-Hasanî 1992-1993, 38-40.
72 Shaykh al-Qardâwî quotes here Sûrat al-Mumtahina, verses 1 and 8-9.
73 Al-Qardâwî clearly stands in the tradition of the reformists' reformulation of Islamic political theory mentioned earlier. This involves, among others, the interpretation of the *jihâd* as a strictly defensive institution. Cf. Peters 1979, 135ff; Sadan 1980, 103-104). Such views imply also the abolishment of the age-old concepts of *Dâr al-Islâm* and *Dâr al-Harb*, etc. See also our discussion below of the views of Mawlawî.
74 This view is based by Al-Qardâwî on Sûrat Al {{c}}Imrân, verse 28.
75 Apud Benomar al-Hasanî 1992-1993, 39-40.
76 "What you ought to know", *Q-News*, 11-17 August 1995, p. 5.
77 Jâdd al-Haqq {{c}}Alî Jâdd al-Haqq (1995), 335-347. The authors would like to thank their colleague, Dr. J. Michot (Louvain-la-Neuve), for having made available to them this important source.
78 Doi 1992, 113-135.
79 Doi 1992, 126.
80 Criticism has been levelled against the *Muslim Manifesto* of Siddiqui, also from the side of Muslim circles. See Raza 1993, 104.
81 UMO, *Why Muslim family law for British Muslims?* London 1983.
82 *The claim to a separate Islamic system of personal law for British Muslims*. In: C. Mallat and J. Connors (ed), "Islamic Family Law", London 1990, 147-166.
83 Vgl. M.I.H.I. Surty, *The sharî{{c}}ah family law courts in Britain and the protection of women's rights in Muslim family law with special reference to the dissolution of marriage at the instance of the wife*. In: "Muslim Educational Quarterly" 9(1991), 59-

68.

[84] Hamidullah 1992, 153-154.

[85] Hamidullah 1992, 154.

[86] Raza 1993: ...

[87] Raza 1993, 84-5.

[88] The author quotes Sûrat al-Nisâ' verse ca. 63 (?): "Yurîdûna an yatahâkamû ilâ 'l-tâghût wa-qad umirû an yakfurû bihi". The same verse was quoted by the religious scholars who, in the twenties, qualified the person who had adopted French nationality as an apostate (see Benomar al-Hasanî 1992-1993, 36; see also Al-Jazâ'irî 1989, 40).

[89] Khamlîshî 1994, 458-63.

[90] Al-Jazâ'irî (1988).

[91] Remmelenkamp (1995).

[92] Ibidem, 82-86.

[93] We fail to understand why Remmelenkamp does not mention the names of these imams, the exact dates of the emissions of the local weekly radio-program directed towards Moroccan Muslims in Amsterdam during which they publicly expressed their views, nor even the name of the radio station involved (cf. Remmelenkamp 1995, 86-91).

[94] Shadid, 1979, 216.

[95] Ibidem, 245.

6

Muslim Attitudes Towards Political Activity in the United Kingdom:
A Case Study of Leicester

Ahmed Andrews

In May 1995 an edition of Derby's Evening Telegraph (Derby 1995) carried a report that stickers had appeared in an area of the city heavily populated by Muslims urging them not to vote in the impending local government elections. The stickers read "None of the electoral parties in Britain represent Islam. Don't Vote It's Haram." The report quoted a Muslim candidate in the Derby election as saying that the stickers were an attempt to "divide the Muslim community", while a Muslim councillor said, "I will be urging people personally to take part in the democratic process and vote."

Although this event was an isolated incident, and was seen by many in Derby to have been carried out by a group called Hizb ut-Tahrir, it raises a series of interesting questions for an observer of Islam in the United Kingdom. Firstly, Is it Haram (forbidden) for Muslims to take part in elections in which no Islamic parties are taking part, and if so on what is this view based? Secondly, if it is Haram, why do so many Muslims take part in the political process in the United Kingdom, joining all the main British political parties and becoming local councillors? Finally, as most Muslims in the United Kingdom are of South Asian origin, how do Muslim attitudes towards the electoral process compare with those of Hindus who share the same political history of the Indian sub-continent?

Islamic constitutional law

Muslims writing in support of the concept of the Islamic state argue that the principle of Islamic government lie in the Qur'an, and they look to

Medina under the leadership of Mohammed in 622AD as being the model (see for example Maududi, 1980: 158-71). Khan (1985: 2-3), states that "The ultimate objective of Islam was to establish peace and order in accordance with Islamic justice within the territory brought under the pale of its public order, and to expand the area of the validity of that order to include the whole world." He continues by saying that Islamic political theory splits the world into two divisions; the territory of Islam (*dar al-Islam*), comprising of Islamic and non Islamic communities that had accepted Islamic sovereignty, and the rest of the world regarded as the territory of war (*dar al-harb*). He continues by saying that, "Even in its early period Islam entered into peaceful arrangements with communities beyond its frontiers in accordance with a set of rules and practices, before some of those communities were brought under its sovereignty.", and he makes the point that it does not follow that hostilities need occur (Khan, 1985: 3). He argues that it is possible to preach Islam in *dar al-harb*, and that Muslims may carry out their lawful business outside the boundaries of *dar al-Islam*, adding that a Muslim entering *dar al-harb* was under an obligation to respect the authority of that territory, and observe its laws, as long as he remained there enjoying the security granted by safe conduct or treaty with Muslim authorities. It is on this basis, therefore, that an argument might be developed supporting the political participation of Muslims in a non-Islamic society.

Writing on government within *dar al-Islam*, Abdal'ati (1978: 146-57) explains that sovereignty in the Islamic State belongs to God, not to the people, and that the people only exercise sovereignty due to the trust placed in them by God. He further states that, "The ruler... is only an acting executive chosen by the people to serve them according to the Law of God."; and adds that, "The aim of the Islamic state is to administer justice and provide security and protection for all citizens... in conformity with the stipulations of God in his constitution, the Qur an." In response to those Muslims who argue for the concept of an Islamic state, it should be remembered that even before the death of the fourth Caliph, Ali ibn Talib, the early Muslim community was torn by civil war which lead to the break up of the community into a series of Sultanates. This resulted in what Hussain (1992: 18) sees as the "two-way process of political participation between ruler and ruled" being replaced by an authoritarian regime "whereby the state existed for the Sultan."

Despite the claims made by Muslim scholars for the concept of the Islamic state, Schacht (1964: 76) observes that, "the state as envisaged by the theory of Islamic law is a fiction which has never existed in reality". Coulson (1964: 120-34), adds support for this view, arguing that by the Abbasid period supreme power had moved away from being vested in the Caliph, with the *qadis* (judges of Islamic courts) coming under the political control of dynastic rulers. He adds that the effect of this was the prevention of "the only sure foundation and real guarantee for the ideal of the *Civiitas Dei*", and claims that a system was created that came very close to the division between secular and religious courts. The result of this development was that although the *qadi* still represented God's law, he was subservient to the ruler, with the only limits upon the *de facto* power of the ruler being his own conscience. It is this configuration of power which prevailed in Mughal India.

Muslims in South Asia under Muslim and British rule

It appears from Hardy's (1972: 3-4) account of the arrival of Islam in the Indian sub-continent that Muslim rule was established by a professional immigrant elite supported by further migration. This was further aided by conquest and conversion. It was not until AD 1555 that the Mughal conqueror, Humayun, supported by the Safavid empire in Iran, sowed the seed of an Indian empire, while it's final frontiers were established by Aurangzeb (1658-1707 AD). Following the death of Aurangzeb the Mughal empire saw two wars of succession and unrest among both the holders of military and civil appointments. The result of this was that by the 1740's the empire had undergone considerable contraction. Moreover, a series of disputes meant the consistent weakening of the last vestiges of the empire, which by the opening of the nineteenth century saw the British entrenched in Bengal, Bohr and Boskier. Delhi itself was annexed by the British in AD 1803.

The break up of Mughal empire did not, however, mean that the Muslim ruling *elite* were automatically ousted from positions of authority, and it was the *Ulama* (Islamic scholars), rather than the aristocracy, that were to see their position in society undermined. Under Mughal rule the court had employed members of the *Ulama* as educators of the entire nobility, and they had also staffed the judiciary and overseen the charitable work of the empire. Metcalf (1982: 19), writes that, "Leading members of the ulama ranged from those who acted as prayer leaders at a town mosque to the most influential of courtiers. The intellectuals among them were sought out as adornments to the various entourages of the nobility." She also says that the *Ulama* had taught *fiqh* (law) supplemented by studies of commentaries on the Qur'an and *Hadith* (recorded traditions of the Prophet Mohammed).

According to a number of scholars the eighteenth century saw demands for a classical Arab Islam; demands which, under British rule, were to unite most of India's Muslims who would otherwise have been divided by class, education, language and regional culture. Significant among them is Shah Wali-Ullah of Delhi who "forms the bridge between medieval and modern Islam in India" (Ahmad, 1964: 201). He shared the Arab reformer Abd al-Wahabb's view that Islam as a religio-ethical force was disintegrating, and that there were only two forms of ultimate authority, the message of the Qur'an and the *Hadith* (Jones, 1989: 51). Wali-Ullah felt that it was for Islamic scholars to remove error and restore a purified Islam by applying *ijtihad* (individual reasoning) to the study of these authorities, although traditionally the Sunni *Ulama* believed that following the formation of the four Sunni schools of jurisprudence *ijthad* was no longer applicable.

As a result of growing British influence, Shah Wali-Ullah's successors found themselves acting as "internal caliphs" to a Muslim community under alien rule, and his son Abdul-Aziz started instructing students to live in adherence to the practice of the Prophet by reference to the *Hadith*, along with a familiarity with the Qur'an. By AD 1803 Abdul-Aziz and his followers were faced with the British in control of Delhi and vast tracks of the Indian sub continent. Even though there was nominally an emperor, the last vestiges of a Mughal empire had gone, and, in many people's view, along with it any claim that the Indian sub-continent was still a Muslim land.

Both Metcalf (1982: 48-49) and Hardy (1972: 31-60) note that the effects of early British rule were felt gradually and unevenly. One effect being that employment in government service, a one time prerogative of scholarly Muslims, was now in the hands of aliens. The change which most upset pious Muslims, however, related to the administration of law, whereby Muslim law "was transformed into Anglo-Muhammadan law, in which central issues such as the law of evidence and the interpretation of offenses against the state were not Muslim but British." (Metcalf, 1982: 49). Abdul-Aziz responded to this new situation by issuing a *fatwa* which, although ambiguous, was understood by some Muslims as being a declaration that India was no longer *dar ul-Islam,* meaning that it was no longer under Islamic political control and a place of peace; rather it was now *dar ul-harb*, a place of war under non Muslim rule (Jones, 1989: 52).

Metcalf (1982: 50-51) says that the ambiguity of this *fatwa*, "derived in part from the lack of clear consensus within Islamic law on what constituted *dar ul-harb*"; for within classical Islamic thought Muslim countries could only wage war on non-Muslim neighbours if Muslim law was not in force with regard to matters of worship and the protection of the faithful. She argues that Abdul-Aziz's *fatwa* only implied that a state of *dar ul-harb* existed, and that he did not press the point, "by showing that there was a Muslim ruler to whom the faithful (of the Indian sub-continent) could shift allegiance". She further states that he only sought to show that the state could no longer provide the structure capable of implementing Islamic law, and that only the *Ulama* could offer "direction to the faithful on such issues of civil behaviour as trade, inheritance, and family relations, as well as on more narrowly religious matters" (ibid). The debate over this *fatwa* continued right up to the time that the British left India. It influenced ideologies of various Islamic movements in the sub-continent, and still influences debates among South Asian Muslims in the United Kingdom.

The granting of separate electorates to Indian Muslims came in 1909 with the reserving of seats in the regional and central legislatures to community groups on the basis of religion. This grew out of the concept of religion as a basis for community, which in turn emerged from a ten yearly census starting from 1871 (Jones, 1989:184). The result was that within the Hindu, Sikh and Muslim communities organisations appeared which sought to represent religious interests within a British controlled political system. One such group was the All India Muslim League, later to become the Muslim League, which was to campaign for the creation of the Muslim, but not Islamic, state of Pakistan.

In AD 1919 the *Ulama* of the Deoband had founded the political party *Jam'iyyat al-ulama-i Hind* (Society of the ulama of India), which, although according to Hardy (1972: 246), supported the demand for a completely independent India, considered "Muslim's religious freedom to keep their own distinctive culture to be more important than Muslim's political freedom." *Jam'iyyat al-ulama-i Hind* was, therefore, against the idea of a Muslim state, perceiving the Muslim League to be seeking a worldly rather than a religious government for Pakistan (Hardy, 1972: 244). Some *Ulama*, however, supported the notion of Pakistan, and founded the *Jam'iyyat al-ulama-i Islam* in support of the Muslim League. They argued that the way to prevent Pakistan from being run by "irreligious Muslims" was for "religious men to join the League and thus ensure that Pakistan would be in the right hands' (Hardy, 1972: 24). A third party, made up of *Ulama* who supported what Gellner (1992) has termed a "Folk Islam" rather than the high Islam of the scholar, were also supportive of the demand for Pakistan, and mobilised politically under the *Jamiat ul-Ulama-i Pakistan.*

The only group to call for an Islamic state was *Jamaat-i-Islami*, which was founded in 1941 by the Muslim journalist Abul Ala Maududi (1903-1979), and which has been called by Robinson (1988:19) "a prime example of Muslim fundamentalism'". In founding his party Maududi stressed the need for it to be different from other Muslim parties, claiming that the only ideology capable of replacing both capitalism and socialism was Islam, but that the right ideology needed a righteous party (Maududi, 1942: 158). His vision was that of an Islamic state ruled over by an *Amir* (ruler) elected by a *shura* or religious *elite*, which had been elected by the righteous (see also Andrews 1993). Although opposed to the Muslim League and the formation of the state of Pakistan on the basis that the former was a secular rather than an Islamic state, civil unrest in East Punjab shortly after independence forced Maududi and his followers to seek asylum in newly created Pakistan. Once there he campaigned for the replacement of the Pakistan Penal Code and other British based statutes with Islamic Law, and he, along with many of the *Ulam*a, played a significant role, in the formulation of the 1956 Pakistan constitution (see Maududi 1960).

Three key points emerge from this history. Firstly, Muslim rule in India was never based on a theory of an Islamic state as propagated by writers such as Abdal'ati or Maududi; rather the Mughal empire was dynastic and feudal, with overall power resting in the emperor, but with a degree of local autonomy for the landed aristocracy. The *Ulama* were themselves dependent on the patronage of the court, and the whole ethos of government models outlined by Coulson earlier in this paper. Secondly, following the advent of British rule in the sub-continent, the *Ulama* found themselves without a role in society and became the guardians of the Muslim conscience and culture. Although they withdrew from contact with the British, they appear in the main not to have been antagonistic, falling short of calling India under British rule *dar al-harb*. Finally, the majority of Muslim leaders, including the *Ulama*, became involved in a political system controlled and modelled on British lines.

It is this history, supporting as it does the views expressed earlier by Coulsen and Schacht, rather than the concept of the Islamic state, that I suggest offers the best understanding of South Asian Muslim political activity in the UK. Rather than seeking explanations of current events by referring to Islamic law, or theories of an Islamic state, it is perhaps better to concentrate on way in which power became centralised within the Indian sub-continent as a result of the unplanned yet structured outcomes of the "interweaving of the intentional action of countless more or less powerful interdependent groups and individuals over several generations" (see Elias: 1982). This paper argues that it is such action that has been central to the long-term development of Muslim and Hindu political activity, and that it is the study of such configurations of power that helps observers to understand the questions stated in the introduction. With these views in mind we now move on to consider Muslim and Hindu political activity in the United Kingdom by reference to a case study of Leicester.

Muslim and Hindu political activity in Leicester

According to the 1991 census there are 64,076 people of South Asian origin in Leicester, made up of 60,362 ethnic Indians, 2,663 Pakistanis and 1,051 people of Bangladeshi origin (see Rooney and O Connor, 1995). Estimates of religious affiliation suggest that 16.6% of this population is Sikh, 62.15 % Hindu and 21.79% Muslim (see also Leicester, 1983 and Narain, 1995). Moreover, as this author has argued elsewhere, the Hindu and Muslim populations are spatially segregated between certain key Wards within the city, due to their desire to live within their own communities supported by their own community institutions, and due to 'Hindu Estate Agents' keeping Muslims out of Hindu dominated areas (see Phillips, 1981 and Andrews, 1995).

Table 1. Hindu and Muslim Names As a % of Electors in Belgrave and Highfields Wards 1991		
Ward	*Hindu*	*Muslim*
Abbey	28.00	2.79
Belgrave	27.38	1.02
Crown Hills	32.06	4.00
Rushey Mead	27.18	2.09
Spinney Hill	4.39	38.53
Wycliffe	5.63	39.60

Source: 1991 Electoral Rolls

Perhaps the two representative bodies with the highest public profile in the city are the Federation of Muslim Organisations and the Gujarati Hindu Association. The former, created in 1984, represents approximately fifty local Muslim bodies (Vertovec, 1993: 14), while the latter claims to represent "over fifty Hindu organisations covering nearly sixty thousand people" (Weller, 1993: 253). Unlike Bradford's Council of Mosques, which was created by the Bradford city authorities in the 1980's, Leicestershire's Federation of Muslim Organisations was formed out of a purely local Muslim initiative, and represents a united Muslim voice in the city, engaging with "the City and county authorities" (Vertovec, 1993: 14-15). Among its successes it can include its campaign for the provision of Halal meat in public institutions, such as schools and hospitals, and the building of Europe's only *janazgah* (small funeral mosque) in a public cemetery. The Gujarati Hindu Association, which was founded in the 1970's, numbers among its achievements the establishment in the city of annual celebrations on Indian Independence Day; Gandhi's birthday; and Navara-tri. It is the generally accepted representative of the Hindu community in the city on matters involving the City and County Councils. In addition to this there are nine Asian councillors on the city council, all of whom are members of the Labour party and five of whom are Muslims (see Jewson, 1995: 108); while as Vertovec (1993) notes, the Chief Executive of the City council and two County councillors are Muslim. Both Hindu and Muslim religious and community leaders encourage participation in the local electoral process, and this study focuses on interviews that were conducted with ten such leaders, five Hindu and five Muslim.

When questioned on whether the Hindu faith had a particular position on political activity, or some form of political theory rooted in the Hindu religion, all the Hindu leaders said that there was no such theory within Hinduism. All those interviewed made the point that Hinduism was a personal faith, and that Hindus were free to participate in western style politics if they so chose. One respondent, a Brahmin, made the point that, under British rule the Hindu community had co-operated with their rulers and had adopted "peaceful democratic methods" when seeking independence for India. He admitted that there was an "extreme Hindu nationalist trend" within India at the present time, but that this was not based on religious doctrine but on the "desire to assert Hindu identity". He claimed that it was the duty of British Hindus to take full part in the democratic process. Another respondent, the secretary of the Gujarati Hindu Associ-ation, supported the above views, making the point that there was no problem for Hindus living in a western secular society. He said that "religion is a matter of private observation which does not conflict with one's public responsibilities."

A representative of one of the temples made the point that Leicester's Hindu community had no choice but to participate in political activity as, having been expelled from East Africa, most of Leicester s Hindus had no other home and had no choice but to fully partake in the British political system. He also confirmed that there were no doctrinal restriction on Hindus taking part in any form of political system, and made the point that, "India was created as secular state, while it was Pakistan that was created on the bases of a religious state." He continued, "India has never claimed to be a Hindu nation, while the sole reason for the creation of Pakistan was that Muslims wanted their own state."

Of the other two respondents, one claimed that India should be a Hindu state, but could not justify his views by reference to any Hindu doctrine. His argument rested only on the fact that Hinduism is the religion of the majority in India. He did, however, say that the religious laws of minorities such as the Muslims should be safeguarded, except where they conflict with the interests of the majority. The final respondent said that "Hinduism is a collective name given to a wide range of beliefs found in the Indian sub-continent, and can not, therefore, have any cohesive political theory based on religious identity." There was not, therefore any problem about taking part in British political activity, or accepting the authority of British government.

When questioned about Muslim involvement in British politics, a representative of the Federation of Muslim Organisations, himself an Imam of one of the mosques, said that, "There is no problem for Muslims participating in politics, we can practice Islam and we have mosques and can pray, so Muslims should vote and take interest in what is going on around them. We have to make the politicians take notice of our needs and this they do when they want our vote." Clearly his reference to the establishment of prayer refers to the debate over the *fatwa* of Abdul-Aziz; and when one realises that the respondent is an Indian Gujarati and a follower of the Deoband, which, as pointed out above, supported the demand for a completely independent India and which saw the protection of religious freedom and Muslim culture to be more important than Muslim political freedom, it is not hard to see how this attitude is based on those of the Deoband and *Jam'iyyat al-ulama-i Hind* mentioned above.

Another representative of the Deoband made similar points, referring directly to the *fatwa* of Abdul-Aziz. He said, "Abdul-Aziz made a ruling which allows us to live in a society providing that prayer is established and that we are not prosecuted for our faith. Here in Leicester we have mosques and freedom of worship. There are other things we would like, such as better facilities for Muslim schools. We can only obtain these things by talking to politicians. I am not sure, however, that we should join a political party like a lot of the Pakistanis." His comments about Pakistani involvement in politics is also significant, as in Leicester it is the Pakistanis who mostly represent the Muslim presence in local politics, providing a number of county and city councillors, even though they are a minority within the city's South Asian Muslim community (see Andrews, 1995).

A third Muslim respondent, this time a Pakistani Imam following the 'Folk' Islam of the Barelvi style of belief, also expressed the view that there was no prohibition to Muslims taking part in political activity providing that it did not conflict with the basic beliefs of the faith (for an explanation of the term Barelvi see Robinson, 1988). He was of the view that religious and political activity were separate, although Muslims have a duty to see that their faith is protected. He saw Muslim participation in politics as being part of their duty towards the wider society, although some observers have seen such activity as being part of Muslim community leaders attempts to raise their status within their own community and the wider society (see for example Anwar and Werbner, 1991).

In my sample of interviewees, one, a Pakistani from the Punjab, was a local councillor. When asked if he saw any conflict between being a Muslim and being a member of the Labour party and a city councillor he said that he did not see why there should be such a conflict. He said, "It is the duty of a Muslim to safeguard their religion, and if Muslims do not take part in local government their interests will not be taken into account." When asked why he stood as a Labour party candidate rather than as an independent Muslim or as a member of the Islamic party of Great Britain, he said that, "Although the Ward (electoral division of a city) I represent has a large Muslim population, there are also white people in the area. I could not have won my seat if I had only represented Muslims. I represent all my Ward, although I also represent Muslim interests." In response the question of whether his beliefs might come into conflict with Labour Party policy, he replied, "A few years ago I might have agreed that there was a possibility of conflict, especially over single sex education, but more recently the party has modified its position.

Moreover, one has to be pragmatic and make concessions in order to promote the greater good of the community."

My final respondent, a member of the UK Islamic Mission, and follower of the teachings of Maududi said that, "Although Muslims desire an Islamic state, this applies to countries that have a Muslim majority. It is the duty of Muslims in the UK to abide the laws of the country, and seek to achieve Muslim interests through making representation to local and national politicians." He added that Muslim should not, however, join British political parties, but shift support according to which party was prepared to meet "Muslim demands".

The attitude of the majority of Muslims in Leicester towards participation in British politics is perhaps summed up by Mohammed Raza, (1991: 36), an Imam from one of Leicester's mosques, who believes that, "... when any community is without political power in the society it is resident in, it is at the mercy of those in power." He argues that political protection for Muslims can only be achieved if "the political elite in power can themselves think about an injustice or inequality suffered by a minority and eradicate it through legal protective measures.", or, if the community suffering an injustice "start exercising political clout and get such laws passed". He argues that although Muslim participation through voting takes place at both local and national levels, it is limited, and that the factors of class, ethnic identity and sectarianism affect Muslim political participation.

Conclusions

This paper started by asking a number of questions, and in response to the first, the Muslim respondents to my survey appear to believe that it is not an *Haram* activity to take part in elections in which no Islamic parties are taking part. In answer to my questions the arguments put forward in support of such activity seems, at least in part, to be based on the *fatwa* of Abdul-Aziz; and judging from the number of Muslims that do participate, such activity appears to have widespread support. The view that involvement in western style political activity is allowed also seems to be supported by the historical precedence of Muslim political activity in the Indian sub-continent, which has been reinforced by the *Ulama* themselves having formed political parties and having participated in western style political activity.

That more fundamentalist groups, such as *Jamaat-i-Islami*, argue that Muslims should not join western political parties appears to carry little influence with the many Muslims who stand as candidates in the UK's political parties; while a group such as *Hizb ut-Tahrir*, which appears to have a following among a section of Muslim youth, and who argues for the total non-involvement of Muslims in the Western political process, is rejected by the majority of the Muslim community. It is interesting to note that such groups as *Jamaat-i-Islami* and *Hizb ut-Tahrir* very rarely attract members that have a knowledge of Islamic law or history; rather they rely on their appeal to disaffected middle class professionals and university students who have often trained in the western sciences and technology (see Kepel, 1994: 13-46). Maududi, for example, was, on the admission of his followers, "A self taught theologian" (Jameelah, 1987:117).

My brief survey seems to suggest that Muslim attitudes towards the electoral process does differ from the attitudes of Hindus, in that the Muslims interviewed appeared to be more inclined to justify their action by reference to religion than did the Hindus interviewed. It must, however, be stressed here that the sample was very small. If the findings are accurate they would seem to support the view that it is the process of history, rather than religious doctrines, that affect attitudes of both Hindus and Muslims towards participation in British politics, with the key factors being the breakdown of the Mughal empire, and the experiences of British rule in the Indian sub-continent. What fundamentalists such as *Jamaat-i-Islami* and *Hizb ut-Tahrir* fail to realise is that religion, even Islam, does not remain static, it is both an instrument of, and subject to, social change. Whether consciously, or unconsciously, religion is constantly being re-interpreted by those who subscribe to it in such ways as will help the adherent to make sense of their social situation. This has happened all through the history of Islam and remains the case. A return to some golden age of religious purity is a dream, one which is often turned to in times of crises.

Finally, in an attempt to address some of the more general questions the following points are worthy of note. Firstly, it is fair to say that although, within the context of the United Kingdom, groups like *Jamaat-i-Islami* (in the form of the UK Islamic Mission), *Hizb ut-Tahrir* and the Islamic Party of Great Britain exist, their activity is very marginal, and at best they act as no more than pressure groups. Most Muslims, and Hindus and Sikhs for that matter, conduct their political activities through the traditional British political parties who appear to encourage both Muslims and Hindus to stand as candidates to the city and county councils. It seems reasonable to assume, therefore, that this pattern will probably continue with both Muslims and Hindus taking part in constitutional politics through membership of the traditional political parties.

With regard to representation at the level of national government, however, I have argued elsewhere (Andrews, 1994) that until the British political system moves away from the first past the post system of election to some form of proportional representation, such as that found in the Netherlands, there is little possibility of Muslims or Hindus being able to gain election to the national parliament on the bases of attachment to a purely religious party. Finally, it should be noted that although the major parties encourage Hindus and Muslims to come forward as candidates in local government elections, it has been noted that there is still little inclination for either Labour or Conservative parties to encourage candidates from these communities to come forward as prospective members of parliament (see Anwar, 1995). There is a possibility that this lack of encouragement could result in a loss of party membership as disaffected members of both the Muslim and Hindu communities seek a more a radical forum from which to fulfil their political aspirations.

7

Settler Political Participation:
Muslim Local Councillors

Kingsley Purdam

This paper focuses on the political identities, activism and experiences of Muslim local councillors in Britain.[1] In the last 10 years there has been a significant increase in the number of Muslims holding the office of local councillor; there are in 1996 in Britain over 160 Muslim Councillors in Britain. The paper attempts to document not only instances of discrimination and exclusion, but also successful mobilisations by Muslims and the wider issues of cultural identity and cultural status raised by such mobilisations. One of the major gaps in research on migration processes and settler experiences is the failure to deconstruct the wider political and social system in which they live. The discussion here centrally questions the structures of *liberal equality* within a so called *multicultural democratic* state: how open is the system? How can it help settlers?

Though little research has been carried out nationally on the political participation of Muslims[2] it is apparent that in comparison with the wider British population they display a high level of activity. This takes a variety of forms: voting; Labour, Liberal or Conservative Party membership; individual and group lobbying, including neighbourhood action groups and professional bodies such as The Association of Muslim Lawyers; street protests; the formation of various interest groups (of varying size and substance) such as the U.K. Action Committee for Islamic Affairs, The Bradford Council for Mosques, An-Nisa Society, The Al Masoom Trust, The British Muslim Association, The Muslim Forum, Muslim Solidarity Committee, The Islamic Foundation, The Muslim Parliament, The Islamic Party of Great Britain. A number of umbrella organisations have also been set up, such as The Union of Muslim Organisations of U.K. and Eire, The Council of Mosques, The National Interim Committee for Muslim Unity, The Supreme Council of British

Muslim Conference. Additionally a number of foreign countries and international organisations such as Hizbut Tahrir, Islamic Forum Europe and The World Islamic Forum have strong bases and networks in the U.K. The British Muslim media is also expanding rapidly, including satellite and cable television channels such as *Asianet*, newspapers written in English such as *Muslim News*, *Q.News* and presses such as *Alkalifah Press*.

It is important to check the assumption that Islam is a uniform homogeneous political or cultural constituency. Islam is not a singular *other*. Muslims invoke various interpretations and rhetorics of Islam to justify and inspire particular political strategies. They operate both inside and beyond the *liberal democratic* system. It is evident that in Britain a majority of Muslim voters vote Labour but within this general alignment there are various political and cultural positionings. Muslims are not an undifferentiated group, they are not, in the language of political science a single-issue pressure group. Identities are more complex than this: they are negotiated, contested, unstable historical positionings. Muslims themselves are debating and contesting exactly what it means to be a Muslim, what Islam means and how it should be constructed and reproduced both in the *West* and in the rest of the world. Strong factions and sects exist both in Britain and internationally as a result of these debates.

This discussion raises wider theoretical issues about the construction and recognition of individual and collective identities such as *Islam* and the *West* which require discussion beyond the scope of this paper. Labels/identities are the means through which culture is contested politically and therefore through which legal rights have to be fought for and potentially recognised. If politics is, following Laswell, "who gets what, when and how?" (Laswell 1936); it is important to ask: who decides who who is? And who decides what resources become contested? Particular discourses of equality such as *Liberalism, equal-opportunities*, *race-relations* and *multi-culturalism* can work to construct and reify difference. State bodies can have a functional role in constructing these categories and therefore in constructing *ethnic* identities (Werbner 1991). For example, in Britain in October 1995 the Muslim media boycotted the Commission For Racial Equality (C.R.E.) - the main spokesbody for victims of *racial* discrimination in Britain - on the grounds that it had consistently failed to support Muslims. Muslims argue that the C.R.E. does not recognise a distinct Muslim religious identity and therefore fails to address the problems that Muslims as distinct religious group face. Similarly, Muslims are critical of the wider discourse of equality in *racial* terms. The 1976 Race Relations Act in Britain which legally protects recognised *racial* groups excludes settlers considered to be defined only in terms of *religious* identities. Muslims have no protection from discriminatory employers.[3] The logic of this remains unclear. Arguably, it is linked to the ideological demands of *secularism* and a desire to force cultural homogenisation. Muslims are directly encouraged to emphasise what can be more constructively termed their *country of departure* identity[4] i.e a *racial* and/or *ethnic* identity over any Islamic identity. Amongst other consequences, this can work to subordinate Islamic needs/interests and also to increase the level of factionalism between Muslims.

Settlers are constructed as the unwelcome guest, while certain discourses of equality reproduce an undifferentiated control identity of *secular white*. The status and an ideal of *white* becomes internalised in all cultures. There is no country called *white* and secularism is in many ways an ideological construct. It is clear that the language through which we understand those around us continues to be dominated by the discourse of those who differentiate and discriminate. This summary is clearly limited but extensive discussion of these issues is available in Bauman (1994); Fuss (1989); Hall (1990, 1992a, 1992b); Mackenzie (1978); Werbner (1991).

Having encouraged the questioning of racial/ethnic categories and the way in which they force a cultural identity and presume a uniformity, it is important not to disempower those who choose or are forced to work collectively with regard to certain issues. The potential collective power of the *umma* should not be underestimated despite the lack of agreement amongst Muslims on what form it should take. In Britain there are a number of key issues which concern Muslims and which they are attempting to resolve by collective action. It is evident that Muslims have interests in common but also shared experiences of exclusion. Muslims assert an Islamic identity in the face of homogenising categories such as *Asian* and *Black*. The term *Asian* can have real creative and reappropriated cultural content, particularly amongst second generation Muslims in Britain, and in discussing common experiences of exclusion experienced by Indian, Pakistani, Bangladeshi and Chinese settlers. However, it also serves to marginalise particular identities. For example, over the issue of Kashmiri independence, Indian nationals can be the most immediate rivals of Pakistani Muslims. The cultural needs of Muslims, Hindus or Sikhs are far from identical. Similarly, many Muslims differentiate themselves from a wider *Black* representation, which though a point of mobilisation, can serve to marginalise specific Muslim concerns (Modood 1988). At a recent meeting of the National Forum of British Muslim Councillors (N.F.B.M.C.) it was agreed that Muslims: *"need to move away from a Black identity and keep our Muslim identity"* (N.F.B.M.C 1995).

Many Muslims are active within anti-racist groups and forums; they feel that they are forced to fight from a broader platform but many have concerns about its limitations. The identity/label *Muslim* encompasses a multiplicity of identities. It is a variously interpreted way of life and a contested strategic cultural and political unity/disunity of history - belief-rhetoric - ideology, but also a discourse of demonization, if and when it is appropriated by the discriminator.

Muslim political participation

An important question related to the actions of Muslim councillors are the political and cultural constituencies in which they operate. It is clear that being a *Muslim* is not their only reason for entry into the system, nor is it the only aspect of their identity; however, it seems to be one of the main reasons for their exclusion. It is to the processes of political inclusion and exclusion as a dynamic of cultural incorporation that I now want to turn.

Electoral participation amongst Muslims in terms of voter registration and electoral turnout has increased significantly in the past 15 years. Research in 1964 suggested that less than half of Commonwealth settlers were registered (Deakin 1965). Subsequent survey data is inconclusive and subject to local variation but points to the increasing level of Muslim registration (Anwar 1984, 1994; LeLehoe 1987). However, recent survey data suggests Indian, Pakistani and Bangladeshi registration is still lower than that for whites; as Anwar argues this is cause for concern (Anwar 1994). Arguably, although there is no documentation of this, Muslims who are registered are more likely to be committed voters, considering the costs and fears many have of being on the electoral register. Research by Anwar and by Johnson supports this thesis (Anwar 1994; Johnson 1990). Party membership amongst Muslims is also evidently increasing. My research shows that many local Labour Parties in areas with a high Muslim population are now under Muslim control.

The increased level of participation amongst Muslims is a consequence of the processes of settlement, the economic security and prosperity of an increasing number of Muslim settlers, improved language and professional skills and the increased experience in working with the British political systems. Participation campaigns targeting Muslims have been carried out by a number of local authorities, community relations agencies and political parties.

The biggest impact of Muslim political mobilisations has been at the local level. As stated, there are now more than 160 Muslim councillors, mainly concentrated in inner city wards of a number of Britain's major cities. The majority have been elected in wards with large Muslim popula-tions, i.e by other Muslims. This raises questions of the nature of political representation and the wider participation of Muslims. Can Muslims represent only other Muslims? How effectively are they representing non-Muslim members of their electoral ward? These questions are beyond the scope of this paper but it is important here to consider the extensive debates in political science over the issue of representation. Particularly important are the discussions by Pitkin and later work by Swain (Pitkin 1967; Swain 1993).

Democracy is at best about majorities, it is majority-seeking. The estimated 1.2 million[5] Muslims in Britain, the largest settler group if we overlook the various heterogenous Islamic identities within this categorisation, are even collectively irrelevant to the wider process of national *democratic* rule. However, it is clear that as a result of Muslim demographic concentration and the British *single member simple majority* system (otherwise known as First-Past-The-Post (F.P.T.P.)) Muslim political participation can still be of direct electoral significance. Hard data is limited, but calculations purely in terms of population numbers produce workable indicators of potential electoral significance. The 1991 Census data suggests that there are more than 20 Parliamentary constituencies which are more than 10% South Asian,[6] with 15 of these wards having more than 20% South Asians. There are over 50 local wards with more than 30% South Asians, 38 wards of which are more than 40% South Asian. More detailed data relating specifically to Pakistani, Bangladeshi and Indian electoral significance is not yet available. Early findings from my research suggests that in the 1992 General Election Pakistani and Bangladeshi Muslims could have changed the outcome of at least 14 marginal parliamentary constituencies. In the British democratic system, which is characterised by low voter turnout, particularly at local elections, and often by small parliamentary majorities of less than twenty MPs, Muslims and certain other settler groups have a potentially significant power base.[7] It is apparent that Muslims are increasingly realising this, as are the political parties reliant on their votes. Conversely the British F.P.T.P system is unfavourable to diffuse, dispersed political alliances such as the support for the Liberal Democrat Party and the Green Party.

It is important to note here how settlers living in countries with proportional representation based systems do not have the same political potential should they seek to act in unity.[8] In countries such as The Netherlands and Belgium for example, the electoral system is less favourable to geographically concentrated settlers. Leman states, for example, that though settlers in Belgium may have a more differentiated party membership, they rarely secure elected office. Settlers are allowed to stand as candidates but have little chance of being elected as votes are transferred, after the first round, to the leading candidates (Leman 1995). The system has no directly elected local responsibility for elected representatives. The geographical dimension to representation if it is there at all is not as strong. Councillors represent parties, not their constituencies and there is less sense of local responsibility. The local state does not therefore present such an opportunity for settler political mobilisation. This difference has potentially significant implications for settler political and cultural mobilisations and therefore for long term processes of *integration*.[9] Additionally, a further consequence of the combined effects of settler demographic concentration and the F.P.T.P system in Britain is that the elected councillors are concentrated in a number of local authorities, thus maximising their potential influence on the policies of their local party and the local authority, as research by Solomos and Back has shown (Back and Solomos 1995).

Councillor profiles

Most Muslim councillors are middle aged men though there are an increasing number of women. In this sense Muslim councillors fit the wider stereotype of local councillors. They have a varied career backgrounds: accountancy, engineering, self-employed; a number are unemployed and retired. Many have wide ranging experience in anti-racist agencies and community action groups. Reflecting the size of the population, more than half of the councillors' *country of departure* is Pakistan, most having arrived in Britain in the late 1950s and mid 1960s. As a result their involvement with the politics of their *country of departure* can be high, this is reflected, for example, in the sustained commitment of many councillors to the issue of Kashmiri independence. An increasing number of the councillors are from Bangladesh, India and Africa. Though there is an overriding claim of loyalty to Islam, what might be termed a *sense of Islam*, there are other competing claims and policy priorities.

An estimated 90% of Muslim political party membership in Britain is affiliated to the Labour Party and 95% of Muslim councillors are Labour councillors. Muslims in general view the Labour Party as more sympathetic to their needs. Amin and Richardson state that Muslim support for Labour is not as strongly associated with class as it is for *white* people (Amin and Richardson 1992). This ties in with early research findings of this project. Predictably, perhaps, most Muslim Labour councillors stated clearly their loyalty to the party they represent and a commitment to the party line. This is to be expected, it is inherent in the party system, it is driven by party loyalty. It is however possible to look beyond this claimed loyalty to actual reasons for individual involvement. Most Muslim councillors stated that they are motivated by concerns of their own *communities*. The following comments by two Muslim councillors are revealing: "I got involved in order to raise issues of concern to the Muslim Pakistani community." "I could not sit back and see the Muslim community as a disadvantaged group."

A commitment to Socialism is not always the primary stated motivation for Muslim involvement in the Labour Party (it is notable that in Blair's new *One Nation Labour,* Socialism is not a clearly stated commitment of many Labour activists). Though a commitment to some form of egalitarian and redistributive society is stated by many councillors it is inspired and framed in terms of Islam rather than Marx. The implications of this are potentially far-reaching, and perhaps, in part, cause of some of the severe tensions between Muslims and a number of local Labour Parties in Britain. It relates to the existence of Muslim political agendas concerning the rights to religious freedom including: protection from discrimination in education, employment and local service provision (Dwyer and Meyer 1995). It is notable that the Labour Party did not provide any leadership to Muslims over their protests against *The Satanic Verses* or more recently over the issue of Voluntary Aided Status Schools.

Muslim Labour Councillors can be characterised as centrist on many Labour Party policies, though on issues such as education, marriage and gender roles there is a strong Conservative leaning.

Increasing but still relatively small numbers of Muslims have switched to supporting the Conservative Party. This increase is difficult to estimate accurately. However, an N.O.P sample survey carried out for the Runnymede Trust found that 8% of Pakistanis and 11% of Bangladeshis supported the Conservative Party (Amin and Richardson 1992). As Anwar has pointed out, the importance placed on self-employment, home owner-ship and family life by many, particularly first generation Muslims, is more in tune with Conservative Party philosophy (Anwar 1994). As stated, many Muslims also own their own businesses of which the Conservative Party is viewed as being traditionally more supportive. The support for the Conservative Party has also developed as Muslims have become increas-ingly disenchanted with the failure of the Labour Party to represent their interests/demands. However, Muslims do not have comparable representa-tion within the Conservative Party. Where they have been selected as council candidates, it has been in unwinnable seats against other Muslims. Muslims, despite real commitment to Conservative policies have arguably been used by the party in an attempt to split the Muslim Labour vote. This

exploitative policy has proved unsuccessful, though it has created antagon-
ism amongst Muslims.

Muslim participation and the local Labour Parties

Outside of the factors discussed above, tensions have developed as a result
of the threat to the position and power of long-serving Labour activists.
Despite the Labour Party being the most open of all parties to Muslims
(and this should not be overlooked) a number of conflictual situations
have developed in various Labour Party branches. They raise broader
questions relating to participation theories and issues such as *discrimination*, *opportunity* and *integration* which I will attempt to address.

A number of cases require documenting:

Muslims activists have been accused of recruiting members in order to
secure the selection of a Muslim candidate in Manchester (Gorton),
Preston (Central) and London (Tower Hamlets); of using council funds to
bribe Labour Party members in order to secure support for a Muslim
Labour candidate in Birmingham (Sparkbrook, Ladywood) and Bradford
(University ward).

There have also been several instances however where the national
party has intervened to protect the selection of a Muslim council seat
candidate, who though selected by local party members was subsequently
rejected by the local party hierarchy. As a result, in certain wards, selected
Muslim candidates have been forced to stand against senior local Labour
activists standing as Independent Labour candidates.

Legal action has been taken by both sides in all cases and the Labour
Party has suspended a number of local parties in Birmingham and Walsall,
suspended a number of individual Muslim councillors and barred a
number of Muslim Labour Party members. The Labour Party is also
proposing to introduce new rules controlling party membership and voting
rights.

I do not intend to dwell on the specific details of each case; most
remain in the hands of the courts. It is apparent that problems have
developed in almost all constituencies where there is a significant Muslim
population and in which serious attempts are being made to gain Muslim
representation in the Labour Party. Difficulties in Birmingham and Not-

tingham date back to the early 1980s. I propose here to focus on the more general relationship between the Labour Party and Muslims, and the councillors' experiences of representation.

The Labour Party has actively sought to recruit Muslim and other settlers in order to increase support. Before Blair's leadership the decline and fragmentation of Labour Party membership in the 1970s and 1980s was causing serious instability in the party both in financial terms and regarding the party's political outlook. Difficulties have been exacerbated by the failure to gain office in the last 16 years.[10] A number of recruitment drives have been initiated in recent years and advice books have been sent out to encourage all members to attract new supporters. This targeted recruitment can be traced back further to the early 1970s and 1980s when Afro-Caribbean people were actively recruited as a means by which membership could be built up without threatening the balance of political control (Jeffers 1991). It is arguable that certain Muslim councillors now fulfil a similar role.

Though Muslims have responded to these recruitment drives in large numbers, it is apparent that the Labour Party executive at both local and national levels are not enthusiastic for Muslim members to climb the party hierarchy and gain positions of power. As stated, at the local level many long-serving Labour Party loyalists feel their positions to be under threat. Anonymous comments from a number of Muslim Labour Party councillors are inconclusive but revealing: "New members should be welcomed if there is a commitment to political theories...if there is not and block membership is only in order to tip the balance, then the Establishment, both Labour and Conservative, becomes cautious."

"More Muslim members, okay! Provided they all vote for white candidates - otherwise perception is taken as fact - politics of fear.

"The impression you get is one of *what do these men with beards and their women understand about socialism?*".

"The Labour Party has used Asians - so have the Tories - it is time Muslims and Indians built strong bases with membership drives and beat the bastards at their own game."

"In some cases individuals from the Muslim community have done this for their own personal gain....but I think largely they are allegations to discredit Muslims."

"Frankly speaking, we have not learnt how to become acceptable members. We do not join in time, we do not attend meetings, we recruit members who do not have time or interest and we believe in block membership which causes suspicion."

The current tensions remain unresolved. The distinction between party-driven recruitment and Muslim-led membership drives has not yet been clearly or convincingly established. Party politics is about calling in support as it is required; this is the basis on which the House of Commons functions. When Muslims adopt such tactics it is more visible, and they have been accused of corruption. Membership applications are closely scrutinised and checked with electoral registers. These procedures are, it seems, not as far reaching for membership applications whose names are not indicative of a Muslim identity.

The causes of the many tensions are complex. Arguably, problems have developed as a result of the Labour Party's and Labour Party activists' resistance to the advancement of Muslim politicians. Investigations by the electoral registration officer into recruitment in Birmingham (Small Heath) found no irregularities. In Birmingham (Sparkbrook) a local government ombudsman report dismissed the allegations of the misuse of council funds and in Manchester (Gorton) a second internal Labour party report found that the party had wrongly banned a number of new Muslim members. Almost all Muslim councillors state that they have experienced some form of discrimination within their local political parties. A number document systematic dirty tricks campaigns.

As stated, at the local level certain conflicts reflect a simple contest for power. A number of actions by the national party office suggest that the Labour Party leadership does not want to be seen to have too many Muslim members. This relates more generally to a view of Muslims as an electoral liability and the fear that Labour will lose *white* votes. Successful Muslim councillors have had to progress against this national backdrop of discrimination. Specific discrimination extends from questions of candidates' abilities and competence to their questionable constituency/party loyalty. Part of the party's concern over Muslim candidates lies perhaps in the way in which Muslims are identifiable by name. Potential voters, it is feared, may be put off at the last moment by the name on the ballot paper. A number of councillors stated that they felt that in candidature applications, and also in other areas of their lives such as job applications, their names can be the basis on which their forms are rejected. Muslim and other settlers whose names and heritage remain un-Christianised and un-Anglicised by slavery and colonialism, in this sense carry an added basis for exclusion compared with certain other settlers. Muslims in Britain have to overcome the stereotype not only of the *Black* other but the religious - enemy - terrorist other (Sit 1996).

Muslims become subject to the consequences of the political party playing what is unhelpfully termed the *race-card*. However, voting alignment is more complex. The small number of councillors who have been successful in non-Muslim areas are proof that Muslim candidates can attract non-Muslim Labour voters; just as a Muslim candidate will not always bring in Muslim votes. For example, a number of Muslim Conservative candidates standing against sitting *white* Labour M.P.s have failed to secure significant Muslim votes in numerous local elections in Birmingham, Bradford and Manchester. Muslims do not simply vote for Muslims. The Islamic Party of Britain (I.P.B) has failed to retain its deposit in any of the parliamentary or European elections in which it has put forward candidates, despite the fact that all the candidates were contesting constituencies with significant Muslim populations.

Muslim party membership is growing. Many local Labour Parties in areas of high Muslim population have several hundred Muslim members. Some have more than a thousand. In this sense Muslims constitute a new grass roots Labour movement. However, this increased membership is widely viewed by other Labour Party members with suspicion. Many councillor candidates were selected as a result of the support of local constituency Muslim members, having failed to receive the support of their party MP or the local party leadership. There is evidence, therefore, that a number of Muslim party activists have been forced into recruiting members in order to support their campaign for selection in the face of resistance from non-Muslim members.

Further questions

Many issues raised by the research are beyond the scope of this paper. However in conclusion it is important to indicate the key areas still to be considered. Firstly, the impact of the increased representation of Muslims remains undocumented. Early research findings suggest that the councillors are playing a key role in negotiating with the state agencies. Successful negotiations have been made concerning service provision, particularly in rendering local authorities more responsive to Muslim needs.

Secondly, it is important to locate Muslim councillors in relation to the wider Muslim population. The councillors have largely been elected by Muslims but to what extent are they providing leadership for Muslims? Do they represent a challenge to the leadership provided by the Mosques? There is some evidence that many of the councillors distance themselves from the mosque. To what extent is this happening? What compromises, if any, have the councillors had to make in order to advance in the system? One councillor, despite proudly identifying himself as a Muslim revealingly stated: "It took me five years to be thought of as one of them and then some other Muslim attempts to get involved and polarises the party along Muslim and non-Muslim lines."

Thirdly, what political agendas do the various councillors have? Which Muslim views are being represented? To what extent does the system and the Muslims that have gained a foothold *inside* it police the entrance of other Muslims? What potential is there for unified action at the local and national level?

There are increasing signs of factionalism in local Labour Parties between different Muslim groupings. Although this is yet to be documented, one councillor stated: "I would like to become a member of Parliament but I don't have a chance at all. My own *Black Brothers* will be the first to chuck me out."

The absence of a movement of even one or two Muslims into national government remains a symbolic and real sign of exclusion. Local government has traditionally been a training ground for national politics. With the increasing numbers of experienced local Muslim politicians the election of a Muslim M.P is long overdue but imminent.

Fourthly, is it possible to talk of what might be termed a *new Muslim politics*? Increasing attempts at unified action and cooperation are being made through the National Forum of British Muslim Councillors, a recently formed network organisation. Other regional bodies have also been set up such as the North West Pakistani Councillors Forum.

Finally, and more generally, it is important to discuss the ideology of *democracy* and in particular the British *democratic* system in more detail. *Democracy* claims to equalise all citizens. In this sense it is a metaphor for fair government. The concept of a *democratic* state is a signifier of Western (post) colonialist modernity. Yet to what extent does it exclude and marginalise particular issues and particular individuals/groups. To what extent does it compromise? To what extent does it deliver?

In conclusion, it is evident that political incorporation is an important indicator of wider acceptance of settlers as part of what it is to be British. Muslim entry into the British political system has been problematic. The Labour Party has allowed greater representation to Muslims than any other political party in Britain. However, there is still evidence of exclusion and discrimination against Muslims within the party. Muslims have been forced to mobilise and organise with little outside support. Perhaps as a consequence Muslims are increasingly realising their collective political potential within the party system. Muslim local councillors are providing the key to increasing Muslim political organisation and to realising some of their autonomous political potential at the national level. In the British first past-the-post-system it is clear Muslims have perhaps the most advantageous system for maximising their collective political power. Muslims often marginalised in a discourse of the hegemonic cultural majority, actually according to this cultural discourse, constitute in certain localities a political majority. Though the discourse that distinguishes minority from majority simplifies the forces and processes of identification at work, Muslims acting collectively are in a position to significantly influence, if not determine, the election result in many local wards and in a number of parliamentary wards. The wider consequences of this are yet to become fully apparent.

Notes

[1]   This paper is an initial report of research into Muslim councillors in Britain. The research was conducted by national postal survey, interview and the shadowing of particular actors. The final report will be published in the Autumn of 1996.

[2]   Important work has been carried out by Anwar (1994) Solomos and Beck (1992) (1995) however they do not focus on Muslims directly. Valuable area studies on Muslim *communities* have been carried out see Vertovec (1994); Werbner (1991). Also see Lewis (1994).

[3] Jewish settlers have such protection on the basis that they have been accepted as a *racial* group.

[4] The phrase *country of departure* is used here in an attempt to step outside the biologically deterministic discourse of *country of origin*. The discourse of *origin* prioritises the issue of *where you are from*. It arguably reproduces and reinforces notions of categorization and lineal enlightenment development which culturally pedestals the country of settlement. Cultural identities are more complex than this and the prominence of *origin* conceals the processes of history and cultural change.

[5] The actual figure is disputed by Muslim groups who suggest it could be as high as 2.5m. The 1991 British Census, though it does not record Muslim identity directly arguably provides the most accurate data. It is this figure which is used here.

[6] The category of *South Asian* is not particularly helpful here and has been criticized by a number of policy advisors, welfare rights workers and a number of theorists as an academic invention. See for example Modood (1988). *South Asian* describes here people of Indian, Pakistani and Bangladeshi origin; clearly these people are not all Muslims, however the figures can be used to provide a rough indication of Muslim geographic and therefore political concentration. Sources: 1991 Census, National Ethnic Minority Data Archive (N.E.M.D.A).

[7] The 1991 Census data reveals that a significant percentage of the Muslim population is under 18. Increasingly the Muslim population will be composed of those born in Britain and as the settlers come of age this can only serve to increase their political potential. For data see the National Ethnic Minority Data Archive, Center for Racial and Ethnic Studies at Keele University, England and also Ballard and Kalra 1994.

[8] Proportional representation is used to describe a number of differing *democratic* political systems. It is clear not all proportional representation systems lack a geographical constituency, for example the German and Australian systems. Though arguably however even in these systems the local dynamic of representation is not a strong as in the British F.P.T.P system.

[9] *Integration* is used here to describe a process of participation, a process of change for more recent settlers and for earlier settlers; we are all settlers. Public culture norms should be contested, should be permeable, more reflective of the changing nature of British society. Recent settlers are part of this process, certain aspects are retained certain aspects are lost. This is essentially the present situation but there has to be greater control of the content of the exchange and the way in which public culture becomes public.

[10] Membership problems perhaps reflect wider long term shifts in Labour Party support base see Gyford (1985).

8

Riots, Representation and Responsibilities

The Role of Young Men in Pakistani-Heritage Muslim Communities

Stacey Burlet & Helen Reid[1]

A series of events took place in the Manningham area of Bradford, a Northern industrial city in Britain, over a period of three days in June 1995. People belonging to the Pakistani-heritage Muslim community[2] gathered to protest about the arrest of four youths and the treatment of community members by the police. During these protests, property and business premises, largely 'white'-owned and non-Muslim-owned, were damaged and many more arrests were made.[3]

The events were widely reported in the national and local media as 'riots'.[4] Young men belonging to the Pakistani-heritage Muslim community were singularly blamed as the perpetrators of these 'riots' and were accused of a lack of civic loyalty. Moreover, because the youths did not immediately respond to calls for calm from 'community leaders'[5] they were "portrayed as a monolithic and angry group, caught between two cultures, who were using violence as a means of empowerment" (Burlet 1995: 21).

In the aftermath of the 'riots', grassroot members of the community expressed frustration and anger with the way in which they, and particularly male youth, were represented in the media. Many see the 'riots' as an expression of the difficulties associated with being a young Pakistani-heritage Muslim male in Bradford in the 1990s, and believe there is an urgent need to tackle the problems of deprivation and discrimination suffered by the community as a whole. In addition, many argue that new mechanisms of negotiation and representation, both inside and outside the community, need to be developed to meet the specific needs of male youth.

These different and contrasting interpretations mean there is confusion about the way policymakers should respond to the events. This paper will attempt to clarify this confusion. To do this, it will examine how new and appropriate mechanisms for community representation might be developed. This analysis will be based on a detailed examination of the events which occurred, preceded by some background on why the protests took the form they did. To initiate this examination, the role and lifestyle of male youth in the Pakistani-heritage Muslim community and the social and economic infrastructure within which they live will be described.

Bradford's Pakistani-heritage Muslim community

Bradford Metropolitan District is multiethnic and multifaith. Approximately fourteen per cent of the Bradford population have South Asian heritage. This shared heritage is sub-divided by national heritage and religious affiliation. Communities have their roots in Bangladesh, the Punjab areas of Pakistan and India, Gujarat in India, and Mirpur in Pakistan,[6] as well as being Hindu, Muslim and Sikh. The largest of all Bradford's South Asian heritage communities is the Pakistani-heritage Muslim community.

As a result of early settlement patterns[7] two thirds of Bradford's South Asian heritage population now live in four wards of the city. This clustering has certain advantages. Prejudice is minimised, for example, as very few white people live or create employment in these areas. More positively, residents have been able to build up a social infrastructure which supports community needs. This includes food and clothes shops as well as religious buildings. Thirty mosques and nine mosque schools have been established, for example, to serve the needs of Muslim communities (Lewis 1994: 58). The concentration of South Asian heritage communities in specific wards has also ensured the election of councillors who represent community interests.

These wards are among the poorest in Bradford, however. The Manningham ward, where the 'riots' took place and where ninety per cent of residents are Pakistani-heritage Muslims, has been designated by the local Council as one of the ten most economically and socially deprived areas of Bradford (City of Bradford Metropolitan Council a. 1993: 3). Deprivation is reflected in many ways. One indicator is housing, which is officially recorded as overcrowded and of poor quality in Manningham. Fifty per cent of all households, for example, have no central heating compared with thirty-seven per cent in the metropolitan district as a whole (City of Bradford Metropolitan Council a. 1993: appendix).

Raminder Singh also points out that more able community members have moved, and continue to move, to more affluent areas of the city, leaving behind the less able, such as the elderly and the unemployed. Those moving include a large proportion of Hindus and Sikhs (Singh 1994), thus creating "substantial Muslim residential zones" (Lewis, 1994: 62). This process of 'ghettoization', has meant that limited communication between people of different religio-cultural backgrounds takes place, as they have few opportunities to meet.[8]

Many Manningham residents are actively involved in efforts to improve the quality of life in their neighbourhood. Most recently, they have undertaken localised action to remove prostitution from Lumb Lane, a road which runs from the city centre and through the Manningham area of Bradford. The road has had a long association with prostitution and this has been a source of aggravation to local residents who have had to put up with used condoms and empty syringes on their streets, as well as harassment of female residents. Since the early 1980s, local residents have campaigned for an end to prostitution in their neighbourhood, with the support of the local mosque and newspaper. These campaigns included mass lobbying of local government and running a neighbourhood watch scheme (Siddique 1993: 119-126). Despite these efforts, prostitution increased in Manningham during early 1995 (Weale 1995: 5). The perceived inability and/or unwillingness of the police to control the trade, led some residents to form a direct action group to actively discourage prostitutes from Lumb Lane (Narayan 1995: 8). This took the form of street patrols which were carried out by both 'white' and 'Asian' residents, and young men, in particular, were heavily involved in this campaign (McElvoy 1995: 15). The street patrols were effective as most prostitutes left Lumb Lane at this time.

Before focusing on the immediate frustrations of male youths which formed an immediate backdrop to the 'riots', it is worth noting that the young people of Manningham have been disproportionately affected by unemployment and a lack of resources. Youth unemployment in Manning-ham is thirty-seven per cent, compared with twenty-two per cent in the metropolitan district as a whole and thirty-one per cent in Thorpe Edge. Thorpe Edge is a predominantly 'white' area which has also been desig-nated by the local council as one of the ten most socially and economical-ly deprived areas of Bradford (City of Bradford Metropolitan Council a. 1993: 17).

Youth unemployment means that many young people have little or no money to spend on recreation. While most young unemployed women, by tradition, have chores to occupy them at home, many young men in Manningham are spending their 'free' time on the streets. This situation is exacerbated by the lack of any council-funded youth clubs or activities in Manningham. The net result is that a strong and highly politicised male youth culture has been developing in the area which includes an element of opposition to mainstream British culture.

Immediate frustrations of male youths

The above descriptions of socio-economic deprivation and social isolation explain some of the frustrations which triggered the 'riots'. More specific frustrations were also part of the build up and are crucial for understand-ing the conflict. These factors include the increasing alienation of male youth and worsening community relations with the police.

In recent years some sections of the youth population have become increasingly alienated from mainstream society as a result of discrimina-tion and disempowerment. Many at the grassroots believe that discrimina-tion has created an informal system of apartheid in Bradford and point to higher unemployment rates amongst themselves in comparison to their 'white' peers,[9] as well as continued separation in social settings, as evidence of this. One young woman, for example, expressed the latter issue as, "white people go to English fish and chip shops and Mirpuris go to Mirpuri fish and chip shops". This situation has both politicised and alienated many young people who are increasingly aware of their rights and what racial equality should mean. Their daily experiences of prejudice have sparked off demands for representation, justice and equality. These demands are meant to be facilitated by existing bodies such as the Commission for Racial Equality Council[10] and the Council for Mosques (CfM),[11] backed up by local councillors and the 'Asian' business community. Many youths feel these mechanisms are inadequate, however, and designed to keep them disenfranchised. One young man, for example, stated that he and his friends were no longer willing to cooperate with decisions made without them if they did not agree with the potential outcome as, "elders are increasingly out of touch with our reality of unemployment and racism." This has led to an increasing feeling of disempowerment amongst some sections of youth.

Poor youth-police relations also formed part of the immediate backdrop to the 'riots'. In particular, a newly built local police station is viewed as symbolic of the police's attitude to the community. Local residents refer to it as 'Fortress Lawcroft' because it is situated on a hill, surrounded by high walls and looks as if it has been designed to withstand a siege (Bodi 1995: 7). One 'white' male police officer even claimed "if the rest of Manningham burns to the ground, it will stand."

There have also been widely voiced allegations of police harassment over a number of years which has had a negative impact on community-police relationships. For example, frequent use of stop and search legislation, which legally entitles the police to search anyone they believe has committed or is about to commit a crime, is referred to locally as the 'Stop and Grab policy'.[12] There is also a widespread belief that the police are regularly involved in assaulting people while they are in custody and extracting false confessions from them.

Many local people believed such unofficial policing tactics intensified in frequency during the direct action campaign on Lumb Lane (Naum 1995: 6). Male youths, in particular, believed the police were annoyed that the street-patrols managed to remove prostitution from the area, something the police had said could never be achieved. They were defiantly pleased with their achievements on Lumb Lane, arguing that the streets of Manningham were no longer "a dumping-ground for Bradford's problems".

An account of the conflict

On the evening of 9 June 1995, a local resident contacted the police about a noisy game of football being played by two youths. Two police officers arrived at the scene and attempted to arrest the youths. The situation escalated and five other officers were called to the scene. All seven of these officers were later accused by some community members of using unnecessary force in both their arrest of the youths and their handling of the situation. They were said to have charged at onlookers with batons and a dog, torn a female relative's dress and assaulted her baby (when the officers pursued one of the youths into her house), and arrested two other young men for asking why the initial youths were being arrested.[13] These allegations, and particularly the one concerning the young mother, led certain members of the community to seek redress about alleged police brutality and demand the release of the youths held at the Manningham police station. They also allege that they were prevented from entering the police station when they tried to make a formal complaint. During this period another ten people were arrested and riot police arrived at the scene. A dynamic of tension began to evolve after this, with more members of the community arriving at the police station, some to support the protest and others to find out what was happening. By the end of the evening, approximately fifty people had gathered outside the police station and were faced by riot police.

The next day, following a meeting between the police and community representatives,[14] the Assistant Chief Constable refused to release the fourteen people who had been arrested or initiate an inquiry into police action. By the evening, the number of protesters outside the police station had increased to approximately three hundred, as had the number of riot police. The police allege that some of the protesters rioted, smashing windows, throwing petrol bombs and setting cars on fire. Some eyewitnesses countered that rioting began with a spiral of reciprocal violence. They allege that first the riot police charged at protesters using batons and dogs, and a minority of the crowd retaliated by throwing bricks. This in turn provoked the police to use more force and so on. Some local people also suggest that it was trouble-makers from other cities such as Manchester and Leeds rather than local residents, who were responsible for damaging property.

On the third and final day of the 'riots', demonstrators were allowed to protest on a piece of wasteground close to the police station. This concession, combined with a multifaith, multiethnic peace march by eight women who stood between the riot police and the protesters, calmed tempers down.

Local responses to the conflict

A diversity of opinions were expressed by community leaders, representative bodies and at the grassroots, during and after the protests. Although the majority of 'community leaders', the police and local councillors expressed their shock at the events,[15] many local councillors actively called for calm and for negotiations between youths and the police. In addition, they and elected members of parliament called for the charges against those initially arrested to be dropped, and for an official inquiry to investigate both the causes of the conflict and the policing of it. A few local and national government representatives also publicly condemned the initial incident which triggered the 'riots' and spoke of long-standing police brutality towards youths in the area.

These responses contrast with those of senior police officers, many of whom blamed the 'riots' on a generation gap within the Muslim community. Norman Bettison, Assistant Chief Constable, for example, said in a press statement: "The youths seem to be rising up as much against society and elders as against the police. The police are the anvil youth is beating out its frustration and anger on. Youth seems to be alienated from every conceivable part of the community from which it is drawn" (Wilkinson 1995: 2). Similarly, Ruth Billheimer, a local councillor and member of the West Yorkshire Police Authority Complaints Committee, voiced comparable ideas about youths increasingly using violence as a means of gaining independence (Telegraph and Argus Reporters 1995: 5).

Such comments have angered many members of the Pakistani-heritage Muslim community who see this as a deliberate attempt to mask the issue of policing and they are determined that debate on the policing of the 'riots' will not be silenced. Although the police have established a police-youth forum to aid communication between the two groups and agreed to an investigation by the independent Police Complaints Authority in the aftermath of the conflict, many at the grassroots expect the investigation will lack impartiality and be uncritical of police actions.

Similarly, the decision to arrest thirty-eight people on a variety of charges following the investigation of video tape footage by a team of detectives (set up during the conflict, with the aim of catching "the ringleaders of the riots") has not been welcomed by everyone at the grassroots.[16] Although the majority of community members condemn the violence which took place, in retrospect they can understand why the youths resorted to such measures (Cohn 1995: 24). One elderly man stated, for example, "if the police won't do anything, then they [the youth] have a right to protest in a way that will be noticed."

A smaller proportion of community members also voiced the suspicion that those 'community leaders' who publicly supported the arrests (on the grounds that violence should not be seen to be rewarded) were typical of an elite trying to hold onto a power-base that was no longer guaranteed. An illustration of this occurred during the 'riots' when two local councillors and a representative of the CfM (known 'community leaders') tried to address the crowd and call for calm. Their pleas were shouted down by chants of "police puppets" and allegations of bribery.

In contrast, many women have focused their responses to the conflict on gender relations within the community. They argue that the exclusive presence of men in the disturbances is symptomatic of a macho religio-cultural identity which brings up male youths to believe that they are more important than women and exclusively in charge of the honour of the community. Many women subsequently believe that the youths were showing off in the 'riots' and were not seriously trying to achieve anything. Indeed, a substantial number of women have spoken out against being branded as 'militant' and 'extremist' because of male behaviour. One middle-aged woman argued, for example, that "women wouldn't smash up shops, we direct our energy towards peaceful action." In another example, a group of Muslim women started a petition in the week following the incident. The petition stated, "as women we feel sad about what happened at the weekend. We want everyone to listen to each other. We want peace" (Cohn 1995: 24).

The conflict has also provided impetus for Muslim organizations to attract supporters. Some 'community leaders', for example, have called for the creation of a single body to represent the views of Muslims at national and local levels of government. This body would include representatives from the clergy, intellectuals, professionals and different Islamic sects and would, therefore, be able to claim the support of the majority of British Muslims. In this way 'militants', who are presently seen as dominating media coverage, would no longer be viewed as being representative of the whole community (Evans 1995: 5). It is possible, however, that the conflict may actually help to strengthen the position of more exclusive groups. Just after the 'riots', Hizb-ut-Tahrir,[17] a radical Islamist group, for example, held a meeting in the area with the aim of finding new supporters among the disaffected.

On a positive note, the willingness of many people to act for peace was illustrated by their attendance at the mela, an annual festival of the performing arts, two weeks after the 'riots'. This year many people predicted there would be trouble, while others saw it as an opportunity for healing wounds. For example, Champiak Kumar, an organiser, said, "This is just what we need now - a way of people getting together" (Wainwright 1995: 11). His optimism was well founded as people mixed together peacefully during the two days of festivities.

Implications for future community representation

In the aftermath of the conflict, there have been calls for the direct involvement of male youth in the representation of the Pakistani-heritage Muslim community in Bradford. This is based on the twin ideas that responsibility and respect would provide the youth with a public platform for their opinions as well as a means of bringing about change. It is thought that this will be viewed positively by the majority of the youths and will provide the minority who 'rioted' with a peaceful alternative to violence. This suggestion has implications for future relationships both inside and outside the community.

Devolving power and resources to male youth would involve present 'community leaders' giving up a proportion of their own power. They may or may not be willing to do this. It will largely depend on whether they approve of the mechanisms proposed and how these might reflect on their own work. They may feel that devolving power would be divisive and limit the community's effectiveness in negotiations with others. The local government, for example, would have to negotiate with a variety of representatives whose views might be potentially conflictual. It is also important to remember that 'community leaders' have negotiated effectively on behalf of community needs in the past. For example, they managed to introduce the provision of halal meat in county schools. If power is to be successfully devolved, therefore, past achievements must be acknowledged and the experience of present 'community leaders' must be utilised for the common good.

Many members of the community's other subgroupings are also unsure about the proposed changes in community representation. They are concerned that the changes may be exclusive to male youth and their interests, and not aimed at increasing democratization within the community. Many women, for example, do not feel they are currently represented by 'community leaders' because the vast majority are male and many are conservative in outlook. These women would subsequently like to have more decision-making power or direct representation. Simply including male youth representatives into decision-making mechanisms might, therefore, draw accusations that people are only listened to if they use violence.

Another issue is that working to represent a section of the community takes time, commitment and preparation. To be a successful representative requires specialist understanding and skills, such as knowledge of legislative procedures, debating etiquette and canvassing techniques. Since few young men have these skills at present they would need time to develop them if they are to become effective representatives. In the short-term it may, therefore, be more practical to maintain the present system of 'community leaders', but encourage them to directly consult subgroup representatives before negotiating outside the community. In the long-term, education needs to be provided so that future generations can learn about the political system and be active in it from an early age.[18]

It is also essential to ensure that mechanisms are developed whereby youth leaders are chosen to be representative of the views and opinions of the youth community at large. This would prevent highly skilled and organised groups, like Hizb-ut-Tahrir, from capturing all youth representative vacancies because no other youth groups could effectively challenge them.

However, electing a few representatives is not going to resolve the deeper problems associated with boredom, deprivation and alienation. This is particularly relevant given the extremely limited resources made available by local and national government to alleviate them. Although the creation of youth clubs and youth activities would help to support these young men by providing entertaining and satisfying recreational facilities, these are not the only measures required. The youths need to be taken seriously and gain the respect of their community, as well as wider society. To do this they need to have access to training and/or educational facilities that can support them in finding employment and enable them to make a greater contribution to their community and the local environment.

Change is also required outside the Pakistani-heritage Muslim community if young men are to be directly represented in Bradford. The incident which directly preceded the 'riots' was the result of conflict between the police and some young members of the community. Although the actual 'riots' are the subject of a local government inquiry, it would be prudent in the interim to assume that both the male youth and police have a responsibility for improving youth-police relations and admitting where past misunderstandings and mistakes have been made. The establishment of the police-youth forum has the potential to provide a means whereby good communication might be achieved. For this to be realised, however, the police must be prepared to respond constructively to issues raised by the forum. Police officers also require training that sensitises them to the issues that concern male youths and have caused past tension. These issues include deprivation, racism and religious prejudice.

Conclusions

The 'riots' in Bradford raise the twin issues of responsibilities and representation in multiethnic, multifaith societies. Local and national governments need to develop new ways of encouraging active citizenship to meet the expectations of all people in society. This will require education and training to equip more people with the skills necessary for participating in formal political processes. The police also require training so they are able to fully serve all citizens in an equal way. This training should aim to sensitise them to particular groups of citizens of whom they may have had little previous experience. In addition, police officers who continue to discriminate against certain members of the public on the basis of their religio-cultural affiliation should be actively reprimanded, and ultimately dismissed.

There are also demands for increased democratization within South Asian heritage communities. For these to be met in the short-term, present 'community leaders' need to listen to a diversity of grassroots' opinions and, in the long-term, a proportion of their power needs to be devolved to others in the community. If male youths want a proportion of this power, they must become effective political actors. This will involve potential youth leaders equipping themselves with the required skills, and a small minority accepting that violence is an inappropriate means of affecting change.

It must be remembered that the conflict which took place in Bradford could have happened anywhere in Europe where distinct communities suffer from deprivation and discrimination. This poses challenges for both policymakers, academics and those at the grassroots who are interested in creating more representative societies.

Notes

[1] Stacey Burlet and Helen Reid gratefully acknowledge the financial support of the Economic and Social Research Council and the Rowntree Trust in funding their respective research projects. They would also like to thank all of the interviewees, Frank Hanley and Tom Gallagher for their time, as well as Ian Davis and David Herbert for their helpful comments.

[2] This description has been used to denote British citizens who are Muslims and belong to a community with Pakistani cultural heritage.

[3] The cost of the 'riots' has been estimated at over one million pounds, this includes a 360 thousand pounds policing bill (Palmer 1995: 2).

[4] The events taking place in Bradford were described as 'riots', but this description is contested on two grounds. First, those involved in the events argue that their aim was to protest against police brutality and the violence which occurred was a reaction to later developments. Second, it is argued that the number of people involved and the scale of the events - where, for example, the main arena of the 'riot' was one street which is approximately a kilometer long - do not merit the description of 'riot'.

[5] The term 'community leaders' refers to both elected local government representatives and non-elected business, religious and social leaders.

[6] According to the City of Bradford Metropolitan Council's District and Ward 1991 Census Digest, 62,243 people have South Asian heritage in Bradford: 45,280 from Pakistan, 11,713 from India, 3,653 from Bangladesh and 1,597 from other 'Asian' countries (City of Bradford Metropolitan Council b. 1993: Table 5,12-13).

[7] Today's communities are mostly comprised of the descendants of men who came to work the night shifts in textile mills and foundries from the late 1950s onwards. Although the men were used as cheap labour (to make the maximum profit for British

investors), they themselves needed to earn enough money to support their families and to save enough to buy land "back home". As a result, the men tended to settle in the inner-city, close to their work and kinfolk, where cheap housing was available. In more recent years, community members have also suffered from a lack of access to mainstream credit facilities, which has meant that the main way families can buy houses is through borrowing relatively small amounts of money from moneylenders or relatives. This has perpetuated initial settlement patterns.

[8] Opportunities are largely limited to the interfaith movement and the mela. The mela is an annual two day festival organized and partially funded by the 'Asian' business community. This is an international celebration of the performing arts held in the center of Manningham. It is widely attended by members of different communities and seen as a yearly testimony to Bradford's good multiethnic relations.

[9] The potentially negative impact of discrimination on 'black' and 'Asian' youth (and particularly male youth) was submitted as evidence to the House of Commons Employment Committee by both Bradford Metropolitan Council and Bradford Metropolitan Community Relations Council. Evidence provided by the latter stated: "racial discrimination and negative attitudes of private employers towards blacks [sic] is a major cause for concern. Discriminatory practices of employers contribute a great deal to the problem of unemployment. They have not shown any real interest in offering help to improve the situation ... The Department of Employment, having all the facts before them, has failed to act" (HMSO 1986: 3).

[10] The Racial Equality Council was established in 1966 as a link between local and 'Asian' agencies, and as a forum for raising concerns about discrimination. It is credited with influencing the local authority to adopt a formal race relations policy in 1981.

[11] In the 1970s, religious leaders of the Muslim community formed the Bradford Council for Mosques (CfM) to represent all Muslims in Bradford, particularly on occasions or issues pertinent to relationships with non-Muslim groups. The CfM also represents Muslim communities on issues of national concern and negotiates with the representative bodies of other communities at times of conflict. Following the events at Ayodhya (India) in 1992, for example, when a 16th century mosque was demolished by Hindu nationalists, community relations between Hindus and Muslims in Bradford were strained. The CfM played a functional role in calming local Muslim anger in Bradford by acting as negotiators with Hindu community leaders (Burlet and Reid, 1995).

[12] Under the Police and Criminal Evidence Act 1984, the British police were given extensive powers to 'stop and search' both persons and vehicles for stolen and prohibited articles on the basis of 'reasonable cause' (Leigh 1985: 169). Although this legislation has mostly affected young men in Bradford, a 'white' Manningham resident also pointed out that it is not unknown for the same police officers to "routinely stop and search respectable looking middle-aged men going to pick up wives from work".

[13] See N. Cohn's article for a good example of how the initial incident was interpreted differently by eyewitnesses and those involved (Cohn 1995: 19-24) .

[14] Non-police personnel present at this meeting included an elected member of parliament, a representative of the Bradford Council for Mosques (CfM), local government representatives and youth representatives.

[15] Paradoxically, many commentators have stated in the aftermath of the events that although the riots were not expected, they were surprised that a "localized explosion of anger ... had not happened before" (Lewis 1995: 767).

[16] The charges included arson, violent disorder, indecent assault, conspiracy to commit arson, theft, and possessing offensive weapons.

[17] Hizb-ut-Tahrir's understanding of Islam includes the creation of an international Khalifa (Islamic government), even if this requires the use of force. The organization has been opposed by a variety of non-Muslim groups. For example, the National Union of Students (NUS) has criticized the organization on the grounds of homophobia and anti-Semitism, and some mosques in Britain have banned it because of the overtly political nature of their meetings (Public Eye 1995).

[18] There has been a progressive centralization of power in Britain from the late 1970s onwards and this has had a negative impact on mechanisms of local democracy. This has led to a reduction of public participation in the political process, which is particularly marked among the working classes (and includes a high proportion of Pakistani-heritage Muslims). For example, even though fourteen per cent of Bradford's citizens have South Asian heritage, they represent less than two per cent of the total local representatives elected.

PART III

Identities and Integration

9

Living as a Muslim in a Migration Country

Moroccan youngsters in the Netherlands

Cécile Nijsten

The future of Islam in the Netherlands now lies largely in the hands of the second generation of migrants. In comparison to the first generation they have the advantages of better language skills and better knowledge of Dutch society, they are better educated and moreover they have probably made a decision to stay in the Netherlands, something the first generation never really did. In other words some of the structural barriers for the integration of Islam in the Netherlands are decreasing (Shadid & Van Koningsveld, 1991). However structural barriers related to the host society still exist. Prejudice, stereotypes and discrimination on the part of the autochthonous population is one of these structural barriers. A negative image of Islam is presented in the media and public and political discussion about the position of Moroccan and Turkish minorities in Dutch society concentrates on issues like the position of women in Islam, the wearing of the headscarf, the founding of mosques and Islamic schools.

On the basis of research among the second generation of Muslim immigrants in France, Belgium and Great Britain Saint-Blancat (1993) formulates several hypotheses about the future development of Islam in these migration countries. She observes that among these young Muslims a relatively small group is attracted by radical islamism that manifests a strong political militancy. On the other hand an equally small group shows tendencies towards secularization, but the largest group is formed by Muslims that adhere to their religion in a 'silent way' and show no inclinations towards political manifestation as Muslims, or towards obtaining a special legal status.

In the Dutch situation several research projects point in the same direction.

Rooijackers (1992a; 1992b) detects tendencies towards secularization among young Turkish Muslims in the Netherlands. This is in line with the findings of Feddema (1991; 1992) who concludes in research on young Moroccan and Turkish men that the main development among these young men can best be characterized as secularization, and not as islamization. On the basis of research among young men, Sunier (1994) suggests that there is a tendency among young Muslim Turks towards orientation and integration in Dutch society while at the same time holding on to their Islamic identity. Bartelink (1993) concentrates on the religious attitude of Moroccan women living in the Netherlands. She observes that the largest group is formed by women who live their religion in what can be called a traditional way: for them to be a Muslim and a Moroccan is self-evident and they have few contacts with Dutch society. However, in particular among young well educated women and young women that participate in the work force, Bartelink detects tendencies to reinterpret Islam influenced by living in the Netherlands. A small group turns to the Koran and the hadieth to find answers to questions concerning the position of women in Islam, and an even smaller group shows tendencies towards a more liberal interpretation of their religion.

In this paper we concentrate on young Moroccan Muslims living in the Netherlands. First we present material concerning their religious commitment and pay attention to the relationship between religious commitment and socio-cultural integration. In the context of this conference their views on and concerns about the future of Islam in the Netherlands are of relevance, as well as their interest in Dutch politics and willingness to acquire the Dutch nationality. In describing this, we hope to find some preliminary answers to the question of the future of Islam in the Netherlands and to the question whether Islam can be a mobilising force in political formation and participation of Muslims.

Method
Subjects

Data were gathered in interviews with 91 young Moroccans -46 men, and 45 women- of the 'second generation', that is: children born from parents that migrated to the Netherlands. Some of them are born in the Netherlands; most came to this country at a fairly young age. The average age of migration is

7.5 years, the average duration of stay in Holland is 12.9 years. Only youngsters between the ages of 17 and 26, who attended school in the Netherlands for at least five years participated in the research. Mean age is 19.9 year.

In three cities we obtained a list of Moroccan youngsters of the required age. Subjects were taken at random from these lists, and approached to participate in the research project by mail, telephone and/or by visits to their home. The response rate was satisfactory: more than 70% of the approached youngsters, that met the criteria to take part in the research, agreed to be interviewed.

Method

As said above data were gathered in interviews. These structured in-depth interviews consisted of open-ended and closed-ended questions and a limited number of paper and pen questionnaires. Interviews were in Dutch and the interviewer was a Dutch female.[1]

Variables

To measure religious commitment we made use of the multi-dimensional model of religion as developed by Glock and Stark (1965). A large number of questions were asked concerning this subject. In this paper we will concentrate on observance of ritual practices, acceptance of religious beliefs, and agreement with Islamic cultural norms and values. In addition we present material about the importance the subjects attach to their religion.

Concerning the observance of ritual practices we asked questions about observance of the fast during the month of Ramadan and observance of the obligation to pray five times a day and about foodprohibitions concerning the drinking of alcohol, the eating of pork and the eating of meat that has not been ritually slaughtered. A mean score was computed on these five items.

Religious belief was measured by asking whether the subjects affirmed the control elements of the Islamic creed (Allah, prophecy of Mohammed, divine origin of the Koran, angels and day of judgment). Subjects could answer these questions with 'yes', 'unsure' or 'no'. A mean score was computed.

To measure attitude towards Islamic cultural norms and values the 'Islamic cultural tradition scale' (Rooijackers, 1992) was used. This scale consists of 12 items concerning Islamic norms and values, in particular attitudes towards male-female relations, parent-child relations, rules of dress etc. Some examples of items are 'a Muslim should treat other Muslims as brothers and sisters', 'children should always obey their parents'. Several items concern the role of women like 'it is the task of a woman to stay at home and take care of the children', 'Islamic women should remain virgin until marriage' and 'Islamic women have to wear a headscarf'. On these 12 items a mean score was computed.

In measuring socio-cultural integration we distinguish structural participation, social participation, affective orientation and ethnic identification.

Structural participation refers to being involved in the work process or attending school, as opposed to being unemployed or being a housewife. As most subjects are still rather young, most attend school full-time (59.3%), only 17% work full- or part-time outside the home, and 24% is unemployed or housewife.

Social participation was measured by asking whether they had Dutch friends, visited them at home, or received them as visitors, and whether they ate with them. A mean score of 1.8 was found (range 1.00 to 3.00). Social participation of one third if the subjects can be classified as low, and of one fourth as high, the others have an intermediate position.

For measuring affective orientation towards living in the Netherlands, we made use of the 'subjective-integration-scale' developed by De Jong en Van Batenburg (1985). In its original form this scale consists of 14 items measuring the degree in which subjects feel themselves at home in Dutch society. For instance subjects are asked to indicate on a five point scale whether they feel at home in Dutch society, have intentions to settle in this country permanently. In analyzing this scale we found that only 8 items form a reliable one-dimensional scale. On these 8 items a mean score was computed. Affective orientation of these young Moroccans is rather high: mean score of all subjects is 3.58, indicating that most of the youngsters have a positive attitude towards Dutch society.

To determine the ethnic identification we asked them to indicate in percentages to what extent they feel they are Moroccan and to what extent they feel they are Dutch. Almost all youngsters said they felt partly Moroccan and partly Dutch. Only eight subjects said they felt 100% Moroccan. Of the others a large majority felt more Moroccan than Dutch, only six subjects had the feeling they were more Dutch and one fifth answered 50% Dutch, 50% Moroccan.

Regarding the aim of this conference we also report on the attitude of these youngsters towards politics, in particular in relation to religion. Subjects were asked whether they intend to vote in the next elections. Almost one quarter has no intentions to vote, some are not sure yet and the others said yes. We also asked whether they consider changing their legal status of foreigners by acquiring the Dutch nationality. 15 Youngsters already have the Dutch nationality, of the others almost 30% has no intentions to change their legal status of foreigners.

In addition we asked several open questions concerning the position of Islam in the Netherlands: views and concerns about the future of Islam in this country, perceived barriers for living in this country as a Muslim and wishes they have on this subject.

Results
Religious commitment

All youngsters say that their religion is of some importance to them: the vast majority considers Islam very important (71%) and only six youngsters (7%) say that their religion is not important in their lives, but not unimportant either. A considerable number of interviewees have trouble in motivating this answer. For a lot of members of the second generation being a Muslim appears as self-evident in their lives: they were born and raised as such, live in Muslim families and intend to pass on this religion to their children when the time comes. Others make clear that they idea of being an atheist is not an option: they consider Islam important because one has to believe in something. Some youngsters wrestle with the problem of perceiving themselves as a Muslim but not living by the rules this religion sets. Others say that they do not feel the need to follow all the rules although they consider it important to be a Muslim. They say that it is enough to be a Muslim 'at heart' and not in 'outer appearance' or in following foodrestrictions or other rules and obligations of being a Muslim.

Belief stands high. Scores on the index of belief can range from 1.00 - indicating a high degree of belief- to 3.00 -indicating a low degree of belief.

A range was found between 1.00 and 2.80, with a mean score of 1.14.

As was to be expected more variance is found on the ritualistic aspect of religion. The vast majority (80%) says to fast during the whole period of Ramadan. Only eight youngsters do not partake in the fast. Fasting during the month of Ramadan is not only seen as a religious ritual -not to partake in it is associated with not being a Muslim- but also as a social and family event. In this respect not to fast is seen as excluding oneself from the family and the Moroccan community. This is underlined by the fact that half of the youngsters who have left the parental home and live alone or together with a non-Muslim partner, do not feel obliged to follow this religious and social rule, as opposed to only one in six of the youngsters that live with their parents or a Moroccan partner.

Praying five times a day is an obligation that appears to be much more difficult to fulfil for these young Muslims. Almost 60% of the subjects never prays, and only six youngsters say to pray five times a day. Almost 60% of the male respondents never visits a mosque and only 11% goes at least ones a week.The women that pray, pray at home. In general praying is associated with a higher age or with a later stage in life. Most youngsters are of the opinion that the religious rules concerning praying should be followed strictly. In their experience it is not enough to pray once a day or whenever you can: to pray means to pray five times a day at prescribed times. Since a lot of our interviewees visit school or partake in the work force, they have decided to postpone the fulfilling of this religious obligation. Moreover, in the parental home the pressure to pray is not nearly as high as the social pressure to partake in the fast.

Of the rules on food and drinking, the prohibition on eating of pork is the most generally observed (78%), followed by the rule not to drink alcohol (63%). 44% Never eats meat that is not slaughtered ritually. It are mainly young men that associate with Dutch peers outside the parental home, that do not follow the Islamic restriction concerning drinking alcohol. Some do not see drinking alcohol and partaking in the fast during the month of Ramadan as a contradiction. They are of the opinion that drinking alcohol is allowed as long as you make sure that your body is 'clean' when you start fasting. This is achieved by not drinking forty days before the month of Ramadan.[2]

So in some ways these members of the second generation make a distinction between the various ritual obligations of their religion in the way that Saint-Blancat (1993) describes: individual practices like praying, and collective or family practices like the fast. It are mainly the collective and family practices that are observed by these youngsters.

On the 12 items of the Islamic cultural tradition scale a mean score was computed and subjects were classified in three groups: 32% agrees with these Islamic norms and values, while 39% is opposed to them. The other 30% have an intermediate point of view.[3] In particular the wearing of a headscarf and norms concerning the relations between partners in marriage are on the whole met with disagreement. Norms concerning the relationships between parents and children are generally approved of.

In summary: Islam seems to be important to almost all young Moroccans in our research. A large majority has no doubts concerning religious beliefs. In this respect it seems that living in a non-Muslim context has hardly any influence on religious commitment. However there seems to be a decline in ritual practice. Also traditional views about relations between men and women, and the position of women in Islam are not endorsed by a lot of youngsters. We might interpret this as the first signs of a secularization process. However this conclusion has to be taken with some precautions, since as lot of interviewees say to associate the strict following of Islamic rules with a later stage in life, and a lot of them intend to start fulfilling these obligations after marriage or when they get older. In this context it is interesting to note that subjects that are married practice their religion more, and that a majority of our subjects considers it important to raise their own children as Muslims.

Living as a Muslim in the Netherlands
The relationship between religious commitment and socio-cultural integration

In tables 1 and 2 we present results about the relationship between aspects of religious commitment and socio-cultural integration. There is no relation between the four aspects of religious commitment and structural participation. Affective orientation is only related to 'traditionalism'. The more one agrees with Islamic cultural norms and values, the less one has the feeling to be a full member of Dutch society.

Table 1. Pearson correlations between four aspects of religious commitment and three aspects of socio-cultural integration

	Social participation	Affective orientation	Ethnic identity
Importance attached to religion	-.23*	-.13	-.25*
Belief	-.16	-.03	-.25*
Ritual participation	-.31**	-.14	-.38**
Traditionalism	-.40**	-.28**	-.43**

Table 2. Analysis of variance between four aspects of religious commitment, an structural participation, political participation and willingness to acquire Dutch nationality

	Structural participation N=91	Political participation N=78	Attitude towards naturalization N=71
Importance attached to religion	n.s.	n.s.	n.s.
Belief	n.s.	n.s.	n.s.
Ritual participation	n.s.	n.s.	sign: p.001 group 1 (no) mean: 1.39 group 2 (yes) mean: 1.93
Traditional	n.s.	n.s.	n.s.

Social participation is negatively related to several aspects of religiosity. The more one has contact with Dutch friends, the less importance one attaches to Islam, the less one practices the rituals and the more one disagrees with Islamic cultural norms and values.

Also there is a negative relation between ethnic identification as Dutch and all four aspects of religious commitment. The more one feels Dutch, the less importance one attaches to religion, the less one affirms the belief statements, observes ritual practices and agrees with Islamic cultural norms and values.

Religious commitment is not related to the intention to vote and there is only one significant relationship with the willingness to acquire Dutch nationality: ritual practice of the subjects that are willing to become Dutch is lower then of the others.

We may conclude that these young Muslims will go on to consider their religion important in some way and to accept Islamic beliefs. At the same time they consider themselves as part of Dutch society and participate at school and on the labour market and intend to vote in Dutch elections. However, when they come into closer contact with Dutch society and the more they start feeling Dutch, religious commitment undergoes changes. Ritual practice appears to be in decline and in particular Islamic norms concerning the position of women and relations between men and women change. These are precisely the issues that are a source of prejudice and stereotypes on the part of the autochthonous population of the Netherlands. Now we take a look at what these youngsters say about living as a Muslim in the Netherlands: what do *they* think the future of Islam in this country will be, do they encounter difficulties in this respect and what changes would they like to see in Dutch society to make living as a Muslim in this country easier?

Being a Muslim in the Netherlands
Aspirations and fears

A large group (39%) foresees a decline in Islamic religion: they are of the opinion that Moroccan youngster will in the end loose their religion, if the trend they discern now among their peers continues. A small group (15%) shows concerns about the attitude of the Dutch -and sometimes the world- towards Islam. They are afraid that conflicts between Muslims and non-Muslims will arise and refer for instance to recent attacks on mosques in the Netherlands, to the rise of right-wing extremist parties and to the negative image that is presented of Islam in the media. Others (35%) see the future of Islam in the Netherlands in a more positive way. They are of the opinion that the attitude towards Islam on the part of the Dutch is becoming more and more understanding.

When asked whether they consider it more difficult to be a Muslim in a non-Muslim country half of the interviewees said yes, a small group said it is more difficult in some respects and less so in others. Three out of ten youngsters are of the opinion that it makes no difference. It turns out that these different evaluations are unrelated with religious commitment, socio-cultural integration, or attitude towards politics.

When looking more closely at the reasons these youngsters give for their initial answer, the following picture appears. In table 3 we present these motivations. We expect differences between men and women in this respect.

Table 3. Categories in answers to the question "Do you consider it more difficult to be a Muslim in Dutch society than in Morocco?"						
	Total (N=87)		Men (N=44)		Women (N=43)	
More difficult because of the absence of structural provisions	16	18%	9	21%	7	16%
More difficult because of contact with Dutch peers	37	41%	26	59%	11	26%
More difficult because Dutch do not accept Muslims	12	13%	1	2%	11	26%
Makes no difference because you	24	26%	10	23%	14	33%
Makes no difference -or is easier- because Muslims in the Netherlands are more strict	11	12%	5	11%	6	14%

A large group (41%) encounters difficulties in being a Muslim in a non-Muslim context because they are without the almost automatic support in practising their religion that they encounter in Morocco. Some of them say they are tempted by their contact with Dutch peers to do things that are forbidden in Islam (like drinking alcohol). A small group is of the opinion that there are no structural provisions for Muslims in the Netherlands (18%). They refer to the absence of places to pray for women, the lack of Islamic schooling, discrimination of women wearing a headscarf at work and the fact that they have to work or visit school at the time of religious holidays or the Friday noon prayer. Another small- but interesting- group says they do not feel accepted when living their religion (13%). This feeling is almost in all cases associated with the wearing of the headscarf.

Among the youngsters that are of the opinion that it is not more difficult to live as a Muslim in the Netherlands a rather large group (26%) is of the opinion that it makes no difference. If you really want to, you can be a Muslim wherever you want, and some of them say that living in the Netherlands has made them more aware of their religion and more convinced. Others (12%) say that Moroccan Muslims in the Netherlands are more strict and adhere to their religion more than Muslims living in Morocco.

We find that in the group that has feelings of not being accepted, all but one of the subjects are women, and in the group that says that coming into contact with Dutch people makes it more difficult to live as a Muslim more than two thirds is male. The other three groups are equally distributed among men and women. Since one of the issues in the public debate about Muslim minorities in the Netherlands concentrates upon Islamic rules and regulations concerning women it is not surprising that in particular women have the feeling they are not accepted when showing in the public domain that they are Muslims.

When asked whether they want things to change in Dutch society so it will be easier for them to live their religion, 16 youngster have difficulties in answering this question: it is a topic they have never thought about (see table 4).

Table 4. Categories in answers to the question "Do you want any changes to come about in Dutch society so that it will become easier for Muslims?					
	Total (N=75)		Men (N=38)		Women (N=37)
No changes	36	48%	24	63%	12	32%
Structural changes	10	13%	6	15%	4	11%
Cultural changes	22	29%	5	13%	17	46%
Muslims should change	7	9%	3	8%	4	11%

In the answers of 75 others we find four categories. A rather large group (48%) says that the structural provisions for Muslims in this country and attitude of the Dutch government towards Muslims are satisfactory. Seven youngsters (9%) are of the opinion that Moroccan Muslims living in the Netherlands should have no expectations and claims in this respect, instead they should try and actively adjust themselves to Dutch society. Some are opposed to Islamic schools and the founding of mosques.

Only a rather small group (13%) says they wish structural changes: more mosques, possibilities to get a day off on religious holidays or provisions for praying at work or at school. Others (29%) say that they would like to see more cultural changes come about: namely that the Dutch learn more about Islam and try to understand this religion more, or that the rather negative view of Islam that is presented in the media is substituted by a more positive view of their religion.

Here again we might expect that in particular women wish for cultural changes, since the debate concerning the position of Islam concentrates in some ways on them.. This is confirmed: 63% of the male subjects are satisfied as opposed to 32% of the women. It is mostly women that want to see cultural changes come about (46% of the women give this answer, and only 13% of the men). This leads us to the question whether these women are more in agreement with Islamic cultural norms and values. Contrarily to this expectation we find that this is not the case.

For these youngsters there are hardly any specific issues that they would try to get on a political agenda. In the opinion of most of them Muslims have succeeded in getting the provisions they need to actively practice their religion. Their concerns -if there are any- concentrate on the society at large and on the media: they wish for a more positive view of Islam and more understanding on the part of the Dutch. These seem to be in particular concerns of women, not surprisingly since the public debate and the negative image of Islam mostly concentrates on issues concerning women.

Conclusions

We find indications for a secularization process: that is to say observance of ritual practices and agreement with Islamic cultural norms and values seems to be in decline. In this respect our findings are in line with those of Rooijackers (1992a; 1992b) and Feddema (1991; 1992). As indicated before, this has to be taken with some precaution however. A lot of youngsters say they intend to start living by Islamic rules when they get older or get married and have children. And besides the percentage of youngsters that do not fast during the month of Ramadan is still rather small.

We can conclude that religious commitment and socio-cultural integration are partly negatively related. Forming friendships with Dutch peers and having the feeling to be at least part Dutch are associated with lower degrees of religious commitment. It is not possible to conclude what is cause and what is effect; it is equally plausible to assume that social and identificational integration lowers religious commitment as to say that a lower religious commitment fosters social participation. Since we find that religion and ethnic identity are strongly related, we have doubts concerning the hypothesis of Sunier (1994) that Islamic and ethnic identity will become separated and that young Muslims will perceive themselves as Dutch, while at the same time feeling Muslim. Our results point in the direction that when youngsters start feeling more Dutch, a decline in religious commitment can be expected.

In the context of this conference the fact that structural participation and political participation are not related to religious commitment is interesting. The policy of the Dutch government is directed towards the structural integration of minority groups. Our results seems to point in the direction that it is possible to combine structural participation with a Muslim identity. However a lot of our interviewees have not yet reached the point in their lives where they enter the labour market, and since unemployment among young migrants is several times higher than unemployment among Dutch youngsters (CBS/ISEO, 1994), we cannot predict what will happen when these young Moroccans are confronted with difficulties in finding a job. The fact that a positive attitude towards Dutch society -affective orientation- and religious commitment can go hand in hand however leads to an optimistic view about the possibilities be a Muslim and feel part of Dutch society.

On the whole these youngsters are satisfied with the opportunities they get to live as Muslims in this country. They show no inclinations to strive for more structural provisions for Muslims, and a small group is even opposed to this. Their fears concentrate on the attitude of the Dutch towards foreigners and the negative image of Islam that is presented in the media. They wish for more positive information and a more balanced view of Islam and its adherents. A substantial number of these young Muslims is opposed to certain so-called Islamic practices that Dutch public opinion finds reprehensible and in particular young women have the feeling that it is time that the negative image that is presented of them as Muslim women is changed.

Notes

[1]   Namely the author of this paper.
[2]   Buitelaar (1993) also encounters this deviant interpretation of Islamic rules in an ethnographic study of Ramadan in Morocco.
[3]   Classification scheme: 1.00 through 2.24 is 'agree', 2.25 through 2.74 is 'intermediate' and 2.75 through 5.00 is disagreement.

10

Ethnic Identity and Cultural Orientation of Second Generation Turkish Muslim Migrants:

Consequences for Minorities Policy

Jan van der Lans & Margo Rooijackers

Since World War II the techniques of system analysis have become increasingly important in political science. The concept of the system provides a broad framework for studying society as a process of ceaseless interactions of interest groups within the state, and politics as that part of the overall social system whose activities involve steering these interactions in the right direction. During the last decades, the influx of large numbers of Mediterranean migrant workers not only changed the demographic map of Western countries but also made new demands for the political system. Especially because of the high birth rate in migrant families,[1] minority groups came into being. Although politically less influential than other sections of the population, as new interest groups they change the interplay of forces in society which burdens the overall social system with new problems. The fact that minority groups are distinct in nationality, language, culture, religion and economic function segregates their members from the rest of the society and gives rise to prejudice. The minority itself is likely to respond with strong attitudes of group loyalty, which again increases the chances of conflicts with other interest groups. Actually, the public debate concerning the Turkish and Moroccan minorities is focused on issues that are connected to their deviating religion: the growing number of mosques, the foundation of islamic schools, the restrictive prescriptions for women with respect to clothing and behaviour. In the eyes of many members of the indigenous population, features like these mark off muslim minorities as a distinct and even threatening interest group and are considered impediments to their integration into society.

The makers of government policy, who feel responsible for an equitable distribution of social goods as well as for the prevention of conflicts between interest groups, are faced with a choice by this situation. One line of policy should be to provide facilities (on the domains of education and religion) that enable each interest group to maintain its cultural identity. Another line of policy however should be the advancement of social integration of minority groups into society, to benefit the social and economic well-being of the system as a whole. It appears logical to expect that a policy supporting cultural characteristics will reinforce segregation, however, and hinder the policy of social integration. Whether the two lines of policy are really counteractive, however, has not yet been empirically assessed.

During the eighties, the decision-making of Dutch authorities with respect to minority groups was inspired by the first line of policy, which was laid down in the *Minderhedennota 1983*. Recently, the emphasis has shifted.Now, policy is aimed at emancipation of minorities (Smeets a.o., 1995).[2] Priority is given to the removal of economic deprivation and of lags in cognitive and linguistic development, whereas the maintenance of cultural identity is left to the minority groups themselves. Obviously, this shift of policy has been encouraged by the growth of negative attitudes towards strangers that is apparent from the electoral success of some political parties.

A well-considered policy requires a clear insight into the cultural orientation of minority-groups. Instead of being static, it is liable to transform in connection with the shift of generations. Most of the empirical research dealing with ethnic groups has been focused on intergroup attitudes and on adaptation problems (Rooijackers, 1994). Far less studied have been the attitudes of minority group members towards their own group and its cultural traditions (Phinney, 1990). While members of the first generation of migrants stick to their cultural traditions in order to secure a feeling of safety and self-respect, it is generally assumed that members of the second generation, as an effect of interactions with peers from the dominant group during their formative years, will increasingly take over the life-style of the dominant culture and abandon values and practices of the parental culture. However, intercultural contacts may also have quite another effect. As a result of psychological processes of social comparison, minority group members may become aware of their low social status and of the impossibility to change their destiny. In coping with feelings of powerlessness, they may seek to maintain a positive selfregard by identifying exclusively with their own group and by proudly cherishing distinctive cultural features.

In this paper we will present data on the cultural orientation of second generation Turkish muslim migrants in The Netherlands, obtained by interviews. The term 'cultural orientation' refers to culture as *modus operandi* or *habitus* (Bourdieu, 1977). Using the concept of ethnic identity, we will compare two groups of second generation members that differ in ethnic orientation. Central point of discussion will be whether these two groups also differ in attitudes towards rules of conduct of the parental culture, in religious involvement and in everyday practices that are indicative for integration into the Dutch society.

Method

Subjects

Data have been obtained from interviews with a sample of 80 young adults (40 men and 40 women), who were identified as members of the second generation of Turkish migrants in The Netherlands. To be classified as second generation, a subject had to meet two criteria. Firstly, to have been born in The Netherlands of Turkish parents or having migrated to this country for the purpose of family-reunification. Secondly, he or she should have attended a Dutch school for at least five years. The majority of names and addresses were drawn at random from lists, obtained from the municipal register of two cities, of all local inhabitants of Turkish nationality belonging to the age-group of 17-25 years old. Some additional subjects were obtained from schools in a third city. All subjects were approached by mail, telephone or by visiting the addresses. The responserate was satisfactory. In approximately two-thirds of the addresses at which youngsters lived who met the criteria for selection, they agreed to participate in the research.

Subjects (or their families) came from all over Turkey with an overrepresentation of the regions Central-Anatolia and East/South-East Turkey. On average, the subjects had resided in The Netherlands for 13 years. An unanticipated difference in religious denomination emerged; besides 66 Sunni's there appeared to be 14 subjects with an Alevi background.

Instruments

The instrument used was a structured in-depth interview that consisted of open and closed questions. A large questionnaire was devised in order to obtain data on four domains: social network, social-cultural orientation, religious involvement (knowledge, attitudes, ritual practice), and psychological well-being. Moreover, questions were asked about the subject's migration history, level of education, civil status and employment. Ethnic identity was assessed by self-rating. All subjects were asked to express in percentages to what extent they felt themselves as Turkish and as Dutch. Measured in this way, ethnic identity is conceived in accordance with Tajfel's definition of social identity: "that part of an individual's self-concept which derives from his knowledge of his membership of a social group together with the value and emotional significance attached to that membership" (Tajfel, 1981, 255).[3]

In order to measure attitudes towards rules of conduct of the parental culture, a list of 12 obligations familiar to people from islamic countries was presented to the subjects. (Examples: "The reputation of the family should always be respected"; "A woman has to obey her husband"; "Out of doors women should always wear a headscarf"; "It is the man's duty to protect the reputation of his female family members".) They were asked to indicate on 5-point rating scales to what extent they agreed with the obligations.

Regarding life-style, three aspects were distinguished: voluntary participation, linguistic skill, and affective orientation towards Dutch society. A large number of questions served as a basis to construct a measure for voluntary participation in social life: reading Dutch papers, magazines and books, watching t.v. and videotapes, membership of sports clubs, using the possibility to participate in local elections, nationality of friends. Affective orientation towards Dutch society was measured by the Subjective Integration Scale, developed by De Jong & Batenburg (1985). The 12 items of this scale express a positive attitude towards living in The Netherlands.

We used two measures of religious commitment. Firstly, a self-report of the subjective importance the subject ascribed to islam. Secondly, from a large number of interview questions about acceptance of religious beliefs and observance of ritual practices and of some prescriptions of the Shari'a, a homogeneous Scale of Religious Involvement, consisting of ten items, could be constructed (reliability: alpha = .82; average = 14.4; st.dev. = 4.3; min 10, max 26).

Results
1. Ethnic identity

A quarter of the sample reported an ethnic identity that was exclusively or for at least 95% Turkish.[4] For some, even for the two who had been born in The Netherlands, it is a self-evident feeling, a non-reflective attachment. For some a deliberate choice. Some referred to kinship-loyalty, e.g. "I am proud of my grandparents and that I belong to their offspring. I know what they have done and I must try to behave as one of them." For some, it is the outcome of a process of social comparison: e.g. "When I visit Dutch people, I feel that I am a Turk. I see what they do and what I don't do. Then I feel that I am Turkish". This subject could be conceived as an example of "reactive ethnicity" (Ballard, 1979).

Not more than one subject, a twenty-one year old woman, reported an exclusively Dutch identity. An explanation for the complete cross-identification can be found in her exceptional personal history and in the fact that in the period in which she was interviewed, she and her husband were threatened with compulsory remigration to Turkey.

Although the number of subjects that identified themselves as exclusively Turkish is substantial, the majority of subjects labelled themselves as partly Turkish, partly Dutch. Ten (13%) of these bi-cultural (Wong-Rieger & Quintana, 1987) subjects see themselves as equally Turkish and Dutch, but for most of them (73%) the Turkish identity is predominating to varying degrees. Only 12 subjects (15%) labelled themselves as more Dutch than Turkish.

One should be aware of the fact that the data on the ethnic identity option of the interviewed second generation migrants are a picture at a given moment. What is true for human identity in general, goes for ethnic identity too: the concept does not refer to a static but to a variable aspect of the self. Considering the age of the subjects, it can hardly be expected that their self-identification at the interview represents a definitive option. The way in which subjects motivate their bi-cultural option, reveals structural variations, that from the viewpoint of psychological maturity, must be qualified differently. In this context, we cannot elaborate on this. Elsewhere, one of us (Rooijackers, 1994) has distinguished types of multi-ethnic identity , that are qualitatively different in connection with the underlying coping strategy. Here, we will give just two examples. A male subject explained his bi-cultural ethnic identity in the following way: "As a child you just copy the behaviour of people, without being conscious of it. But when you become older, you become more conscious. Now I try to combine the good things of the Turkish culture with those of the Dutch." The next example leaves quite another impression. A twenty year old female said: "Sometimes I feel so in-between that I hate myself for it. Why am I like this? I have not become 100% Dutch nor 100% Turkish and that is precisely my problem." Considered in terms of Erikson's developmental theory of identity formation, the first quotation is indicative of an achieved identity status, whereas the second suggests a state of identity confusion.

Having noticed that the majority of second generation Turkish migrants prefers a dual ethnic identity but that a substantial number feel themselves exclusively Turkish, it is relevant within the scope of this conference to know whether both groups differ with respect to social-demographic factors that might influence their option for ethnic identity. Are there such factors that can be influenced by policy-makers? Also it is important to know whether migrants with a mixed ethnic identity attach less interest to elements of the traditional Turkish culture and show a higher participation in Dutch society than their peers who opt for a mono-ethnic Turkish identity.

To make a comparison, we did not use all the subjects with a Turkish/Dutch ethnic identity in the analysis, but selected a more restricted range of subjects. Only subjects who see themselves for at least 30% Dutch and not less than 25% Turkish have been compared with subjects who feel themselves more than 95% Turkish. The dual ethnic identity-group consists of 40 subjects. Twenty-one of them are male and nineteen female. The comparison group consists of 20 subjects, 11 male and 9 female. So, the two groups do not differ with respect to sex ratio.

2. Comparison of both groups with respect to social-demographic factors

In Table 1, both groups are compared with respect to factors that might have influenced the option for ethnic identity.

Table 1. Comparison with respect to social-demographic characteristics			
	Dual ethnic identity (N=40)	*Excl. Turkish ethnic identity (N=20)*	*Difference = significant*
Born in Turkey	85%	90%	-
Rural (non-urban) origin	62%	55%	-
Average age of migration	5.9	7.4	-
Length of stay	13.9 yrs.	12.7 yrs	-
Present age	19.8	20.0	-
Intention concerning remigration: will stay in The Netherlands will remigrate don't know	 55% 15% 30% (100%)	 25% 65% 10% (100%)	p<.01
Civil Status: married engaged durable friendship no partner	 27.5% 12.5% 15.0% 45 % (100%)	 55% 10% 0% 35% (100%)	-
Nationality partner: turkish dutch	 82% 18%	 100%	-
Job situation: employed unemployed housewife at school	 32.5% 12.5% 5 % 50 % (100%)	 10% 20% 20% 50% (100%)	p=.04
Level of education: Secondary lower level secondary middle level 40% (pre-)university, higher vocational	 45% 40% 15% (100%)	 55% 35% 10% (100%)	-
Religious denomination: Sunni Alevi	 72.5% 27.5%	 95% 5%	p=.01
Has experienced discrimination	56.2%	43.7%	-
Language at home: turkish dutch both other	 56.2% 3.1% 37.5% 3.1% (100%)	 100% 0% 0% 0% 100%	yes

Contrary to expectations, among second generation migrants who opt for a dual ethnic ethnicity there are hardly more subjects that have been born in

The Netherlands. Neither do both groups differ with respect to migration age or length of stay. It is obvious that among the subjects with an exclusively Turkish identity there are more who know for sure that they will remigrate to Turkey. It is surprising however, that some of the subjects with a dual ethnic identity also have the same intention. This might be indicative of the tentative character of an identity option.

Knowing that both groups have an equal sex ratio, the figures with respect to civil status teach us that for young women there is a relationship between being married and opting for an exclusively Turkish identity, while most Turkish young women who feel themselves partly Dutch, indicate that they do not have a durable partnership. As far as durable relationships are concerned (marriage, engaged or friendship), the majority of young Turkish migrants prefer a Turkish partner regardless of their own ethnic identity option.

Regarding job-situation, there is a difference between the groups. The figures indicate a relationship between ethnic identity and employment, unemployment respectively. This is not attributable to the fact that there are relatively more married women in the second group. When these are excluded, the percentage of unemployed among young migrants with an exclusively Turkish identity is twice as high as among those with a dual ethnic identity. It should be remarked however, that it is not possible to conclude which in this case is cause and which is effect. Anyway, the figures do not allow to attribute it to an educational difference between the two groups.

Regarding religious orientation, the figures indicate that it is more likely for Turkish migrants with an Alevi background to opt for a dual ethnic identity than for those from Sunni families.

The most substantial difference between the groups however seems to be the language spoken at home. It appears that all migrants with an exclusive Turkish identity indicated that at home Turkish is the most used language, while 37.5% of the subjects with a dual ethnic identity reported that Dutch and Turkish are used equally at home. Additionally, there is one subject of this group, who reported that Dutch is the most spoken language, and another one who comes from a Kurdish family. Knowing that language is generally considered to be the most important carrier for the transition of culture (Liebkind, 1992) as well as the central vehicle of habitus (Hanks, 1993), we conclude from our data that the cultural praxis in the parental home is one of the predictors of the ethnic identity option of second generation migrants. The data suggest that this is a more decisive factor than level of education.

3. Comparison of both groups with respect to participation in dutch social life

We expect that second generation migrants from Turkey, who indicate that they see themselves as partly Dutch, are better integrated into Dutch society than their peers who stick to an exclusively Turkish identity. Two measures were available to check whether the facts validate this expectation, first the Voluntary Participation Index, and second the scores on the Subjective Integration Scale.

Six interview questions have been used to construct the Voluntary Participation Index: whether or not the respondent regularly reads Dutch papers and/or books, is a member of a non-Turkish sports club and/or other association, whether or not he will vote at the next elections, and the nationality of friends. The average sumscores in Table 2 indicate that subjects with a dual ethnic identity did not give evidence of being generally more involved in Dutch society than subjects with an exclusively Turkish identity.

Table 2. Involvement in Dutch social life				
	average	st.dev.	T	P
Index of Voluntary Participation (reading, membership of clubs, voting, Dutch friends)				
dual ethnic identity subjects (N=40)	4.4	1.1	1.02	.31
exclusively Turkish ethnic identity Ss (N=20)	4.1	1.2		
Subjective Integration Scale				
dual ethnic identity subjects (N=40)	3.8	.52		<.001
exclusively Turkish ethnic identity Ss (N=20)	2.8	.52		

The majority of all interviewed youngsters said that they never read books, neither Turkish nor Dutch. More subjects with a Turkish ethnic identity than with a dual ethnic identity regularly read a Turkish paper. In both groups this is done by a minority however. A substantial number of young migrants say to vote when there are elections. Among those with a partly Dutch identity, their number is slightly higher than in the comparison group. A similar picture was found with respect to inter-ethnic friendships. The majority of young migrants report to have Turkish as well as Dutch friends. In the dual ethnic identity group this is more frequent than in the exclusively Turkish group. Surprisingly enough however, no less than a quarter of the subjects who feel themselves partly Dutch, said to have no Dutch friends. It turned out that none of the female young migrants participates in a sports club. One of them said that she now occasionally went to the swimming pool when only women are allowed, but nearly all female respondents never play sports. Some indicated that they should like to do it but would not get permission from their parents.

With the second measure, it becomes more obvious that subjects with a dual ethnic identity considered themselves better integrated in Dutch society (Table 2). While there are hardly any differences between the groups with respect to the kinds of actual behaviour that is measured by the Index of Voluntary Participation, the attitude statements of the Subjective Integration Scale characterize better that young migrants who opt for a dual ethnic identity feel more attracted to living in Dutch society than migrants who stick to an exclusive Turkish identity. They more strongly agree with items like: "More and more I feel I belong to the Dutch"; "I want to stay on in The Netherlands", and more strongly disagree with statements like "I prefer not to have contact with the Dutch"; "If conditions are favourable, I'll leave". It is also interesting to see, however, that both groups without any difference strongly agreed with items like "I can get along well with the Dutch"; "I am totally accustomed to The Netherlands"; "Most Dutchmen accept me." Although we can conclude that migrants, who feel partly Turkish partly Dutch are better integrated into Dutch society, it would be erroneous to say that second generation members with an exclusively Turkish identity do not feel integrated. The adherence to original ethnic identity does not necessarily interfere with a positive orientation towards the migration society.

4. Traditional values and norms

In this section, we will examine the attitude of second generation members towards some cultural-islamic values and norms. It concerns values and norms that generally are repudiated by the Dutch and often provoke negative prejudice and even discriminative reactions towards migrants from muslim countries. In the interview, a list of twelve items was presented, referring to norms such as the reputation of the family, being obedient to one's parents, and special prescriptions for women like wearing a headscarf, staying virginal until marriage, obeying their male family members. All respondents were asked to indicate on a 5-point scale whether they agreed or disagreed with any of the items. We expect that the stronger second generation migrants feel attracted to Dutch culture, the more likely they are to abandon traditional norms.

The statistical analysis showed that, bar one, the items formed a uni-dimensional measure. The scale may therefor be conceived as a homogeneous measure of the concept Traditionalism. Comparison of the average scale scores of both groups proves, that subjects with a dual ethnic attitude in general do have a less positive attitude towards traditional norms than subjects who opt for a Turkish identity (Table 3). However, they do not reject any of the items, bar two, namely the obligation for women to wear a headscarf and to obey their husband. It should be remarked that with respect to the virginity norm they are equally positive as subjects with an exclusive Turkish identity.

Table 3. Attitudes towards traditional norms and values				
	average	st.dev.	T	P
Traditionalism Scale dual ethnic identity subjects (N=40) exclusively Turkish ethnic identity Ss (N=20)	2.7 2.0	1.0 0.8	2.72	.008

5. Religious commitment

In relation to particular traditional norms, their islamic religion also gives rise to negative attitudes towards Turkish and Moroccan migrants. It is not in the least because of the deviating characteristics of islam, in comparison to the familiar christian institutions, that the general population goes on to see them as foreigners. Whether the government should promote material, legal and other cultural facilities in the domain of islam or not, is a continuous issue of political debate. Whether religious involvement of muslim migrants is really negatively related with the speed of social and cultural integration, has hardly been investigated, however.

If this relationship exists, then we may expect to find a difference in religious involvement between second generation migrants with a dual ethnic identity in comparison with those sticking to an exclusively Turkish identity.

Table 4. Religious commitment				
	average	st.dev.	T	P
Importance attached to Islam in one's personal life (1 = very important; 5 = very unimportant) dual ethnic identity subjects (N=40) exclusively Turkish ethnic identity Ss (N=20)	2.6 1.8	1.2 1.1	2.34	.02
Scale of Religious Involvement (belief and observance) (10 = very involved; 26 = not involved) dual ethnic identity subjects (N=40) exclusively Turkish ethnic identity Ss (N=20)	15.6 12.6	4.9 2.6	2.56	.01
After exclusion of Alevi subjects				
Importance attached to Islam in one's personal life (1 = very important; 5 = very unimportant) dual ethnic identity subjects (N=29) exclusively Turkish ethnic identity Ss (N=19)	2.1 1.8	.98 1.1	1.04	.30
Scale of Religious Involvement (belief and observance) (10 = very involved; 26 = not involved) dual ethnic identity subjects (N=29) exclusively Turkish ethnic identity Ss (N=19)	13.4 12.6	3.1 2.6	.85	.39

As said already in the section on methods, the concept religious involvement was measured in two ways: a question to each respondent to indicate how important islam is for him/her, and also a scale measuring religious belief and observance of ritual obligations. As Table 4 shows, the scores of subjects with a dual ethnic identity on both measures indicate a significantly smaller religious involvement compared to subjects with an exclusively Turkish identity. Viewed separately, their religious involvement is generally quite high, however.

The standard deviation scores make plain that the multi-ethnic group is more heterogeneous with respect to religious involvement than the other group. While 80% of the mono-ethnic subjects reported islam to be an important, even very important element in their personal life, one in four subjects in the dual ethnic group qualified it is personally irrelevant. Knowing however, that this group comprises a considerable number of Alevi's, we presumed this to be the main explanation for the difference. As shown elsewhere (Van der Lans & Rooijackers, 1992; 1994), the attitudinal variance found with respect to religious beliefs and practices can be mainly reduced to historical cultural differences between Sunni- and Alevi-muslims. When we restrict the analysis to subjects with a Sunni background, the remaining subjects with a partly Dutch ethnic identity appear to be equally high in religious involvement as subjects with an exclusive Turkish ethnic identity.

This finding leads to an important conclusion. There is no reason to assume a relationship between the speed of integration of young migrants into Dutch society, and their commitment to islamic religion. Neither is there an indication that religious involvement slows down the speed of integration nor that integration fosters secularization. Not the option for ethnic identity, which we assume to be indicative of social-cultural integration, explains the differences found between young migrants in religious involvement, but a socio-historical factor that has nothing to do with migration.

Conclusions

In all Western societies that have changed from monocultural to multicultural in the last few decades the societal system has been subjected to pressure. The harmony between the needs of the citizens on the one hand and social institutions, such as legislation, labour market, educational and medical facilities, on the other has been disrupted. For policy-makers, who have the task to restore the balance of the societal system, it is indispensable to be well-informed about the direction in which the cultural orientation of minority groups is developing.

The concept of ethnic identity is a workable tool to study changes in the social self and cultural orientation of minority group members. Although the definition and explanation of ethnic identity is still a much debated issue among sociologists, anthropologist and psychologists (Van Soest & Verdonk, 1984; Phinney, 1990; Liebkind, 1992), the concept provides a method to study the dynamics of segregation and integration on the level of the person. In order to be of predictive value however, the range of options for ethnic identity should be larger. Because of the fact that there were few subjects in our sample who have shifted to a predominantly Dutch identity, the differences between the comparison groups with respect to the indicators of change, were generally small.

Several results of our investigation shed new light on the cultural orientation of second generation Turkish migrants. First, the evidence that differences in social-cultural identification are not related with migration history but primarily depend on the language spoken in the parental home. This reinforces the expectation that with the shift of generations a dual ethnic identity or a mono-ethnic Dutch identity will be found more and more.

Furthermore, it is revealing that young migrants who prefer to stick exclusively or dominantly to a Turkish ethnic identity, do not participate to a lesser degree in the Dutch society than young Turks who consider themselves as partly Dutch. Although the latter scored higher on the measure of Subjective Integration, it is not true that the former see themselves as not or badly integrated in Dutch society: the average scores of the Turkish youngsters with an exclusively Turkish identity point out that they feel at home in Dutch society. A mono-ethnic choice for a Turkish identity does not necessarily mean segregation.

On the other hand it appeared that young Turkish migrants who see themselves as partly Dutch, do not repudiate the cultural heritage of traditional behaviourial codes, but go on to conform, except for the rules that are restrictive to women.

The most conspicuous finding is that in our sample young migrants who gave up their exclusively Turkish identity and shifted to a partly Dutch identity, are not less committed to Islam and in general continue abiding by its rituals and behaviourial rules. Contrary to other observers (Shadid and Van Koningsveld, 1991; Feddema, 1992), we have not found evidence that a process of secularization has started.[5] Asked for the reasons for their religious commitment, three kinds of motives dominate the answers.

A frequently heard answer is that the islam serves as a moral grip and a guiding principle in their way of life. Others say that religion provides support in coping with suffering and misfortune. Some confess that religious commitment is a kind of insurance for life in the hereafter. While most respondents with an exclusively Turkish identity account for their religious conviction by referring to their upbringing, it is remarkable that none of those with a dual ethnic identity mentioned this justification. Those who still are devoted believers, emphasized that this is a matter of conscious choice.

The majority of the religiously committed young migrants think it harder to be a good muslim in Holland than in Turkey. Yet, many of them evaluate the societal conditions for muslims as satisfactory. Only a minority (22%) want more facilities. Of the issues mentioned spontaneously, the most frequent was a liberalization of the restrictions with respect to the *adhan,* the public call to prayer, which for many muslims in Western countries is a symbol of religious freedom (Landman, 1992). Twice mentioned were more Q'uran-lessons as well as more facilities for prayer in workplaces. No one expressed the wish for more islamic schools. Several young migrants raised objections to it, however.

In our opinion it would be wise for politicians to listen carefully to the opinions and prospects of the second generation, especially those who have decided to stay. Results of our investigation indicate that there are (now at least) still many among them, who opt for a Dutch ethnic identity without giving up their cultural heritage. Governmental support in maintaining that heritage would prove more helpful to their integration process than a policy frustrating their cultural needs. Whether migrants and their offspring will feel at home and whether they will be incorporated into the society, will greatly depend on the degree in which they will perceive that they have the same rights and possibilities as the indigenous population, while at the same time not being forced to give up the traditional cultural resources of their self-respect.

However, it is not only a matter of respect for feelings. A policy directed at preservation of the migrant culture can also be defended by rational arguments. The cultural heritage provides a shared system of meaning and representations, that will enable social interaction and communication and hold together social networks (Wertsch, J.V. & Lee, B., 1984; Moscovici, S., 1984). When on the other hand social networks fall apart because shared meanings have disappeared, then people will become uprooted, a situation that facilitates mental disorder and social pathology.

Notes

[1] While during the period of 1990-1992 the autochthonic population increased with 0.8%, the minority groups of Turks and Moroccans in The Netherlands increased with 17% each. The age-group of 0-15 years old is relatively larger among the Turks (34%) and Moroccans (39%) than among the autochthonic population (23%). Source: Smeets, H. a.o., 1995.

[2] Revealing is the fact that in official documents the long-established concept "minderhedenbeleid" has been replaced by the term "allochtonenbeleid".

[3] This rating procedure seems to be a more precise measure than just asking the subject which ethnic label from a list of alternatives applies most to him/herself, a widely used procedure in research on ethnic identity, as became obvious in a recent review article (see Phinney, 1990).

[4] Comments, given by the subjects, support the primordial as well as the situational viewpoint, used by social scientists in explaining ethnic phenomena (Liebkind, 1992).

[5] Our finding with respect to religious commitment seems to contradict that of Feddema after his empirical research into the socio-cultural orientation of Turkish and Moroccan boys in three Dutch cities (Feddema, 1992). On basis of observation and interviews of Turkish boys from the same age-range as our sample he concluded that the majority of them is not religiously committed but shows a secular orientation. Fewer respondents in his sample than in ours reported a regular observance of the prescribed practices of prayer, visit of the mosque, and fast. The difference in research setting might play a part here. Feddema obtained his data through group-interviews in youth clubs, whereas our respondents were interviewed individually at their place. Apart from that, also Feddema classified 69% of the Turkish boys as "regulars" with regard to religious practice and not more than 2% as non-religious.

11

The Impact of Radical Islam on the Political Attitudes of First Generation Moroccan Muslims in the Netherlands

Frank Kemper

According to popular opinion in the West, Islam and democracy belong to different worlds. Indeed, genuinely democratic states are rare in the Muslim world (Kazancigil, 1991). Moreover, the only viable opposition movement is to be found in radical Islam which seems at odds with western concepts of democracy. On the other hand, there are others (Addi, 1992; Haleber, 1989; Hooglund, 1992) who maintain that the rise of radical Islam is an expression of a great need for democracy in the Islamic countries. For that reason there would not be any ground for fear of Muslim extremism on behalf of the Muslim migrants within the western democracies. The purpose of this paper is to investigate the impact of radical Muslim movements on the political attitudes of Moroccan Muslim migrants in the Netherlands.

Fundamentalism and Islamism

Before doing this, I would like to clarify the concepts of fundamentalism and Islamism I will be using. I will follow Bruno Angelet (1990), who -among others- reserves the label of "fundamentalism" for the Islamic revival movement that restricts itself mostly to the moral conduct and purity of the faith, such as the Muslim Brothers founded by Hassan Al Banna. The fundamentalist movement did not seek to control the economy or the state. It confined itself to trying to influence the nationalist leaders ruling the Arab world after the decolonisation. To a radical minority this was not enough.

Following writers like Sayed Qotb, they want to restore the Muslim world to its former glory by purifying the state, economy, culture and science of all western and other non-Islamic influences. Their struggle is one for independence from the former colonial powers. Angelet uses label of "Islamism" to describe this political movement that calls for a radical Islamization of the entire society.

There is no sharp contrast between fundamentalism and Islamism. The Moroccan Islamist Abdessalam Yacine for example sees as the ultimate aim of the movement the establishment of a second caliphate that unites all Muslims on earth. But first a generation of devoted Muslims has to be bred, an intellectual vanguard able to lead the masses back to the pure faith (Chekroun, 1991). So, the ethical revival of fundamentalism is just the first step in the political programme of Islamism.

Islamism and political participation

The year 1979 marks the beginning of a new era in the Muslim world in two ways. It was the start of a new century, the year 1400 of the Islamic calendar. It was also the year in which western scholars were completely taken by surprise by the Islamic revolution in Iran. From that moment on, the Islamist movement gained strength throughout the Muslim world.[1] Headlines in the western newspapers attested to the growing fear of a new political force that seemed able to mobilize vast masses of people against modernity and the western way of life. Radical Islamists took a violent stand against the western concept of civilization that hitherto had been the model for progress in the world. The movement was opposed to cherished values like civil liberties and the parliamentary democracy.

Explanations of the phenomena were soon offered. Some argued that the rapid pace of modernisation had created a crisis of identity to which the Islamic utopia offered a solution (Heper, 1981; Dessouki, 1982). Others suggested that, after decolonisation, ideologies of western origin such as liberalism, nationalism and socialism had failed to establish legitimate political rule and therefore created a crisis of legitimacy. (Tibi, 1983; Dekmejian, 1985). Still others mentioned the socio-economic context of the growing popular discontent in the Muslim world (Ayubi, 1980; Halliday, 1982-83; Yasini, 1988).

A topic which deserves more elaboration concerns the position of the Islamists on political participation. While they present the "Islamic state" as an alternative to the secular western democracy, there is no consensus amongst Islamist thinkers as to the features of this state. The Islamic state seems to derive its power to reign from an almighty God and it needs no authorization by the people. It rules by the divine law of the sharia, which is a perfect law and suitable for all times and all occasions. Therefore there is no need for any popular consultation. Yet the Islamic state in Iran knows a parliamentary structure, the *majlis*, the representatives of which are chosen in free elections. Any citizen who abides by the narrowly described rules of Islamic conduct is free to run for elections. In western eyes it is these rules of Islamic conduct that are antagonistic to the civil liberties of a democratic society. In Iran these standards of behaviour are shared by the overwhelming majority of the predominantly rural population, as they are in other traditional Islamic countries. Hooglund (1992) points out that the Iranian example of a democratic structure, that respects traditional Islamic values, is the real threat to the autocratic regimes of the Arabic peninsula.

So instead of a total rejection of democracy, the mass appeal of radical Islam might be fed by a need for democracy, be it within the boundaries of the faith. There are other authors whose analyses amount to the same conclusion. Ron Haleber (1988) for instance links the rise of the Islamist movement in Morocco to the erosion of its system of political hegemony. For centuries the king and his religious charisma were able to integrate the force of tribal dissidence and popular Islam and the opposing force of urban centralisation and official Islam. In recent years the old networks of solidarity that were at the base of this structure have eroded, due to the booming population, the urban migration and the mass-unemployment. Millions are locked out of the hegemonical play that used to guarantee the political stability in the country. It is the Islamist opposition that tries to become their spokesman by attacking the whole system on religious grounds. Moroccan intellectuals like Mohamed Tozi and Mohamed Darif and politicians of the left-wing opposition have therefore recently urged for the legalisation of the Islamist movement in Morocco (van Veen, 1995), in order to integrate the Muslim opposition in the political system.

In a similar vein the Algerian sociologist Lahouari Addi (1992) pleads for free elections in his country, including the participation of the outlawed

Islamist party (Front Islamique du Salut, FIS). He says that the FIS entertains a totalitarian utopia that denies the existence of social differences and diverging interests and therefore leads to bloodshed. Once in power the movement would be confronted with reality. Which, according to this writer is the strongest antidote to any utopia.

Islamism in the European democratic countries

So if Islamism is an expression of a need for democracy, what are its chances in a western democracy? Nowadays in Europe there are millions of Muslim migrants. While most of them do not have the right to elect their representatives in parliament, they enjoy the civil liberties of a liberal democracy. They are free to practise the type of religion of their choice, to express their views and to associate freely. But they are also exposed to the way other citizens practise their civil liberties. They are confronted with the use of alcohol and women dressing and behaving in a manner that violates traditional Islamic standards. They might fear the impact of this lifestyle on their own children. On the one hand, the spirit of repression that caused the rise of Islamism in the Arab world is lacking. On the other hand, the anti-western rhetoric of Islamism might appeal to traditional Muslim migrants who witness the sharp contrast between the western way of life and their own traditional values. Moreover, if they want to join fundamentalist or Islamist associations, they are free to do so.

Schiffauer (1988) shows that religion for Turkish migrants in Germany is no longer as self-evident as it was in their homeland. Among Turkish migrants there is a religious diversity that facilitates a personal commitment to movements or parties that have limited freedom of movement in Turkey itself. Kepel (1994) notices a growing popularity of fundamentalist movements amongst the Muslim youth in France. On the other side Saint Blancat (1993) suggests a growing secularist tendency amongst the younger generations. Radical Islamism in France would be confined to a small minority of the older generation. But the great majority of the elderly would combine a pious fundamentalism with an open attitude to French culture and society.

In the Netherlands, some authors have suggested that the permissive society does not supply a fertile soil for the growth of radical Islamism

(Abderrahman, 1987). Landman (1990) sees a better future for a moderate type of fundamentalism that seeks to integrate itself in Dutch society.

In this paper I will present a description of the attitudes of the first generation of Moroccan Muslim migrants in the Netherlands towards the Islamist movement. Furthermore, I will analyze the relationship between these attitudes and religious commitment, ethnic orientation and a number of indicators of social background and migration history.

Method

The data were collected in structured in-depth interviews as part of a study into the religiosity, ethnicity and psychological well-being amongst Moroccan migrants. The sample consisted of two groups of subjects: a random sample of 34 male Moroccan inhabitants of the two cities (Utrecht and Nijmegen), age 40 and older; and a random sample of 20 male Moroccan school teachers in the same age group. The purpose of including this last group was to enable a comparison between the average migrant worker, whose educational level consists of unfinished primary school and the small intellectual elite of Moroccans who completed a secondary education. All subjects were interviewed individually in the respondents' residence or, in the case of the teachers, at school. The language used during the interview was either Dutch or Moroccan Arabic, according to the respondents' fluency in Dutch. The interviews were conducted by myself, a Dutch male.

The data pertaining to the topic of Islamism consisted of the answers to questions about the compatibility of the sharia and the secular Dutch law; the preference for an Islamic school; the appreciation of Koranic corporal punishment and sympathy for the Islamist movement in Algeria (FIS).[2]

Religious commitment was assessed by probing into the ritual behaviour (prayer, fasting, pilgrimage etc.), moral consequences (abstention of alcohol, pork, interest on loans etc.), knowledge of the Muslim creed (the 5 pillars of Islam; belief in God, his books, his angels, his messengers, judgement day etc.), the attitude towards popular Islam (visits to holy shrines, the use of suras as charms etc.) and the attachment to the mosque-community (contact with imam, meeting friends at the mosque etc.). Furthermore a measure of overall religiousness was created, being an amalgamation of the different dimensions of religious commitment.

Ethnic orientation was explored using questions about traditional habits and values (dress, domestic interior, gender segregation etc.); by asking about relations with Dutchmen (neighbours, colleagues) and the orientation on Dutch society (naturalisation, voting in local elections, watching Dutch news bulletins on TV etc.).

Finally, the social background and migration history were indicated by items concerning education, unemployment, age, length of stay, rural/urban origin, and the vernacular of the respondent (Berber or Arabic speaking).

Results

Indicators of Islamism

As table 1 shows, the majority of the migrant workers as well as the teachers does not have a problem with living in a non-Muslim environment. They see no contradiction in following the prescriptions of the sharia and abiding by the Dutch law at the same time. A minority sees contradictions, but does not object to adapting to the Dutch law. Only a few object to the Dutch law for its incompatibility with the sharia.

While the migrant workers in general do not seem to oppose the Dutch way of life, a large number of them likes to secure a Islamic education for their children by favouring separate Muslim schools. Half of the respondents assumes a neutral stand on this topic. They applaud the facilities given to the Muslim population to found their own schools, but they do not want a separate Islamic education for their own children. The majority of the teachers is opposed to the establishment of separate Islamic schools. This is no surprise, as the Islamic school might be considered as a token of disapproval of the type of school they themselves work in.

One of the aspects in which the sharia diverges most from the western liberal values is its insistence on corporal punishments. The stoning of adulterers and the handcutting of thieves have contributed to the anti-Islamic sentiments in the West. Yet radical Islamists urge for an unconditional application of these sanctions in Islamic countries. Among the migrant workers almost 40% agrees with them, while one third strongly disagrees. About one quarter seeks to compromise between the two by stressing the exceptional conditions under which corporal punishment is to be executed. Handcutting for instance should only be allowed in Islamic countries with a proper level of social equality, education, employment and medical care. Among the teachers only 15% approves of the corporal punishments and two third disapprove.

The most direct indicator of Islamist sympathies is the attitude towards the Islamist opposition in Algeria, which has been in the centre of public attention for the last 5 years. Here a remarkable contrast becomes manifest between the migrant workers and the teachers. While the latter are more inclined to pro-western viewpoints than the former, they are also more outspoken in their sympathy for the Islamist opposition in Algeria.

Table 1. Indications of Islamist tendencies among first generation Morrocan males in the Netherlands				
	Migrant workers		Teachers	
Compatibility of Dutch law and the Sharia				
- Adapts to Dutch law	5	15%	6	30%
- Sees no contradiction	26	76%	10	50%
- Objects to Dutch law	3	9%	4	20%
	34	**100%**	**20**	**100%**
Attitude towards Islamic schools				
- Against separate schools	3	9%	12	60%
- Neutral	17	50%	6	30%
- In favour of separate schools	14	41%	2	10%
	34	**100%**	**20**	**100%**
Attitude towards corporal punishments in the Sharia				
- Rejection	12	35%	13	65%
- Conditional approval	9	26%	4	20%
- Unconditional approval	13	38%	3	15%
	34	**100%**	**20**	**100%**
Attitude towards the Islamist movement in Algeria (FIS)				
- Opposes FIS	7	21%	4	20%
- Does not want to take sides	15	44%	6	30%
- Sympathizes with FIS	12	35%	10	50%
	34	**100%**	**20**	**100%**

The opponents of the FIS amount to one fifth of the migrant workers and teachers alike. But half of the latter sympathizes with the FIS, compared to only one third of the former. The migrant workers prefer to keep aloof: 44%

of them does not want to be involved in controversial matters and prefers to mind their own business. After the old Islamic custom they praise God without expecting much of worldly powers.

Among the migrant workers, the attitude towards the FIS coincides with all other indicators of Islamist sympathies, as is illustrated by the results presented in table 2.[3] FIS opponents show a willingness to adjust to the Dutch ways in stead of holding on to the prescriptions of the sharia; they disapprove of the Islamic school and they reject corporal punishments. The FIS adherents hold contrasting visions, while the neutral group tends to occupy the middle ground.

Table 2. Differences between FIS-sympathizers, FIS-opponents and neutral respondents on other indicators of islamist tendencies

	Migrant workers		Teachers	
	t-value	P-value	t-value	P-value
Sharia				
Anti-FIS - Neutral	-3,83	,001***	-0,75	,478
Anti-FIS - Pro-FIS	-2,64	,017**	-1,45	,174
Neutral - Pro-FIS	-0,11	,914	-0,70	,499
Islamic school				
Anti-FIS - Neutral	-1,63	,120	-0,16	,881
Anti-FIS - Pro-FIS	-3,24	,005***	1,54	,149
Neutral - Pro-FIS	-1,01	,323	2,18	,047*
Corporal Punishment				
Anti-FIS - Neutral	-1,39	,181	-1,17	,275
Anti-FIS - Pro-FIS	-2,84	,011**	-1,66	,123
Neutral - Pro-FIS	-1,83	,079	-0,47	,647

* P < .050; ** P <.020; *** P <.010

Among the teachers on the other hand, there is hardly any difference between the pro-FIS and the anti-FIS respondents. The one exception concerns the attitude towards the Islamic school; FIS-adherents differ from the neutral teachers in their *rejection* of separate Islamic education. This remarkable conclusion is not as contradictory as it might seem at first. As we shall see later on, teachers do not sympathize with the Islamists for religious, but for secular political reasons. Preference for the FIS to them is isolated from other aspects of Islamism.

Islamism and religiousness

What are the differences between FIS-sympathizers and FIS-opponents when it comes to religious commitment? Among the migrant workers there are apparent differences in religious commitment, as table 3 shows.

Table 3. *Differences between FIS-sympathizers, FIS-opponents and neutral respondents in religious commitment*				
	Migrant workers		*Teachers*	
	t-value	*P-value*	*t-value*	*P-value*
Overall religiousness				
Anti-FIS - Neutral	-2,64	,016**	-1,12	,294
Anti-FIS - Pro-FIS	-3,53	,003***	-1,59	,139
Neutral - Pro-FIS	-0,65	,519	-1,08	,292
Ritual dimension				
Anti-FIS - Neutral	-1,17	,255	-1,19	,270
Anti-FIS - Pro-FIS	-0,73	,478	-1,39	,189
Neutral - Pro-FIS	0,46	,647	-0,59	,586
Social dimension				
Anti-FIS - Neutral	-0,96	,350	1,11	,914
Anti-FIS - Pro-FIS	-2,49	,023*	0,57	,583
Neutral - Pro-FIS	-1,85	,076	-0,78	,447
Moral dimension				
Anti-FIS - Neutral	-1,92	,069	-0,99	,354
Anti-FIS - Pro-FIS	-2,68	,016**	-0,39	,701
Neutral - Pro-FIS	-1,06	,299	0,26	,799
Knowledge dimension				
Anti-FIS - Neutral	-0,27	,789	0,63	,545
Anti-FIS - Pro-FIS	-1,34	,198	1,24	,243
Neutral - Pro-FIS	-1,52	,142	0,51	,617

* P < .050; ** P <.020; *** P <.010

As for the overall degree of religiousness, the pro-FIS respondents are more or less in line with the neutral ones, but both differ significantly from the anti-FIS migrants workers. When it comes to ritual obligations or their knowledge of the Muslim creed the FIS-adherents cannot be distinguished from their fellow Muslims. However, the pro-FIS faction is more strict in their moral conduct and they have a stronger attachment to the mosque community than the anti-FIS respondents. As for the teachers, there is no difference at all in religiousness between FIS-adherents, their ideological opposites and the neutral category. This is all the more striking considering their level of religious commitment, which is far below the average of the migrant workers. For instance, 92% of the migrant workers abstain from drinking alcohol, compared to 70% of the teachers; 85% of the migrant workers visit the mosque weekly, while only 30% of the teachers do and 65% of the migrant workers consider the headscarf for women a religious obligation, compared to 20% of the teachers. This justifies the conclusion that Islamist sympathies among the migrant workers are closely linked to their religious attitudes. To the teachers it is not religious zeal that explains the appeal of the Islamist movement. In fact, many mention their dissatisfaction with the present generation of nationalist rulers in the Arab world as a reason for their preference.

Islamism and ethnic orientation

It might be expected that FIS adherents are attracted to the anti-western rhetoric of Islamism. Support for the Islamists might be an expression of the fear for the western way of life threatening the values of traditional muslims. However, the results presented in table 4 do not support a withdrawal from Dutch society. There is a slight tendency among pro-FIS migrant workers to be more attached to traditional habits and values, but there are no differences in the number of relations with Dutch neighbours or colleagues.

Neither is there a significant difference in preference for segregated neighbourhoods. On the whole, there is a strong opposition to living in an Moroccan enclave: 53% would like to have more Dutch neighbours, 41% is indifferent and only 6% of the migrant workers would rather have more Moroccans living in their street. As for the Moroccan teachers, there are no differences when it comes to the indicators of ethnic orientation.

Table 4. Differences between FIS-sympathizers, FIS-opponents and neutral respondents in ethnic orientation				
	Migrant workers		*Teachers*	
	t-value	*P-value*	*t-value*	*P-value*
Habitual dimension				
Anti-FIS - Neutral	-1,69	,110	0,11	,918
Anti-FIS - Pro-FIS	-2,16	,047*	0,83	,422
Neutral - Pro-FIS	-0,50	,619	-0,91	,380
Relations with Dutchmen				
Anti-FIS - Neutral	-0,46	,649	0,48	,636
Anti-FIS - Pro-FIS	-0,63	,534	0,20	,847
Neutral - Pro-FIS	-0,29	,771	-0,32	,754
Preference for segregated neighbourhoods				
Anti-FIS - Neutral	-2,07	,052	0,48	,636
Anti-FIS - Pro-FIS	-1,58	,133	0	
Neutral - Pro-FIS	0,96	,348	-0,62	,547

* P < .050;   ** P <.020;   *** P <.010

FIS supporters and opponents -migrant workers and teachers alike- cannot be differentiated on the basis of their general orientation towards Dutch society, as can be concluded from table 5.

Table 5. Differences between FIS-sympathizers, FIS-opponents and neutral respondents in orientation to Dutch society				
	Migrant workers		Teachers	
	t-value	P-value	t-value	P-value
Overall orientation Dutch society				
Anti-FIS - Neutral	-0,35	,734	-0,47	,648
Anti-FIS - Pro-FIS	-0,45	,656	-0,17	,870
Neutral - Pro-FIS	-0,03	,980	0,14	,895
Voting in local elections				
Anti-FIS - Neutral	-2,40	,026*	0,73	,486
Anti-FIS - Pro-FIS	-2,69	,016**	0,17	,865
Neutral - Pro-FIS	-0,16	,876	-0,76	,458
Reading Dutch newspapers				
Anti-FIS - Neutral	-1,40	,178	-3,19	,013**
Anti-FIS - Pro-FIS	-0,95	,356	-1,34	,205
Neutral - Pro-FIS	0,52	,606	0,37	,719

* P < .050; ** P <.020; *** P <.010

Among the migrant workers the attitude to Dutch politics is one of indifference. According to Dutch legislation, foreign inhabitants are allowed to participate in elections at the local level. Still, the interest in voting is not high. Only 37% of the migrant workers claims to vote. However, the ones who oppose the Islamists show significantly more political involvement in Dutch society than the FIS-supporters and the neutral category. The anti-FIS teachers differ from the neutral ones in that they read more Dutch newspapers.On the whole, Islamist sympathies do not coincide with an opposing attitude to Dutch society. The anti-Islamists show more interest in Dutch politics, while the others are more or less indifferent.

Islamism and social characteristics

The only difference in social characteristics among the migrant workers is in the vernacular of the migrant workers opposing the FIS. They tend to be more Arabic speaking than the neutral group. As to urban background, age and length of stay in the Netherlands, there are no differences between Islamist supporters, their opponents and the ones who keep aloof.

Table 6. Differences between FIS-sympathizers, FIS-opponents and neutral respondents in social characteristics (BEGIN)				
	Migrant workers		Teachers	
	t-value	P-value	t-value	P-value
Urban/rural origin				
Anti-FIS - Neutral	0,43	,673	0,73	,486
Anti-FIS - Pro-FIS	2,07	,054	-0,19	,852
Neutral - Pro-FIS	1,67	,108	-1,24	,237
Berber/Arabic speaking				
Anti-FIS - Neutral	2,31	,032*	0,73	,486
Anti-FIS - Pro-FIS	1,40	,180	1,73	,865
Neutral - Pro-FIS	-0,76	,458	-0,76	,458
Length of stay				
Anti-FIS - Neutral	0,96	,498	0,18	,860
Anti-FIS - Pro-FIS	-0,53	,603	0,44	,668
Neutral - Pro-FIS	-1,61	,119	0,20	,845
Age				
Anti-FIS - Neutral	-0,84	,410	0,15	,886
Anti-FIS - Pro-FIS	0,56	,579	1,54	,149
Neutral - Pro-FIS	1,79	,086	1,52	,150
Differences between FIS-sympathizers, FIS-opponents and neutral respondents in social characteristics (END)				
	Migrant workers			
	t-value	P-value		
Educational level				
Anti-FIS - Neutral	-0,96	,350		
Anti-FIS - Pro-FIS	-0,62	,542		
Neutral - Pro-FIS	0,45	,654		
Unemployment				
Anti-FIS - Neutral	1,52	,144		
Anti-FIS - Pro-FIS	1,77	,095		
Neutral - Pro-FIS	0,36	,719		

* P < .050; ** P <.020; *** P <.010

The same goes for the teachers, among whom there are no clear social markers distinguishing the three categories. As the educational level of the migrant workers is generally low and unemployment high,[4] it might be interesting to note that neither education nor the employment status of the migrant workers provides any ground for distinguishing between the ones with Islamist sympathies, the ones opposing and the neutral category.

The teachers could not be compared on these criteria, since all of them completed their secondary education and -due to the sampling method used- all of them were employed at the time they were interviewed.

Conclusions

Radical Islam is generally considered as a movement opposing the western concept of democracy, whereas others suggest that it is the need for democracy in the Islamic world that gave rise to the Islamist movement. Therefore muslim migrants in western society would not be attracted to Islamism, as they participate in the civil liberties of western society. On the other hand, the western way of life might pose a threat to the habits and values of traditional Muslim migrants, making them receptive to the anti-western rhetoric of Islamism. In this paper I presented the results of a study among older male Moroccan migrant workers in the Netherlands. I contrasted this group with a sample of older Moroccan teachers, representing the small intellectual elite within the Moroccan community.

While a third of the migrant workers seems to sympathize with the Islamist movement and only 20% opposes it, the largest group prefers to stay aloof from political matters. The attitude towards the Islamistic movement is closely linked to their religious commitment, the migrant workers opposing it tend to put less emphasis on moral conduct and have less social attachment to the mosque community than the ones in favour of Islamism.

Opponents distinguish themselves by their lower overall level of religiousness compared to all other respondents.

By contrast, half of the teachers sympathize with the Islamist movement and again 20% is opposed to it. Their sympathy is not a matter of religious commitment, as they exhibit a lower level of overall religiousness, and sympathizers as well as opponents of Islamism cannot be differentiated from one another or from the neutral group on religious grounds. Their preference for the Islamist opposition in the Arabic world is rather an expression of a secular political attitude.

Sympathy for radical Islam cannot be interpreted as a retreat from western society. Among migrant workers and teachers alike, the adherents of Islamism do not differ much from the other respondents when it comes to traditional habits, relations with Dutchmen or preference for segregated neighbourhoods. The involvement in Dutch politics is generally low, although the anti-Islamist migrant workers show a greater participation in local elections than the others do. To conclude, there are hardly any social characteristics distinguishing between respondents with Islamist sympathies and their adversaries, neither among the migrant workers, nor among the teachers.

Saint Blancat (1993) suggested that the religious attitude of the older generation of Muslim migrants in France is one of pious fundamentalism, striving for purity of the faith and moral conduct in the personal realm. The greater majority of them kept aloof from the Islamist movement with its political aims. Her observations are in line with the conclusions of this paper. Among the first generation of Moroccan migrant workers in the Netherlands, pious fundamentalism with its emphasis on personal devotion is widespread. But Islamism as an outspoken political ideology has only limited appeal, remarkably in particular to the more secularised minority of intellectuals. In my opinion, the significance for political participation in Dutch society as yet is nil.

Notes

[1] According to Ahady (1992) the Islamist movement is declining since the second half of the 1980s. He claims that Islamist parties in countries with more or less free elections have witnessed a decline in the popular vote. In other countries the autocratic regimes would have succeeded in suppressing the movement. Moreover, the example of the Islamic state presented by Iran would have caused a decline in its attraction. Ahady's extraordinary conclusion does not take into account the recent electoral success of the Islamist party in Turkey, nor the violent activism of Islamist groups in Egypt and Algeria, that the governments in those countries have not been able so far to repress. The decrease in appeal of the Iranian Islamic state is contradicted by Hooglund (1992).

[2] The interviews were conducted in 1992 and 1993. At that time radical Muslims in Algeria had just taken up the armed struggle against government troops and the police. But is was before the violent campaigns against intellectuals and journalists critical of the FIS took place, and long before violent activism spread to France. I might have asked about the non-violent Islamist movements within Morocco itself, but there were severe

doubts whether these would be known to the migrant workers in The Netherlands, among whom there are many illiterates. The FIS at the other hand has received a large media coverage.

[3] The t-test is a statistical method that gives an answer to the question whether a difference found in the mean scores between to groups is in fact just a coincidence. The larger the difference (t-value), the smaller the chance that it is produced by coincidence (p-value). In this table and the ones to follow I will compare the respondents in sympathy of the FIS with the respondents taking a neutral stand, and both are compared to the respondents opposing to the FIS.

[4] Of the migrant workers in the sample, only one fifth had followed at least some years of secondary education, while a quarter had not attended any school. At the time of the interviewing, more than three quarters of them were unemployed or stopped working due to ill health.

12

In the Name of the *Umma*:

Globalization, 'Race' Relations
and Muslim Identity Politics in Bradford[1]

Seán McLoughlin

Of the estimated one and a half million people living in Britain who identify themselves as Muslims, roughly 50,000 are settled in Bradford, a city in the north of England noted for its now largely redundant woollen textiles industry (Lewis: 1994). A majority of these people are first generation labour migrants from Mirpur district in Pakistani administered Azad Kashmir and their families.[2] The 1991 census illustrates the numerical significance of people identifying themselves as Pakistanis in Bradford. It also shows that Pakistanis are increasingly British-born and that they suffer from amongst the highest levels of structural deprivation in the city.[3] Moreover, like other minorities, British-Pakistani-Muslims are constructed as "outsiders" by right-wing nationalist discourses and experience discrimination and attack in such diverse forms as the refusal of religious holidays at work; harassment on the street and the enforcement of punitive immigration legislation that separates families across continents. In this paper I want to explore how British-Pakistani-Muslims represent their concerns about respect and justice in Britain where "race", culture and difference are central to politicised debates about national identity. Arguing that resistance begins with the articulation of new possibilities outside the hegemonic order defined by majority excluders, I examine how Muslim minorities' identifications with other Muslims internationally as part of the *Umma* (the trans-national community of Muslims) can provide one basis for resistance to exclusion in Britain.

While my concern is to consider how and when a Muslim subject position is prioritised over all others in Bradford, I also want to acknowledge that there are multiple possible identification positions from which resistance to exclusion might be articulated. There is also the possibility of an identity politics of the margins that constructs cross-constituency alliances. I understand all identification positions - be they based on religion, culture, class, gender, or "race" - as socially constructed. The representations of identity and belonging that we all make are always contingent. Therefore I do not want to suggest that people who produce a Muslim subject position in one context are not engaged in making different identifications in other contexts. I make this intervention because I understand claims to authenticity by one segment of any constituency as representing a hegemonic operation that routinely peripheralises others. Therefore while it is important to acknowledge Muslim resistance to exclusion in the name of the *Umma*, it is equally important not to valorise essentialist representations of Islam that often silence the voices of other Muslims. Indeed in an attempt to point up the ways in which alliances can be made between different positions, it is important to mention that an emerging Muslim charity sector has begun to make connections with wider society in Britain through various fund-raising campaigns.[4]

In an attempt to explore these issues I describe a "Charity Dinner for Bosnia and Kashmir" held in Bradford after *'id ul-fitr* (the festival at the end of the month of fasting, *ramazan*) in 1994. The dinner was organised by local Muslim businessmen who were frustrated that human rights abuses against Muslims in Bosnia and Kashmir were continuing unchecked by a post-communist "new world order" defined and enforced by the United States. This construction of world "peace" in terms of apparently "universal" norms of law and order often seems in fact to be inimical to the interests of non-Westerners. So at a time when Islamist movements in the Middle East and North Africa are imaged as the new security threat to Western interests in the world, the state of affairs in Bosnia came as no surprise to the organisers of the dinner. In the accounts of the speakers who addressed the gathering before dinner, the idea of the *Umma* produced Muslims - whether they might be in Bradford, Bosnia or Kashmir - as a community that should be unequivocally bounded in solidarity against a hostile world outside. They debated how through unity and a self-reliant activism, grounded in a view of the world distinctive from the status quo represented either by the British establishment or the United Nations, Muslims might best generate an empowering alternative to their current local-global oppressed status.

It is crucial to note at this stage that a local-global intersection of Muslim interests does not suggest a mobilization of Muslims on a global scale. Rather because identification positions are contingent, unity, even on a national or local level, is difficult to organise. Therefore what is under discussion in this paper is the emergence of temporary and localised political struggles that attempt to imagine their projects through discourses that transcend both local and national belongings. Unfortunately there has been very little ethnographic exploration of why, how and in what contexts Muslims in Britain have imagined a community of resistance to local exclusions in the politicised language of this global *Umma*. One notable exception is Werbner (1994) who has described how Manchester Pakistanis, a relatively economically successful community, supported Saddam Hussain of Iraq during the Gulf War in 1990-1. "Why adopt an apparently anti-local strategy that sets them apart morally from wider British society?" she asks. Crucially she observes that this sort of identification: "makes an oblique ideological critique...it can also be regarded as an allegory which comments on a local set of events, values and power relations. In this sense the local and the global are mutually constitutive" (1994: 216), and that Manchester Pakistanis identified with other Muslims in an international setting to contest their lack of access to political power locally.

My description and analysis of the dinner explores both the potential, and the actual limits, of the idea of a globally connected Muslim community, as one basis for local protest. In the next section I situate my concerns in the context of the Rushdie Affair which can be seen as a defining moment in the process of politicising Islam in Bradford (Modood: 1990). I then examine the literature on minority politics in contemporary Britain in an attempt to set out a theoretical framework within which the dinner can be understood.

The Rushdie affair: Muslim assertiveness and 'race' relations

Muslims in Bradford came to global attention on 14 January 1989. During a demonstration protesting against the publication of Salman Rushdie's novel *The Satanic Verses*, a copy of the book - said to blasphemously defame the character of the Prophet of Islam and his family - was burned by members of the Bradford Council for Mosques in the full gaze of the media.[5] Moreover, on 14 February 1989, the late Ayatullah Khumayni, leader of the Islamic Revolution in Iran in 1979, issued a *fatwa* (an authoritative opinion in Islamic law promulgated by a specialist, a *mufti*) calling for the death of Rushdie for blasphemy. The outraged liberal establishment in Britain and beyond defended Rushdie's freedom of speech. Accounts of the irrational, fanatical, intolerant Muslim "outsider" and renewed calls for the assimilation of such errant minorities emerged in academic, media and state discourses. The ensuing debates and arguments re-played themes that have long been central to the West's imagination of itself as defender of what it sees as the universal values of the post-Enlightenment: rationalism, liberalism and diplomacy.[6]

The Bradford Council for Mosques was created in 1981 by the local council under the rubric of multiculturalism. As a publicly-funded channel for the representation of Muslims in Bradford, it was a part of packages initiated in the wake of urban uprisings by black people in Brixton and Toxteth during the early 1980s. Religion was thought by state agencies to be a means for elders to calm the potentially rebellious youth in Bradford. It was reduced to a force for social control and cement while little account was taken of its power as a vehicle for social protest. The Rushdie Affair changed all that. As Ballard (1992) argues, the "race relations industry" in Britain has followed a deprivationist paradigm, based on reductionist sociological models of class, that has been too deterministic in presuming that minorities can not resist exclusion *per se*, let alone in terms of religion.

The burning of *The Satanic Verses* in Bradford was a reaction to the failure of a national Muslim lobby to successfully argue that the book should be banned. In October 1988 Muslim organizations in Britain were informed of the contents of the book by their co-religionists in India. The UK Action Committee on Islamic Affairs (UKACIA) was formed to take up the campaign. However it soon became apparent that Muslims did not have the power to make a telling political intervention. This was a barometer of their excluded status in British society. So disillusioned with attempts to make the British establishment listen was the Council for Mosques, that it felt impelled to subvert its incorporated status and burn the book. It had alerted the media to its intention in the hope of generating a broader debate about Muslim pain. However coverage of events succeeded only in "covering up" (Said: 1981: xi) how little journalists and commentators making Muslims known to wider society, actually knew about Islam in Britain. The result of this was to further isolate Muslims from wider society. Given the backlash against Muslim self-defence strategies the Council for Mosques made a public statement disassociating itself from Khumayni. It proceeded to focus its concerns through UKAC-IA which in April 1990 unsuccessfully attempted to argue in the High Court that the blasphemy laws in Britain, that currently protect only Christianity, should be reformed and extended to Islam.

Reflection on the polarization between Muslim and "race" relations interpretations of the book-burning and *fatwa* is crucial to understanding how minority agendas for social justice may be represented in the late 1990s. As Siddique (1993: 172) notes, "The Fatwa, remarkably, elevated Muslims (in Bradford) from the position of hopeless despair to a position of strength and power". This symbolic moment of Muslim empowerment challenged the institutionalised assumptions about minority responses to exclusion of the "race" relations industry. Modood (1993: 85) has observed the effect of this polarization: "The current temper of British Asian Muslims, partly as a consequence of the injuring and harassing power of The Satanic Verses, is not to seek the common ground, the universal in the particular, but to emphasise difference".

In the next section I want to explore the theoretical literature on why emphasising difference has been understood to be a minority strategy for self-defence in contemporary Britain.

Globalization, ethnicity and identity politics in multicultural Britain: A theoretical framework

Globalization can be understood as a set of processes which cut across national boundaries, making people and institutions experience the world in more integrated configurations of time and space (Hall: 1992). There are now few barriers to effective communication - given developments such as international air travel, satellite television and electronic mail - wherever one might be in the world. Globalization has also seen the emergence of a truly international labour market where migrants from

Britain's former colonies, like the Mirpuris, came from the periphery of the world economy to the core of consumer capitalism, during the 1950s and 1960s post-war boom.

A tendency towards global inter-connection in the contemporary world has not given way to universalistic values however. While the world can increasingly be imagined as a single place there is no doubt that it is (often violently) politically and economically divided, not least along the fault lines created by de-colonization and the post-colonial axis of power that defines "the West" and "the Rest". Hall (1992) argues that a global tendency towards the universalization of the Western project of modernity is matched by the "return" of ethnicity. According to modernist social theory belongings to locality were seen as irrational attachments to the particular that would be eroded by the march of modernization. However the anthropological literature explains why ethnicity is occurring in an increasingly inter-connected globe. Eriksen (1993) refers to ethnicity as a social process that is constructed through *contact* between people in contexts where cultural difference is *made* an important social marker to political ends. Ethnicity therefore describes how people classify themselves in terms of their group relationships. So cultural difference in itself is not the crucial element in the ethnicity process. Anthropologists have understood culture rather as a resource for people to promote group interests through the construction of primordialist ethnic boundaries vis-à-vis the other outside. However ethnicity itself is not a group characteristic, it is not "always there". Rather it is something constructed only in given contexts.

Ethnicity as a social process illuminates the ways in which a majority constructs itself. For example, international migration has brought people from around the world into close contact in Britain. This plurality has had the effect of relativising all cultures, including powerful versions of British culture. Representations of this as something that is fixed in meaning are therefore open to contestation. One response to this fragmentation has been an attempt to re-construct a hegemonic definition of a British national identity by right-wing tendencies. This narration of the nation has rendered migrants "outsiders" on the basis of cultural difference as much as "race". To be black, Asian or Muslim and British is imagined to be mutually exclusive in little-Englander cultural-racist discourses. "They" are routinely identified as a "problem" for British society. In more mainstream representations minority difference is problematised too, as exemplified in BBC Television's Panorama programme "Underclass in Purdah" (29.03.93), where children are allegedly underachieving in school *because* of "their" Muslim culture.

The process of ethnicity is evident too amongst minority resistance to exclusion. As has been noted, the power of a localised politics that speaks in the name of the *Umma* is precisely in its construction of a community that goes beyond the local and the national to the global. Nevertheless many of the observations about the ethnicity process hold good for an analysis of the Islamising of politics in the British diaspora. For example, during the Rushdie Affair Muslims constructed a religious and moral community that imagined a contestant alternative to the dominant values of a British society that excluded them. Ballard (1992) maintains that ethnicity articulates the potential of social networks of culture, religion and kinship as resources for individual and collective strength amongst minorities. Indeed anthropologists working in Britain have maintained that in the struggle for scarce state resources, minority leaders and activists have "fetishised culture" (Werbner: 1991a) in order to represent the interests of minorities in the majority-dominated political arena. However a re-identification with custom or tradition to articulate political concerns is not a traditional reproduction of culture. Rather as Werbner explains, "Culture is no longer an unconscious way of life but an organised ideological agenda" (Werbner; 1991a).

Despite an emphasis in theorizations about ethnicity on the dynamism, situationality and negotiated nature of social identities, in recent years anthropologists working in Britain have been criticised for essentialising the cultural difference of minorities. They have too often failed to intervene in the political discourses of social actors who suggest that there is indeed something immutable about being a Muslim, Pakistani or Mirpuri. Hall (1992) argues that ethnicity was the enemy of anti-racism in 1970s and 1980s Britain because it focused on bounded cultural groups and exoticised cultural difference. This was seen as reactionary, fragmenting the multi-ethnic alliances of black anti-racist politics. Nevertheless, it is important to note that Hall too understands minorities" resistance to exclusion as having emerged through a process of imaginary political re-identification with re-invented histories and cultures. It is this sense of the constructedness of cultural difference, represented in specific debates and conditions of power, that anthropologists have too often been inattentive to.

In response to this criticism, the anthropology of minorities in Britain has made some attempt to confront issues of power. For example, Werbner has emphasised that ethnicity has hegemonic versions, maintaining that ethnic unity is a "fiction" (1991b). Rather extensive alliances are constructed by leaders to unite a community even as it is internally differentiated. For example, Werbner mentions how local and national Muslim organizations united temporarily during the Rushdie Affair to articulate shared concerns about marginalization in Britain. However these organizations routinely compete to represent their own constructions of a Muslim community and often silence other Muslim voices, notably those of women and young men. Werbner (1991a) argues that different ethnic segments can also create alliances which express the common experience of racism, as "communities of suffering". Indeed leaders draw on a variety of strategies, including negotiating reform and mobilising protest, to make their representations.

While Hall (1992) recognises that the category of black has had its silences too, notably for Asians, he still assigns a politicised Muslim subjectivity none of the vigour or strength that he reserves for black representations. He does not problematise the way in which many Western commentators render all Muslim assertion "fundamentalist". He views it as an example of an old essentialist identity trying to restore purity in the face of the Westernization and the confusion of meaning in mixed-up multicultural cities. I want to distance my account of the dinner from interpretations that would stereotype Muslim assertiveness in terms of an intolerant "fundamentalist" threat. As Bhiku Parekh (1992: 9) notes, the term is 'increasingly becoming a polemical hand-grenade to be thrown at those we detest and fear and whom we wish to fight and defeat with a clear conscience'. In contrast to Hall, Modood (1990) notes that the Rushdie Affair crucially pointed up the potential of Muslim identity politics to fight racism. While it is only now that Islamic organizations have begun to seriously address racism as an issue it is also fair to say that Islamic organizations did not feel that anti-racists showed any solidarity with them over *The Satanic Verses*. The dinner that I describe next illustrates that a Muslim identity politics that imagines a global community bounded in resistance to both local cultural-racist narrations of the British nation and hegemonic Western constructions of international law and order, has an important, if contingent, appeal and potential in Bradford.

"Does anybody care?" Imagining the *Umma* at a charity dinner

In early March 1994 Bradford Eid Committee organised a charity dinner held in conference rooms hired from the University of Bradford. Tickets were £10 each and the proceeds went to the twin causes of Bosnia and Kashmir. As Lewis (1994) relates, this organization was formed by a group of nine young businessmen who came together in 1991 to produce more positive images of Muslims through their charity work, given that negative representations of Islam had dominated local perceptions of the Rushdie Affair and the Gulf War. To date the Eid Committee has been engaged in a variety of charity work and also organised the Eid Mela - a South Asian fair with food, rides, music and community information stalls - and established the Fast FM radio station which broadcasts religious programmes during *ramazan*.

This evening of fund-raising was advertised in community centres and Pakistani restaurants with a poster that heralded the question, "does anybody care?" in English and Urdu. The posters maintained that "everyone was welcome" to the dinner and so theoretically addressed all sections of society in Bradford. Indeed the clientele of many Pakistani restaurants is often white and non-Muslim. However on arrival at the dinner it was clear that this was to be an event bounding people on the basis of being Muslim, rather than on the basis of an interest in the multicultural affairs of the city. The white, non-Muslim Lord Mayor had not been asked to preside, as he sometimes was at community events. Instead the organisers had invited speakers, at least two representing notable Islamist organizations in Britain, to address the gathering before the dinner itself. Indeed the evening's speeches would produce an alternative account of agendas for "the Muslim community" to those proposed by the "race" relations industry in Bradford.

By the time proceedings were about to begin probably a few hundred people had gathered. Seating was supposedly gender-segregated with provision made for women at the back of the hall, although as people began to find their seats after prayers in the foyer, some women marched to the front and commandeered those seats for themselves. As the audience waited expectantly for the speeches to begin, the evening's programme opened with a recital of the *qur'an* from chapter *an-nisa'* (The Women). First in Arabic and then in English translation, a section of the chapter making reference to the defence of Islam was read aloud from the stage by an *imam* (prayer leader)[7]. This recitation set the tone for the evening's speeches.

Adeeb, a businessman from Leeds, was the chairperson for the evening. He introduced the event with an explanation of why the event had been arranged. He told us that the organisers had come together after Christmas out of sheer frustration with the fact that after two and a half years of war in the former Yugoslavia, nothing was being done in Bosnia to alleviate the desperate situation of Muslims there. There was a feeling of isolation about his question: "brothers and sisters are suffering...does anybody care?". Adeeb explained that atrocities against Muslims were going on in Kashmir too, under Indian occupation. He acknowledged that the Kashmiri link to the evening's proceedings was special because so many Mirpuri-Kashmiris lived in Bradford. Adeeb continued by thanking the many people that had been of assistance in organising the dinner. Indeed he maintained that at a time when, "we hear so much of Muslim disunity these days - others play on it - this coming together is a good example of co-operation and unity". He was re-enforcing then, the fact that his question, "does anybody care?", was directed at Muslims themselves. They would have to help themselves given the perceived double-standards of the Western powers who had intervened in Kuwait but left Muslims to die in Bosnia. His point was that they could not help themselves unless they were unified. All the speeches echoed these sentiments but ultimately set up a debate about the best method for transforming Muslims' situation in the world.

KHADIJA: Wearing *hijab* (the veil which covers women's hair and body) and darkened spectacles, Khadija struggled forward to take her place on the stage. We were told that she was recovering from a spate of hospital operations to treat injuries sustained in Bosnia. No mention was made of her membership of any particular organization; her's was a testimony based on personal experience. The daughter of a Bosnian-Herzogovian mother and Polish father, she delivered her speech in an ordinary English accent which suggested that she had grown up in Britain. Her speech began as an evocative recollection of Bosnia; its beauty, the night's sky, the mountains and the way in which all these memories had been wiped out by the carnage: "A girl watching the sky is obliterated and her husband and friends are made *shahids* (martyrs) by the murdering Serbs. Their bodies are gone but their souls are with *allah*; they are well now..."

The speech soon moved to the horrific rape of 100,000 Muslim sisters in Bosnia. "The United Nations say that it is not a human rights issue! How does it feel to see your wife or mother or daughter gang-raped before your very eyes? I am sorry if I have offended brothers or sisters" sensitiv- ities. They must face up to it. The victims of rape want to die; they cry and cry until there is nothing left. Some Europeans and Turks (!) offer abortions...What would you do? I know what it is to hate and I hope that those present do not experience what that is like.'

Then the emphasis of her speech shifted from offence at the treatment of Muslims to their need to come together in self-defence. Her delivery was slow, steady and deliberate. Every sentence was solemnly calculated to firmly bond those present with the subjects of the recollection. "We may speak different languages but that does not matter. What matters is that we are all Muslims". Khadija demanded protection from the brothers present for their Muslim sisters. She demanded it for all sisters. "It is your duty". She asked whether any of the brothers present would be in Kashmir fighting for its liberation when she next visited? The Quran speaks of iron and *allah* gives us the right to defend ourselves. We must be armed. The only language is that of the gun barrel. Be proud to be a fundamentalist. Perhaps some feel uncomfortable with the title. But it only means being a basic Muslim. Forget small quibbles between you..."

She concluded with an emotional vote of thanks to the chairperson: "I want to thank you for the 900 lives of Muslims that you have saved by your efforts so far. So and so from Bosnia thanks for his life to the conference convenor."

This was greeted, as were the other speeches periodically throughout the evening, with one of a number of rallying calls: "*takbir*" repeatedly called out for the praise and glorification of God, to which many in the audience enthusiastically replied, "*allahu akbar*" (God is great).

MAJID: Next to speak was the Human Rights Officer of the Muslim Parliament of Great Britain. The publication of The Muslim Manifesto in July 1990 was an attempt, albeit unelected, to propose a "Council of British Muslims" to represent Muslims in Britain along the lines of Board of Deputies of British Jews (1990: 5).[8] Majid, dressed in a suit but with no tie after the Iranian fashion, focused his concern, like Khadija, on Bosnia. Claiming that 80% of human rights abuses in the world were directed against Muslims, his argument was that sending charity, money and food *ad hoc* to suffering Muslims there was not enough: "we are simply fattening our brothers and sisters for their death. There are nearly three million Muslims (sic) in Britain and thirty million (sic) in Europe as a whole...And all of these donating just £1.00 a week, every week, regardless of status would begin a commitment to arming Bosnia and making a strong Islamic state in the heart of Europe."

From here Majid went on to develop two key points: that giving charity should be regular and planned (along the lines of the Muslim Parliament's welfare system of Islam in Britain, the *bait al-mal al-islami*) and that Bosnian-Muslims should be armed and assisted in their bid to defend themselves in *jihad* (to this second end the "Arms for Bosnia Fund", later renamed 'Bosnia Jihad Fund' after the British government deemed that the former was illegal, was established in 1993). Majid then called, like Khadija, for an individual responsibility for activism given the complicity of many Muslim rulers in the West's project of global domination: "The *Umma* is like a body; if one part of the body is pricked then all the rest of the body reacts (quoting al-Bukhari). It is our individual responsibility to act...At *qiyamat* (the day of resurrection and judgement), it is not the King Fahds who will answer for our inaction; it is ourselves. We cannot always blame an *amir* (prince or commander)"

He concluded by informing those present that Muslims in Britain would be next to suffer the West's opposition to Islam. Thus supporting a *jihad* to defend Bosnians and investing in a strong Islamic state in Bosnia, was necessary to defend all Muslims in their future trials in Europe.

IKRAM: The next speaker, Ikram, was a prominent local member of two national organizations that eventually merged in April 1994: (i) Young Muslims UK, which was launched from Bradford in 1984, and (ii) the recently established Islamic Society of Britain. Both organizations are firmly within the Pakistani Islamist tradition of Sayyid Mawdudi and *Jama'at-i Islami* through the parentage of the latter's offspring in Britain, UK Islamic Mission. However in recent years YMUK have been created a distinct organizational and ideological space for themselves in Bradford, reflecting their concern with the experience of Muslims born in Britain (Lewis: 1994).

A young doctor, educated in Britain, Ikram was dressed in an impeccably smart suit and sporting what one neighbour uncharitably called "trendy-Muslim designer-stubble". For Ikram the transformation of Muslims' depressed situation could only come about with a bottom-up process of missionary activity, *da'wa*.[9] This should be their main activity when: "the greatest injury that is being done to the *Umma* is the loss of a generation in Britain. Our children are falling away from Islam. The Muslims are asleep..."

While the materialism and secularism of Western lifestyles was seen as a threat to the faith of young Muslims born in Britain, Ikram also outlined the opportunity that a Muslim presence in Britain presents: offering the invitation of Islam to non-Muslim Britons. He argued that everyone has the right to hear the universalist message of Islam, which itself has a positive contribution to make to the moral and political development of British society. However Ikram counselled that if this message is to be accepted it has to be well presented given the current false images of Islam that dominate the ideas of British people. He recounted for his audience how: "In 1258 the Mongols raided and sacked Baghdad, raping women there too (as was happening in Bosnia). But in the next generation what happened? The Mongols had embraced Islam; they were walking around praying to *allah* and using *tasbih* (prayer beads) in the streets. Islam can overcome the hardest of hearts."

Ikram concluded his plea for *da'wa* amongst Muslims and non-Muslims alike by encouraging the audience to ensure Islam's continued success as the world's fastest growing religion and the second largest religion in Britain through their commitment to a truly Islamic way of life.[10]

SHAKIL: The final speaker of the evening, Shakil, was a white revert (convert) Muslim who was introduced as an "eminent Scottish historian" with a background in the academic study of Islam in universities. Conspiracy against the Muslims was the theme of his talk. He offered an alternative reading of historical and contemporary international relations but after the heavy rhetoric of the previous speeches, here was one shot through with humour that the audience clearly enjoyed. He wove an intricate web which pulled powerful personalities from around the globe into fantastic relationships grounded in their common interest in scuppering the advance of the global Islamic movement. In addition to routine critiques of the West's self-interested intervention in the Gulf during 1990-1, King Hassan of Morocco, had been, he claimed, tutored by the United States' CIA since his childhood. This was why he was their "lapdog". The Queen of England, it was noted, played her own part in the conspiracy as godmother to a number of prominent Serbians. The double-standards of the ruling political establishment in Britain were exposed. Next Shakil wondered why Muslims were surprised at British support for military intervention in the Gulf War but not in Bosnia? "Don't you read the papers?" he asked. He reminded the gathering that the unchaste sexual manners of government ministers is well reported as going hand in hand with their supposed commitment to "the Family". His conclusion called for Muslims to unite in defence of Islam for only then they could they succeed in carrying its message to the world. Thus the evening's speeches came to an end and after *du'a* (supplicatory prayer) we all began to queue in the adjacent hall for dinner.

In the rest of this paper I can only begin to unpack the significance of the dinner for those Muslims who attended the dinner: the organisers, the audience and the speakers. Nevertheless I think that it is important to say something about the following: firstly, why the organisers might have chosen to invite Islamists rather than more mainstream community leaders to address the gathering; secondly, why the audience of ordinary Muslims made a connection with the politics of the speakers; and finally, why the prospects of the Islamist speakers broadening their popular appeal beyond contexts like the dinner would seem to be limited. I shall also attempt to relate these issues to the observations that prefaced my description of the dinner.

Between reform and protest: Muslim dilemmas about representational strategies

For one respondent who had attended the dinner, the event looked like a "race" relations disaster waiting to happen. Faisal, a local "race" relations officer and prominent Muslim activist, was concerned about the way in which the rhetoric of the speeches imagined a Muslim community bounded vis-à-vis the world outside. He contended that even though this was an event something organised to request support from Muslims alone - and not the state or the general public - had the media "covered" the tenor of remarks about *jihad*, an Islamic State or Muslim missionary activity, Islam would surely have been reported as being both aggressively separatist and "fundamentalist". He wondered what could have possessed the organisers, who had begun their charity work with a concern to reform the public image of Muslims in Bradford, to invite speakers with, what he saw as, radical agendas to address the dinner? Faisal argued that given that the backlash against Muslim mobilizations during the Rushdie Affair had isolated Muslims in Britain, organizations like UKACIA were continuing to pursue reformist strategies for change. He maintained that in that light, the organisers' actions were irresponsible and showed them to be bad politicians. In a bid to address Faisal's concerns it is necessary to briefly assess the success of reformist strategies to empower Muslims in Britain.

Since the Rushdie Affair UKACIA and others, including prominent Muslim newspapers like Q-News and The Muslim News, have continued to lobby for "race" relations legislation to be reformed and extended to protect those discriminated against on the basis of religion. However at a time when Muslims have become increasingly visible in a society where cultural-racism is endemic, the law has continued to render them largely invisible. Muslims have still not been delivered legal protection in Britain. The Commission for Racial Equality argues that there should be a separate law to cover religion however very recently, Home Secretary Michael Howard, opted-out of Europe-wide legislation that sought to protect religious minorities from discrimination and attack. He was happy to accept measures on the grounds of "race", colour, ethnic origin and nationality but not religion. This was read in the Muslim press as a cynical refusal to allow any legislation that might see Salman Rushdie prosecuted for "inciting religious hatred".[11] Moreover, around the same time as the dinner, the Home Secretary had advised Muslim organizations to speak with one voice if they wanted to have more influence on government policy making. UKACIA and other umbrella organizations were disappointed that their efforts in that direction had seemingly gone unnoticed and that the government remained indifferent to the complexity of representing Muslims as a homogeneous constituency.[12]

Earlier in the paper I noted how Modood has argued that in the wake of the Rushdie Affair, Muslim representations have been about emphasising difference. He also considers that : "self-confidence is returning but currently is at the stage of assertive independence rather than of a dialogue amongst equals. What happens at this stage, however, could prevent us from arriving at such a dialogue." (1993: 85).

I would argue that like the Rushdie Affair and the Gulf War, the dinner was a space in which an indirect commentary on Muslims' continuing frustration at marginalization in British society emerged. The dinner illustrated the assertive independence of Muslims. It represented a recognition that they must do things for themselves because any faith in the non-Muslim establishment is misplaced. What Modood points up is that if reformist strategies for change do not secure a greater access to power and legal protection for Muslims, they may be driven into a deeper more antagonistic isolation from wider society. While Muslims and all minorities feel that they have a right to participate in the nation, for many it is a case of "I'm British but". Making claims to certain rights on the basis of being British and Muslim involves a hesitation. When told "you do not belong here" one response is to imagine other "homelands". So while the organisers were generally committed to reform, the continued disenfranchisement of Muslims in Britain can be seen as contributing to their decision to invite speakers who could "turn the world inside out" (Gilsenan: 1982) by imagining an empowering alternative belonging to that of Muslims" excluders. Indeed, as a "race" relations officer and a Muslim activist, Faisal was only too aware that his responsibilities to the system of representation established by the state in terms of "race" and ethnicity, often prevented him from articulating an uncompromising sense of disaffection with that status quo (Kalra and McLoughlin: 1996).

Altering marginalization: The potential of Islam's rival universalism

All the speeches privileged the idea of a global Islamic trans-nationality that bounds Muslims over and against their other subject positions. Recall how: Khadija enunciated that Muslims in Bradford had a duty to defend their brothers and sisters in Bosnia and Kashmir; Majid proposed funding an Islamic State in Bosnia to defend all Muslims in an Islamaphobic Europe; Ikram imagined the missionary possibilities of Islam as a universal religion that was now being adopted by twentieth century Britons as it was by thirteenth century Mongols; Shakil outlined conspiracy theories that established a Muslim moral utopia against the moral dystopia of the West. The emphasis was on reaching out from Bradford to realise duties to, and mutual investments in, an *Umma* that transcended attachments to identification positions of nationality and locality, gender and class.

The central message of the evening's speeches, that Muslims in Bradford must defend interests they hold in common with brothers and sisters elsewhere, met with broad approval from the audience. It is also important to note that the dinner was held just after *ramazan* and *'id ul-fitr* when giving charity to other Muslims is incumbent upon all. Muslims in Bradford are constantly reminded of their membership of the *Umma* by sermons at the mosque, the work of Muslim charities and the television coverage that has brought the plight of Muslims in Bosnia into their front-rooms - front-rooms which notably often mark membership of the *Umma* with pictures of white-robed figures doing *hajj* (the pilgrimage) or rugs detailing the *ka'ba* (the black cube in Makka which Muslims pray towards) and other holy places. However ordinary Muslims in Bradford do not argue for an Islamic state in Bosnia or for the necessity of doing *da'wa* in Britain as the speakers did. Rather their connection with other Muslims is routinely produced in terms of sharing pain and showing solidarity. Hence the net result of the evening was to raise a few thousand pounds for charity and not to mobilise the sort of activism the speakers called for.

Living at the centre of Western consumer capitalism but marginalised as a minority both in Britain and in the "new world order" of the West, there is a sense in which Muslims in Britain are doubly alert to the politicization of difference in the contemporary world. It is empowering for Muslims at the margins in Britain to take responsibility for other Muslims be they in Bosnia, Kashmir, Palestine or Chechnya, because despite their marginalization in Britain there is a recognition that theirs is a position of relative privilege. Nevertheless in discussions about the *Umma* with Muslims in Bradford a dread of repatriation is discernible. The idea that because they are Muslim they may indeed be, as Majid suggested, "next" to be forcibly expelled from their European homes, haunts even those holding British passports and born in Britain. This, it was suggested to me by Faisal himself, is one reason, among others, why some minorities still maintain investments in places like Mirpur. I do not claim that this observation explodes the "myth of return" but rather that it signals the importance of suffering as a point of connection between Muslims in Bradford and their co-religionists.

The idea of the *Umma* was sufficient to aggregate Muslims inside the specificity of the dinner context vis-à-vis an often hostile and uncaring world outside. It constructs a good argument with excluders pointing to membership of something somehow bigger and better than cultural-racist representations of the British nation-state. It is something that Muslims in Britain take pride in. This is reflected in the way in which the *Umma* is routinely produced as a metaphor for utopian racial and ethnic harmony in contemporary Muslim discourses. Muslims will explain how it is a diverse and dispersed trans-national constituency numbering at least 900,000,000[13], ranging from Morocco in the West to Indonesia in the East, and how it unites Muslims of all colours and cultures, most manifestly at events like *hajj*. Speaking in the name of the *Umma* can also epitomise a desire beyond a Muslim constituency to say something about the world today from a position that is not centred on the West. Among the reasons why Western claims to be universal have been shown to be local eurocentrisms grounded in a copyrighting of the values of modernity, is the power of the *Umma* to name an alternative source of cultural authority in the contemporary world, Islam (Sayyid: 1994). However as the West has been deconstructed so too must any attempts to capture the debate about Islamic "authenticity". So while the imagination of an *Umma* in contexts like the dinner crucially creates a new space for representation in the contemporary globalised world, that space does not necessarily remain equally open for all Muslim subjectivities to debate what they mean by Islam today.

Altering marginalization? The limits of Islamism's rival universalism

The audience was impressed with the organisers and the speakers because here were Muslims prepared, like the Ayatullah during the Rushdie Affair, to do something about the contemporary situation of Muslims. However the debate as to how Muslims might actually change their local situation, having agreed why they must, has only just begun. As yet the powerful potential of a local political project that invokes a global discourse has not been translated into popular or precise agendas for change in Britain. This situation is also broadly true of the politicization of Islam in the Middle East (Said: 1995). The speakers were united in their claim that Islam is the solution to Muslims' problems in Britain but the dinner also illustrated that there is a struggle over the definition of the boundaries of what Islam should be amongst Muslims.

Islamist attempts at organising Muslim self-determination in the contemporary world have seen an utopian re-invention of Islam as an ideology.[14] Both explanations for, and solutions to, marginalization have been sought on the basis of a re-reading of the sacred sources of Islam (*qur'an* and *sunna*). Thus the accumulation of the diverse experiences of the diachronic community of Muslims throughout history manifest in tradition is rejected for exhibiting *taqlid* (imitation) and *jumud* (stagnation). Islamism is therefore not a conservative reproduction of Islam but a modern example of *tajdid-islah* (renewal). This re-interpretation posits Islam as a universal world system that is in competition with, and ultimately superior to, Western capitalism. In theory Muslims are urged by Islamist ideologues to pursue political power to the end of establishing an Islamic State based only on the blue-print of the *shari'a* (Islamic law). However it was notable that the Islamist organizations that united temporarily to share a common platform at the dinner approached the question of how to translate this project in Britain, where Muslims are a minority, rather differently. Indeed Islamism can not be understood to represent one monolithic tendency.

YMUK's interpretation of *jihad* (exertion, struggle) in terms of *da'wa* was in contrast to the international action and top-down instant institutionalization in Britain proposed by the Muslim Parliament's manifesto. For Ikram, the Islamic state is a distant goal, to be announced only when Muslims - and those yet to take up the invitation to Islam in Britain and beyond - have so thoroughly revived the practice of Islam such as to constitute it organically. So while the Muslim Parliament stresses that "The only survival kit that will work is one that is entirely community based and integrated with a global Islamic movement that protects us..." (1990: 22), YMUK seem more positive about British society as their attempt at producing positive images of Islam illustrates. In Bradford during 1994 the organization of national "Islam Awareness Week" saw information stalls about Islam appear in the town centre; a sponsored walk undertaken for a local hospital charity and a women's day arranged at Bradford Inter-Faith Centre.

The power of Islamism's imagination of a Muslim community resides in its attempt to organise Muslim difference politically vis-à-vis majority excluders with whom Muslims routinely interact. In the multicultural cities of the globalised world Islamists have sought to define and maintain the boundaries of Islam so indissolubly that it is understood to be a complete way of life (Gilsenan: 1982). The speakers shared a concern with translating the multiple and shifting identification positions of Muslims - who are also British, black, Asian, Panjabi, Bradfordian, Pakistani, Mirpuri and so on - into a fixed and set of relations that always prioritises membership of the *Umma*. However even before people had gone home it was evident that mobilising a community is a struggle to agglomerate a variety of criss-crossing but often competing interests. A concern with Bosnia overshadowed events in Kashmir and Arab brothers, who were actively distributing pamphlets about state oppression of Islamist groups like *al-jihad* in Egypt, were told apologetically by the chairperson that there would be no time to give them a platform. Outside the dinner context

Muslim political activity has been organised through the mainstream parties and at local elections Muslims do not mobilise as an *Umma* but for the most part as *biradari-s* ("brotherhoods": patrilineal inter-marrying caste groupings)

For all Islamists resistance to domination and attempts to reform the beliefs and practices of ordinary Muslims go hand in hand. Thus the products of hybrid religious contexts, such as the shrine sufism long associated with Islam in the Indian-subcontinent, is seen as *bid'a* (innovation), a husk that threatens the purity of "true" Islam. The "authentic" kernel of religion is understood to be manifest in a Muslim's conformity to both a prescribed lifestyle and ideology. For example, at the dinner Khadija and Majid called for individual responsibility for activism while Ikram argued that Muslims not positioned as he was must be "asleep". Ultimately, in the Islamist scheme of things, "lapses" of commitment and religiosity by ordinary Muslims are seen as contributing to the disunity and weakness of contemporary Islam. However activism was not a fundamental of faith in the traditional creeds of Sunni Islam.[15] The Islamist reading of Islam which separates religion (Islam) and culture (British, Pakistani) so definitely is particularly attractive to many, but certainly not a majority of, Muslims born in Britain for whom Islamist arguments most adequately address, in a context that fixes non-whites as "outsiders", the need for a framework within which where you are from is less important than where you are going to.

Nevertheless Islamist accounts of Islam routinely represent a hegemonic closure of the possibilities that speaking in the name of the *Umma* presents. Islamist ideological agendas and moral conformity do not exhaust the complexity of debate and practice in Islam. Rather, because Islamists" discourses presume to bound Muslims" belongings exclusively to Islam, they are routinely confronted with ordinary Muslim lifestyles that are unbounded and refuse to conform to their agendas. It is clear that outside contexts like the dinner, Muslims make other identifications, positionings that Islamism's construction of difference - just like any other essentialist politics - ultimately can not speak to. A recognition of these contingencies urges caution when it comes to explaining how ordinary Muslims" interests intersect with the projects of Islamist organizations which are in turn diverse and contradictory.

Conclusions

"We hear so much of Muslim disunity these days - others play on it - this coming together is a good example of co-operation and unity."

I want to draw this paper to a conclusion with reference to the chairperson's opening comments. This paper has not been an attempt to play on disunity in Islam but rather to take his observation that the dinner represented an example of unity one step further. I have argued that Muslim unity can *only* be understood to be imagined in specific contexts such as the dinner, because there are multiple identification positions that Muslim - British - Pakistani - Mirpuri - Bradfordians choose to prioritise in different situations. These constructions are temporary and negotiated, so to understand either Muslim unity or disunity as representing an empirical reality on the ground, is surely to miss the point. Islam should not to be conceived as a timeless and monolithic set of customs and traditions connecting all Muslims for all time. At the other extreme, the notion of a plurality of *islams* is also misleading. Rather I suggest that Muslims must be seen as debating what speaking in the name of the *Umma* means in different contexts that are always situated in certain power relations. In describing contexts such as the dinner it is important to talk about the power and significance of connections between Muslims without suggesting that such positionings are indissoluble. Similarly, it is crucial to comprehend the contingency of adopting such a position without interpreting it as an example of "lapsed" religiosity as Islamists often do. Only cultural-racist stereotypes of the Muslim other and primordialist constructions of Islam feel the need to dichotomise an essential difference between the traditional and the modern; the Islamic and Western; the Muslim and the British; and the *namaazi* (prayerful) and the Bradford City football supporter.

Notes

[1]   This paper is based on research towards the degree of Ph.D. at the University of Manchester. I wish to thank the University and the Economic and Social Research Council for their generous support between 1992 and the present. A version of this paper was presented at Migration and Multiculturalism, a conference organized by ICCR, Vienna at The London School of Economics in September 1995. I am grateful

to participants for their comments.

2   There has long been a surplus of adult male labour in Mirpur. Most migrants have come from rural areas where they had very small farms which provided little more than a subsistence living.

3   The 1991 census processed by R. Ballard and V.S. Kalra (1993), shows 14% of the population of Bradford identified a South Asian ethnicity, while 67% of all ethnicised minorities identified themselves as Pakistanis. Indeed a majority of Pakistanis are under the age of twenty-four years which illustrates that Pakistanis are increasingly British-born. Pakistanis suffered the highest unemployment levels (along with Bangladeshis) of 36%, while white unemployment was 9%.

4   For example, Islamic Relief, a charity established in 1984, now has consultative status with the United Nations; its leaflets sit respectably alongside social security forms and local listings in public libraries; *The Independent* newspaper ran an appeal on behalf of it and other charities in December 1993; its organizers get to be interviewed on national radio without reference to 'fundamentalism'.

5   For useful accounts of events that I am only able to summarize here see Appignanesi, & Maitland 1989; Ahsan & Kidwai 1993.

6   There is a wide-ranging literature on Islam and the European imagination. See for example the seminal, Daniel 1960.

7   See for example *The Koran.* 4:74 - 4:77, Middlesex, Penguin, 1956, translated by Dawood, N.J.

8   The Muslim Parliament, which was inaugurated under the auspices of Kalim Siddiqi's pro-Iranian, pro-*fatwa* Muslim Institute, was produced in the media as a Muslim challenge to the authority of the British Parliament at Westminster. *The Muslim Manifesto.* London, The Muslim Institute, 1990. In a context where Muslims are "disparaged and oppressed" (1990:1) resistance, argues the manifesto, will come only through consensus and top-down self-help institutions.

9   In Bradford during 1994 YMUK organized a range of activities to the end of the revival of Islam: attendance at national residential camps; local study circles; '*id* gatherings with Islamic drama and music.

10   Roy 1994 makes the important point that 'anyone in a Christian environment who converts to Islam is psychologically choosing a sect structure...which thus precludes desire for a mass movement' (1994: 6-7).

11   See Q-News 01.12.95. Q-News is a national Muslim weekly newspaper in English established in 1992.

12   See Q-News 25.03.94.

13   I take this figure from Lapidus 1988.

14   My account of Islamism is based on my unpublished thesis I submitted in part fulfilment of the degree of M.A. in Middle Eastern Studies, at University of Manchester 1991-2.

15   In the Sunnism activism was traditionally not given the centrality to faith that Islamists now accord it. The traditional understanding has always been that as long as the Muslim professed faith s/he would go to *janna* (paradise) on the assumption that only God knows the religious state of a person. See Rippin 1991.

Bibliography

Abdalati, H: *Islam in Focus*. Kuwait, The International Islamic Federation of Student Organisations, 1978.

Abdullah, M.S: The Religion of Islam and its Presence in the Federal Republic of Germany. *Journal Institute of Muslim Minority Affairs*, 10 (1989), 438-449.

--: *Was will der Islam in Deutschland?*, Gütersloh, Gütersloher Verlag-Haus Mohn 1993.

Addi, L: Islamist Utopia and Democracy. *The Annals of the American Academy for Political en Social Sciences* 524(1992), 120-130.

Ahmad, A: *Studies in Islamic Culture in the Indian envionment*. Oxford, Clarendon Press, 1964.

Ahsan, M.M. & A.R. Kidwai (eds.): *Sacrilege versus Civility*. Leicester, The Islamic Foundation, 1993.

Allievi S. & F. Dassetto: *Il ritorno dell'Islam. I musulmani in Italia*. Ed. Lavoro, Roma, 1993.

Andrews, A.Y: *Jamaat-i-Islami in the U.K?* In: Rohit Barot (ed): *Religion and Ethnicity: Minorities and Social Change in the Metropolis*. Kampen, Kok Pharos, 1993.

--: The Inter-Faith Network in the UK. In: M. Foreward (ed.): *Hindo-British Review*. India, Madrass, 1994.

--: A History of South Asian Migration Into Leicester: An Essay on Hindu/Muslim Segregation. In: Jewson, N. (ed): *Migration Processes and Ethnic Divisions*, University of Leicester, The Centre For Urban History and The Ethnicity Research Centre, 1995.

Anonymous: Al-Iqâma fî bilâd al-kuffâr. *Majallat al-Sunna* (published in Birmingham, United Kingdom) Nº 37 (1994), pp.89-92. [Reproduces the opinions of Ibn Taimiyya and Ibn ᶜUthaymîn and Al-Jubrîn].

Anwar, M: *Ethnic Minorities and the 1983 General Election*. London, Commission For Racial Equality, 1984.

--: Ethnic Minorities' representation: voting and electoral politics in Britain, and the role of leaders. In: P. Werbner & M. Anwar (eds.): *Black and Ethnic Leaderships in Britain. The cultural dimensions of political actions*. London, Routledge, 1991.

--: *Race and Elections*. Centre For Research in Ethnic Relations. England, Economic and Social Research Council, 1994.

--: Unpublished Paper presented at the Euroconference on Migration and Multicuturalism, London School of Economics 30 August - 2 September 1995.

Appignanesi, L. & S. Maitland (eds.): *The Rushdie File*. London, Fourth Estate, 1989.

Arnaut, M.M: Islam and Muslims in Bosnia 1878-1918: Two hijras and two fatwâs. *Journal of Islamic Studies* 5(1994), 242-253.

Ayubi, N: The political revival of Islam: the case of Egypt. *International Journal of Middle Eastern Studies* 12(1980) 481-499.

Azmeh, A: *Islams and Modernities*. London, Verso, 1993.

Badran, M: Competing Agenda: Feminists, Islam and the State in 19th and 20th Century Egypt. In: D. Kandiyoti (ed.): *Women, Islam and the State*. Basingstoke, Macmillan, 1991.

Ballard, C: Conflict, continuity and change. Second-generation South-Asians. In: V. Saifullah Khan (ed.): *Minority families in Britain. Support and stress*. London, MacMillan, 1979, 109-129.

Ballard, R: New Clothes for the Emperor. *New Community* vol. 18, 1992.

Ballard, R. & V.S. Kalra: *The Ethnic Dimensions of The 1991 Census. A Preliminary Report*. England, University of Manchester, 1994.

Bartelink, Y: *Vrouwen over Islam. Geloofsvoorstellingen en praktijken van Marokkaanse migrantes in Nederland*. Nijmegen, Proefschrift Nijmegen, 1994.

Bauman, Z: *The Making and Unmaking of Strangers*. Forthcoming, 1996.

Bhatti, F.M: Muslims as Migrants: The Turks in West Germany. *Journal Institute of Muslim Minority Affairs* Winter 1979 and Summer 1980.

Behrman, L.C: *Muslim Brotherhoods and Politics in Senegal.* Harvard University Press, Cambridge Mass., 1970.

--: Muslim Politics and Development in Senegal. *The Journal of Modern African Studies* 15(1977)2, 261-277.

Bencheikh, S: La formation théologique pour les musulmans. In: *La convivance entre chrétiens en musulmans dans les pays méditerranéens.* Séminaire de travail CHEAM/PISAI Rome, 29 Septembre - 1er Octobre 1994, 53-60.

Benomar al-Hasanî, F: *al-Tajannus bayna 'l-ittijâh al-fiqhî wa-'l-buʿd al-hadârî.* Tétouan, Jâmiʿat ʿAbd al Mâlik al-Saʿdî (Shuʿbat al-Dirâsât al-Islâmiyya), 1992-1993, 46 pp. (Mémoire de Licence written under supervision of al-Amîn Bûkhubza).

Binswanger K. & F. Sipahoglu: *Türkisch-islamiche Vereine als Faktor der deustch-türkischer Koexistenz.* Benediktbeuren Riess-Druck, 1988.

Bourdieu, P: *Outline of a Theory of Practice.* Cambridge, Cambridge University Press, 1977.

--: The Social Space and the Genesis of Groups. *Theory and Society* 14(1985), 723-744.

Bredeloup S: Les Sénégalais de Cote-d'Ivoire, les Sénégalais en Cote-d'Ivoire. *Monde en développement,* dec. 1995.

Buitelaar, M.W: *Fasting and feasting in Morocco. An ethnographic study of the month of Ramadan.* Dissertatie Nijmegen, 1991.

Campus A. & L. Perrone: Senegalesi e marocchini: inserimento nel mercato del lavoro e progetti migratori a confronto. *Studi Emigrazione* 98(1990).

Campus A., G. Mottura & L. Perrone: I senegalesi. In: G. Mottura (ed.): *L'arcipelago immigrazione. Caratteristiche e modelli migratori dei lavoratori stranieri in Italia,* Ires-Ediesse, Roma, 1992, 249-275.

Carter D.M: Una confraternita musulmana in emigrazione: i Murid del Senegal. *Religioni e Società* 12(1991), 60-78.

CBS/ISEO: *Minderheden in Nederland, Statistisch Vademecum 1993/1994.* 's Gravenhage, SDU-Uitgeverij / CBS-publikaties, 1994.

Cecconi S: Le associazioni senegalesi di Genova e di Milano. *Studi Emigrazione* 113(1994), 158-178.

Chomsky, N: The Struggle for Democracy in the New World Order. In: B. Gills et.al. (ed.): *Low Intensity Democracy. Political power in the new world order.* London, Pluto Press, 1993[a].

--: Notes on the Culture of Democracy. In: N. Chomsky, *Letters from Lexington. Reflections on propaganda.* Monroe, Common Courage Press, 1993[b].

Christie, C.J: The Rope of God: Muslim Minorities in the West and Britain. *New Community* 17(1991), 457-466.

Copans, J: *Les marabouts de l'arachide. La Confrérie mouride et les paysans du Sénégal.* Le Sycomore, Paris, 1980.

Costa, V: Una pensione senegalese. In: R. De Angelis (ed.): *Ghetti etnici e tensioni di vita.* La Meridiana, Roma, 1991.

Coulon, C: *Le marabout et le prince. Islam et pouvoir au Sénégal.* Pédone, Paris, 1981.

Coulsoñ, N.J: *A History of Islamic Law.* Edinburgh: Edinburgh University Press, 1964.

Cruise O'Brien, D.B: *The Mourides of Senegal: The Political and Economic Organization of an Islamic Brotherhood.* Oxford, Clarendon Press, 1971.

--: *Saints and Politicians: Essays in the Organisation of a Senegalese Peasant Society.* Cambridge, Cambridge University Press, 1975.

--: Sufi Politics in Senegal. In: J.P. Piscatori (ed.): *Islam in the Political Process.*

Cambridge, Cambridge University Press, 1983.

Cruise O'Brien, D.B. & C. Coulon (eds.): *Charisma and Brotherhood in African Islam.* Oxford, Clarendon Press, 1988.

Daniel, N: *Islam and the West: The Making of an Image.* Edinburgh University Press, 1960.

Dara Xitmatul Xadim: La vulgarisation du Mouridisme à l'Etranger. *Ndigel* 21(1990).

Dassetto F. & A. Bastenier: *L'Islam Transplanté. Vie et organisation des minorités musulmanes de Belgique.* Berchem, Anvers, Brussels, Éditions Vie ouvrière, 1984.

--: *Europa: nuova frontiera dell'Islam.* Ed. Lavoro (ISCOS), Roma, 1988; 1991².

Deakin, N: *Colour and the British Electorate, 1964 six case studies.* London, 1965.

Dekmejian, R.H: *Islam in revolution: fundamentalism in the Arab world.* Syracuse, N.Y.: Syracuse University Press, 1985.

Delle Donne, M., U. Melotti & S. Petilli (eds.): *Immigrazione in Europa. Solidarietà e conflitto.* Dipartimento di Sociologia, Università di Roma La Sapienza, CEDISS, Roma, 1993.

Derby: *Evening Telegraph,* 4th May 1995.

Dessouki, A.E.H: *Islamic resurgence in the Arab world.* New York, Praeger, 1982.

Detaille, R: L'Islam en Allemagne. In: M. Arkoun, R. Leveau & B. El-Jisr (eds.): *L'Islam et les Musulmans dans le Monde; Tome I: L'Europe Occidentale.* Beyrouth, Centre Cultural Hariri, 1993.

Diop, A.B: *La confrérie mouride: organisation politique et mode d'implantation urbaine.* Ph.D. dissertation, Lyon, 1980.

--: *La société wolof. Tradition et changement.* Karthala, Paris, 1981.

--: Fonctions et activités des dahira mourides urbains (Sénégal). *Cahiers d'Etudes africains* 81-83(1981a), 79-91.

Diop, M.C: Les affaires mourides à Dakar. *Politique Africaine* 1(1981ᵇ)4: 90-100.

--: Les associations murid en France. *Esprit* 102(1985).

--: Le mouvement associatif africain. In: *Le role du mouvement associatif dans l'evolution des communautés immigrées.* Ministère des Affaires Sociales, vol.II, Paris, 1987.

--: Immigration et Religion: les Musulmans Négro-Africains en France. *Migrations Société* 5-6(1989).

--: Les paysans du bassin arachidier. Conditions de vie et comportements de survie. *Politique Africaine* 45(1992), 39-61.

Diop, M: L'immigration ouest-africaine en Europe. *Etudes internationales* 24(1993)1:111-124.

Dunn, J: *Democracy: The Unfinished Journey. 508 BC to AD 1993.* Oxford, Oxford University Press, 1992.

Dwyer, C. & A. Meyer: The institutionalisation of Islam in The Netherlands and in the U.K: the case of Islamic schools. *New Community* 21, 1995: 37-54.

Ebin, V: A la recherche de nouveaux 'poissons'. Stratégies commerciales mourides par temps de crise. *Politique Africaine* 45(1992), 86-99.

--: Les commerçants mourides à Marseille et à New York, regards sur les stratégies d'implantation. In: E. Grégoire & P. Labazée (eds.): *Grands commerçants d'Afrique de l'Ouest. Logiques et pratiques d'un groupe d'hommes d'affaires contemporains.* Paris, Karthala-ORSTOM, 1993, 101-123.

Ebin, V. & R. Lake: Camelots sénégalais à New-York. *Hommes et Migrations* 1 160(1992), 32-37.

Edwards, J: The Feminist Case for Local Self-government. *Local Government Studies* 21, No 1, 1995.

Elias, N: *State Formation and Civilization*. Oxford, Blackwell, 1982.

Eriksen, T.H: *Ethnicity and Nationalism. Anthropological perspectives*. London, Pluto Press, 1993.

Feddema, R: Perspectieven op migrantencultuur. Een kritiek op het etnocentrisch modernisme. *Psychologie en Maatschappij* 15(1991)1: 47-60.

--: *Op weg tussen hoop en vrees. De levensoriëntatie van jonge Turken en Marokkanen in Nederland*. Utrecht, Jan van Arkel, 1992.

Fierro, M.I: La emigración en el Islam: Conceptos antiguos, nuevos problemas. *Awrâq* 12(1991), 11-41.

Foblets, M.C: De erkenning en de gelijkstelling van de islam in België: enkele actualiteitsvragen in de afwachting van een definitieve wettelijke regeling. S.W.E. Rutten (ed.) *Recht van de Islam* N°.8 (1990), 86-97.

France.- La France et l'Islam. Supplement to *Le Monde* d.d. 13 October 1994.

Fuss, D: *Essentially Speaking. Feminism, nature & difference*. New York, Routledge, 1989.

Gellner, E: *Postmodernism, Reason and Religion*. London, Routledge, 1992.

Gilleband: Harkis Oublie par l'Histoire. *Le Monde* (Paris), July 3-6, 1973.

Gills, B. et al: *Low Intensity Democracy: Political Power in the New World Order*. London Pluto Press, 1993.

Gilsenan, M: *Recognizing Islam. An anthropologist's introduction*. London, Croom Helm, 1982.

Glock, C.Y. & R. Stark: *Religion and society in tension*. Chicago, Rand McNally, 1965.

Gozlan, M: *L'Islam et la République*. Paris: Belfond, 1994.

Gräf, E: Religiöse und rechtliche Vorstellungen über Kriegsgefangene in Islam und Christentum. *Welt des Islams*, Neue Serie, vol. 8, 1963, 89-130.

Gür, M: *Türkisch-islamische Vereinigungen in der Bundesrepublik Deutschland*. Frankfurt-am-Main, Brandes & Apsel, 1993.

Gyford, J: *The Politics of Local Socialism*. London, Allen and Unwin, 1985.

Haleber, R: Marokkaans mozaïek van dominantie en verzet. De hegemonie van de traditie in een islamitisch ontwikkelingsland. *Sociologische gids* 36(1989), 82-103.

Hall, S: Identity. In: S. Hall et al. (eds.): *Modernity and Its Futures*. London: Polity Press in Association with the Open University, 1992.

--: New Ethnicities. In: J. Donald & A. Rattansi (eds): *'Race', Culture and Difference*. London: Sage Publications, 1992[a].

--: The Question of Cultural Identity. In: Hall et al. (eds): *Modernity and its Futures*. London: Polity Press in association with the Open University, 1992[b].

Halliday, F: The Iranian evolution: uneven development and religious populism. *Journal of International Affairs* 36(1982), 187-207.

Hanks, W.F: Notes on Semantics in Linguistic Practice. In: C. Calhoun, E. LiPuma & M. Postone (eds.): *Bourdieu: Critical Perspectives*. Chicago: The University of Chicago Press, 1993, 139-155.

Hardy, P: *The Muslims of British India*. London, Cambridge University Press, 1972.

Harvey, L.P: Crypto-Islam in Sixteenth-century Spain. In: *Actas. Primer Congreso de estudios árabes e islamicos*. Madrid 1964, 163-185.

Heper, M: Islam, Polity, and Society in Turkey: a Middle Eastern Perspective. *The Middle East Journal* 35(1982), 345-363.

Hooglund, E: Iranian populism and political change in the Gulf. *Middle East Reports* 22(1992), 19-21.

Horowitz, D.L: *Ethnic groups in conflict*. Berkeley-Los Angeles-London, University of California Press, 1985.

Hussain, A: *Beyond Islamic Fundamentalism, the sociology of faith and action*. Leicester, Volcano, 1992.

Ibn al-Hâjj al-Sulamî, Muhammad ibn al-Fâtimî: *Is⁽âf al-ikhwân al-râghibîn bi-tarâjim thulla min ⁽ulamâ' al-Maghrib al-mu⁽âsirîn*. Casablanca, Matba⁽at al-Najâh al-Jadîda, 1992.

Ibn al-Siddîq, ⁽Abd al-⁽Azîz ibn Muhammad: *Hukm al-iqâma bi-bilâd al-kuffâr wa-bayân wujûbihâ fî ba⁽d al-ahwâl*. [Tangiers, Matâbi⁽ al-Bûghâz, 1985].

IRER: *Tra due rive. La nuova immigrazione a Milano*. F. Angeli, Milano, 1994.

IRES Piemonte: *Uguali e diversi. Il mondo culturale, le reti di rapporti, i lavori degli immigrati non europei a Torino*. Rosenberg and Sellier, Torino, 1992.

Jâdd al-Haqq, ⁽A.J: *Buhûth wa-fatâwî islâmiyya fî qadâyâ mu⁽âsira*. Vol. 4, Cairo, Al-Azhar, 1995.

Jalal, A: The Convenience of Subservience. In: Kandiyoti (ed.): *Women and the State in Pakistan*. London, Macmillan, 1991.

Jameelah, M: An Appraisal of Some of the Aspects of Maulana Sayyid Ala Maududi's Life and Thought. *The Islamic Quarterly* 31 (2) 1987, p. 117.

Jazâ'irî, Muhammad ibn ⁽Abd al-Karîm al-: *Tabdîl al-jinsiyya ridda wa-khiyâna*. [Paris], no publisher mentioned, [1989], 216 pp.

Jeffers, S: Black Sections in the Labour Party: the End of Ethnicity and Godfather Politics?" In: P. Werbner & M. Anwar (eds): *Black and Ethnic Leaderships in Britain*. London, Routledge, 1991.

Jewson, N: Migrant Populations, Community Divisions and Ethnic Mobilisation. In: Jewson, N. (ed): *Migration Processes and Ethnic Divisions*, University of Leicester: The Centre For Urban History and The Ethnicity Research Centre, 1995.

Johansen, B: Staat, Recht und Religion im sunnitischen Islam - Können Muslime einen religionsneutralen Staat akzeptieren? H. Marré und J. Stüting (eds.): *Essener Gespräche zum Thema Staat und Kirche* 20(1986), 12-81.

Johnson, M: Some aspects of Black Electoral Participation and Representation in the West Midlands. In: H. Goulbourne (ed.): *Black Politics In Britain*. Aldershot, Avebury, 1990.

Joly, D: Les Musulmans dans la Société Britannique. In: M. Arkoun, R. Leveau & B. El-Jisr (eds.): *L'Islam et les Musulmans dans le Monde* Tome I: *L'Europe Occidentale*. Beyrouth, Centre Cultural Hariri, 1993.

Jones, K.W: *The New Cambridge History of India: Socio-Religious Reform Movements in British India*. Cambridge: Cambridge University Press, 1989.

Jong, M. de & Th.A. van Batenburg: Integratie van allochtone leerlingen. In: Jong, M. J. de (ed.): *Allochtone kinderen op Nederlandse scholen. Prestaties, problemen en houdingen*. Lisse, Swets and Zeitlinger, 1985, 125-138.

Kalra, V.S. & Sean McLoughlin: Translating community: mosque-centre, community-mosque. In: T. Modood & P. Werbner (eds.): *The Politics of Multiculturalism in the New Europe: Racism, Identity, Community*. London, Zed, 1996.

Kandiyoti, D. (ed.): Introduction. In: *Women, Islam and the State*. London: Macmillan, 1991.

Kattânî, ⁽A.M. al-: *Al-Aqalliyyât al-islâmiyya fî 'l-⁽âlam al-yawm*. Makka, Maktabat al-Manâra, 1988.

Katzenstein, P: *Policy and Politics in West-Germany. The Growth of a Semisovereign State*. Philadelphia, Temple University Press, 1987.

Kazancigil, A: Democracy in Muslim lands: Turkey in comparative perspective. *International Social Science Journal* 43 (1991), 343-360.

Kepel, G: *Les Banlieues de l'Islam*. Paris, Editions du Seuil, 1987.

234 *Bibliography*

--: *A l'Ouest de Allah.* Paris: Éditions du Seuil, 1994.
--: *The Revenge of God. The resurgence of Islam, Christianity and Judaism in the Modern World.* transl. Alan Braley, University Park, The Pennsylvania State University Press, 1994.
Kettani, M.A: *Inbi'ath Al-Islam fi Al-Andalus.* International Islamic University, Islama bad, 1992.
Khamlîshî, ᶜAbd Allâh al-Tâ'iᶜ al-: *Al-Janna wa-tarîquhâ al-mustaqîm wa-'l-nâr watarîquhâ al-dhamîm.* Rotterdam: Masjid al-Nasr, 1995, 727 pp.
Khan, M.A: *Islamic Constitutional Law.* PhD Thesis, University of Tashkent, 1985.
Khouma, P.A: *Io, venditore di elefanti.* Garzanti, Milano, 1990.
Koningsveld, P.S. van: Some Religious Aspects of the Acheh-War as Reflected in Three unpublished Arabic Documents. In: W.A.L. Stokhof and N.J.G. Kaptein (eds.), *Beberapa Kajian Indonesia dan Islam.* Jakarta 1990, 87-97.
--: Between communalism and secularism. Modern Sunnite discussions on male headgear and coiffure. In: J. Platvoet and K. van der Toorn (eds.), *Pluralism and Identity. Studies in ritual behaviour.* Leiden: Brill, 1995[1], pp. 327-345.
--: Muslim slaves and captives in Western Europe during the Late Middle Ages. *Islam and Christian-Muslim Relations* 6(1995[2]), 5-23.
--: and G.A. Wiegers, The Islamic statute of the Mudejars in the light of a new source. *Al-Qantara. Revista de Estudios Arabes* (forthcoming in 1996).
Landman, N: *Van Mat tot Minaret. De institutionalisering van de Islam in Nederland.* Amsterdam, VU Uitgeverij, 1992.
Landuzzi, C., A. Tarozzi & A. Treossi: *Tra luoghi e generazioni. Immigrazioni africane in Italia e in Francia.* l'Harmattan, Torino, 1995.
Lans, J.M. van der & M. Rooijackers: Types of religious belief and unbelief among second generation Turkish migrants. In: W.A. Shadid & P. S. van Koningsveld (eds.): *Islam in Dutch society: Current Developments and Future Prospects.* Kampen, Kok Pharos, 1992, 56-65.
--: Attitudes of second generation Turkish immigrants towards collective religious representations of their parental culture. In: J. Corveleyn & D. Hutsebaut (eds.): *Belief and Unbelief. Psychological perspectives.* Amsterdam/Atlanta, Rodopi, 1994, 111-133.
Lapidus, I: *A History of Islamic Societies.* Cambridge University Press, 1988, p. xix.
Laswell, H.D: *Politics: Who gets What, When and How.* New York, Smith 1936.
Layton-Henry, Z: *The Politics of Race in Britain.* London, Allen and Unwin, 1984.
Le Lohe: *Ethnic Minority Participation in Local Elections.* Bradford: University of Bradford, 1984.
Leicester *Survey of Leicester.* Leicester, Leicester City Council.., 1983.
Leman, J: *Dialogues at different institutional levels among authorities and Muslims in Belgium.* Conference discussion paper. Leiden University, The Netherlands. Sept. 1995.
Leveau, R. & O. Schmidt di Friedberg: Présence de l'Islam en Europe. In: A. Dierkens (ed.): *Problèmes d'histoire des religions. Pluralisme religieux et laicités dans l'Union Européenne.* Editions de l'Université de Bruxelles, 5/1994, 123-140.
Lewis, B: *Islam et laïcité. La naissance de la Turquie moderne.* Paris, Fayard, 1988.
--: La situation des populations musulmanes dans un régime non musulman: réflexions juridiques et historiques. In: B. Lewis and D. Schnapper (eds.), *Musulmans en Europe,* Poitiers: Actes Sud, 1992, pp. 11-34.
Lewis, P: *Islamic Britain. Religion, politics and identity among British Muslims. Bradford in the 1990s.* London, New York, Tauris, 1994.
Liebkind, K: Ethnic Identity - Challenging the Boundaries of Social Psychology. In:

G.M. Breakwell (ed.): *Social Psychology of Identity and the Self Concept.* London, Surrey University Press, 1992, 147-185.

Löschner, H: *Staatsangehörigkeit und Islam.* Erlangen, 1972.

Lyon, W: Islam in the U.K. In: H. Carr (ed.): *Women: A Cultural Review,* 1995.

Mackenzie, W.J.M: *Political Identity.* Harmondsworth: Penguin, 1978.

Mahler, G: Religiöse Unterweisung für türkische Schüler muslimischen Glaubens in Bayern. In: *Zeitschrift für Pädagogik* 35(1989) 3, 381-397.

Magassouba, M: *L'Islam au Sénégal: demain les mollahs?.* Karthala, Paris, 1985.

Mannûnî, M. al-: *Al-Masâdir al-ᶜarabiyya li-ta'rîkh al-Maghrib. Al-Fatra al-muᶜâsira 1790-1930.* Rabat, Kulliyyat al-Adâb wa-'l-ᶜUlûm al-Insâniyya, 1989.

Manssoury, F. El-: Muslims in Europe: the lost tribe of Islam? *JMMA* 10(1989)1: 63-84.

Masud, M.K: Being a Muslim in a non-Muslim polity: Three alternative models. *Journal Institute of Muslim Minority Affairs* 10(1989), 118-28.

--: The obligation to migrate. The doctrine of Hijra in Islamic law. In: D.F. Eickelman and J. Piscatori (eds.), *Muslim travellers: pilgrimage, migration and religious imagination,* London, 1990, 29-49.

Maududi, Abu A la: *Musalman Aur Mawjuda Siyasi Kashmakash.* Vol.3, India: Pathankot, 1942.

--: *The Islamic Law and Constitution.* trans. and ed. Khurshid Ahmed, Lahore, Islamic Publications Ltd, 1960.

--: *Islam It's Meaning and Message.* trans. and ed. Khurshid Ahmed, Leicester, Islamic Foundation, 1980.

Mawlawî, F: *Al-Usus al-sharᶜiyya li-'l-ᶜalâqât bayna 'l-muslimîn wa-ghayr al-muslimîn.* Bayrout, Dâr al-Rashâd al-Islâmiyya, 1987.

Meier, F: Ueber die umstrittene Pflicht der Muslime, bei nichtmuslimischer Besetzung seines Landes aus zu wandern. *Der Islam* 68(1991), 65-86.

Metcalf, B.D: *Islamic Revival in British India: Deoband, 1860-1900.* Princeton, Guildford, Princeton University Press, 1982.

Modood, T: Black, racial equality and Asian identity. *New Community* XIV 3, 1988.

--: British Asian Muslims and the Rushdie Affair. *Political Quarterly* 61(1989), 143-160.

--: Muslims, Incitement to Hatred and the Law. In: The UK Action Committee on Islamic Affairs (UKACIA). *Muslims and the law in multi-faith Britain.* London, UKACIA, 1993.

Monteil, V: Une confrérie musulmane: les Mourides du Sénégal. In: Monteil, V: *Esquisses sénégalaises.* Initiations et Etudes Africaines, 21(1966), 159-202.

--: *L'Islam noir. Une religion à la conquète de l'Afrique.* Seuil, Paris, 1980.

Moscovici, S: The phenomenon of social representations. In: R.M. Farr & S. Moscovici (eds.): *Social Representations.* Cambridge, Cambridge University Press, 1984, 3-69.

Mu'nis, H: (ed.). Al-Wansharîsî, Asnâ 'l-matâjir fî bayân ahkâm man ghalaba ᶜalâ watanihi al-nasârâ wa-lam juhâjir. *Revista del Instituto Egipcio de Estudios Islámicos.* Madrid 1957, 129-91.

Munson, H: *Religion and power in Morocco.* New Haven: Yale University Press, 1993.

N.F.B.M.C: General Meeting. London. Jan 1995.

Narain, S: Sikhs In Leicester. In: N. Jewson (ed): *Migration Processes and Ethnic Divisi ons.* University of Leicester, The Centre For Urban History and The Ethnicity Research Centre, 1995.

Nielsen, J: A Muslim agenda for Britain: some reflections. *New Community,* 17(1991), 467-475.

Özcan, E: *Türkische Immigrantenorganisationen in der Bundesrepublik Deutschland.*

Berlin, Hitit, 1989.

Panareo, M.R: Donne immigrate tra tradizione e mutamento. Il caso senegalese, seminar on *Incontro tra culture*. Lecce, 20-21 november 1991.

Parekh, B: *The Concept of Fundamentalism*. Occasional Papers in Asian Migration Studies,Peepal Tree Books, 1991.

--: Decolonising Liberalism. In: A. Shtromas (ed): *The End of "ISMS"?* Oxford, Blackwell, 1994.

Parry, G. et al: *Political participation and democracy in Britain*. Cambridge, Cambridge University Press, 1992.

Pateman, C: *Participation and Democratic Theory*. Cambridge: Cambridge University Press, 1970.

Perrone, L: Incontro tra culture: note e riflessioni sulla presenza terzomondiale nel Salento, *La Critica Sociologica* 93-94-95(1990).

--: Cultura e tradizioni nell'esperienza migratoria della comunità senegalese in Italia, seminar on: *Immigrazione extra-CEE in Europa: gruppi etnici tra solidarietà e conflitto*. Roma, 5-7 june 1991.

--: *Porte chiuse. Cultura e tradizioni africane attraverso le storie di vita degli immigrati*. Liguori Editore, Napoli, 1995.

Peters, R: *Islam and colonialism. The doctrine of Jihad in Modern History*. 's Gravenhage: Mouton, 1979 (Ph.D.-dissertation University of Amsterdam).

Piga De Carolis, A: Le confraternite islamiche nel processo di formazione del Senegal, *Politica internazionale*, 2-3(1987), 161-170.

Phillips, D: The Social and Spatial Segregation of Asians in Leicester. In: P. Jackson & S.J. Smith (eds.): *Social Interaction and Ethnic Segregation*. London, Academic Press, 1981, pp. 101-21.

Phinney, J.S: Ethnic identity in adolescents and adults: review of research. *Psychological Bulletin* 108 (1990), 499-514.

Pitkin, H.F: *The Concept of Representation*. Berkeley: University of California Press, 1967.

Poston, L: *Islamic daʿwah in the West. Muslim Missionary Activity and the Dynamics of Conversion to Islam*. New York, Oxford: Oxford University Press, 1992.

Qattân, Manna' el-: *Iqâmat al-muslim fî balad ghayr islâmî*. Published under the auspices of the Union of Islamic Organisations of France (UOIF), Paris. No date. (Mentioned by Kepel 1994, 272 note).

Raza, M.S: *Islam in Britain. Past, Present & Future*. Leicester: Volcano Press, 1992; 1993 (2nd edition).

Remmelenkamp, P: Marokkaanse moslims in Nederland. Naturalisatie en het behoud van de religieuze identiteit. *Religieuze Bewegingen in Nederland* 28(1995), 79-97.

Rippin, A: *Muslims: their religious beliefs and practices*. Vol. one, London, Routledge, 1991.

Robin, N: L'espace migratoire de l'Afrique de l'Ouest: Panorama statistique, *Hommes et Migrations*. 1 160 (1992).

--: Une nouvelle géographie entre concurrence et redéploiement spatial. Les migrations ouest-africaine au sein de la CEE, *Revue Européenne des Migrations Internationales*, 10(1994)3: 17-31.

Robinson, F: *Varieties of South Asian Islam*. Coventry: Centre for Research in Ethnic Relations, University of Warwick, Research Paper No.8, 1988.

Rooijackers, M: Religious identity, integration and subjective well-being among young Turkish Muslims. In: W.A. Shadid & P.S. van Koningsveld (eds.): *Islam in Dutch society: current developments and future prospects.* Kampen, Kok Pharos, 1992[a], 66-73.

--: *Geloven met gesloten ogen. Religieuze identiteit, socio-culturele integratie en subjectief welbevinden bij Turks-islamitische jongeren in Nederland.* KU Nijmegen: unpublished report, 1992[b].

--: Ethnic identity and Islam: The results of an empirical study among young Turkish immigrants in The Netherlands. In: J. Corveleyn & D. Hutsebaut (eds.): *Belief and Unbelief. Psychological perspectives.* Amsterdam/Atlanta, Rodopi, 1994, 99-110.

Rooney, Y. & O. Connor: *The Spatial Distribution of Ethnic Minority Communities In Leicester, 1971, 1981, 1991: Maps and Tables.* University of Leicester, The Centre For Urban History and The Ethnicity Research Centre, 1995.

Roy, O: *The Failure of Political Islam.* London, I.B. Tauris, 1994.

Ruthven, M: *A Satanic Affair: Salman Rushdie and the Wrath of Islam.* London: The Hogarth Press, 1991.

Sadan, J: "Community" and "Extra-Community" as a legal and literary problem. *Israël Oriental Studies* 10, 1980, 102-115.

Said, E.W: *Covering Islam. How the media and the experts determine how we see the rest of the world.* New York, Pantheon Books, 1981.

--: *Travelling Theory. The World, the Text, the Critic.* London, Vintage, 1983.

--: What is Islam? *New Statesman & Society,* 10-2-1995, pp. 20-22.

Saint-Blancat, C: Hypothèse sur l'évolution de l' "Islam transplanté" en Europe. *Social Compass* 40(1993), 323-341.

Salem, G: *De Dakar à Paris, des diasporas d'artisans et de commerçants. Etude socio-géographique du commerce sénégalais en France.* Ph. D. dissertation, EHESS, Paris, 1981.

--: De la brousse sénégalaise au Boul' Mich: le système commercial mouride en France, *Cahiers d'Etudes africains* 81-83(1981), 267-288.

--: Les réseaux ccmmerciaux des artisans colporteurs sénégalais. In: I. Deblé & Ph. Hugon (eds.): *Vivre et survivre dans les villes africaines.* Paris, PUF, 1982, 84-89.

--: Marchands ambulants et commerçants étrangers en France et en Allemagne Fédérale, *Etudes Méditerranéennes* 7(1984).

Salem, I.K: *Islam und Völkerrecht. Das Völkerrecht in der islamischen Weltan schauung.* Berlin: Express-Edition, 1984.

Samb, D: Une majorité musulmane et des minorités religieuses dans un Etat laique: l'expérience sénégalaise. *Conscience et liberté* 39(1990).

Sayid, B: *In Bad Faith.* paper presented at Culture Communication and Discourse. ICCCR workshop, Manchester, 1994.

--: *Bad Faith.* England, Zed Books, forthcoming 1996.

Schacht, J: *An Introduction To Islamic Law.* Oxford, Clarendon Press, 1964.

Schiffauer, W: Migration and Religiousness. In: T. Gerholm & Y.G. Lithman (eds.): *The New Islamic presence in Western Europe.* London/New York, Mansell, 1988, 146-158.

Schmidt di Friedberg, O: Dix ans d'immigration marocaine en Italie: un premier bilan. *Maroc Europe,* oct. 1992, 123-138.

--: Questioni legate alla presenza straniera nella CEE: il caso dei musulmani. In: E.

Granaglia (ed.): *I dilemmi dell'immigrazione. Questioni etiche, economiche e sociali.* F.Angeli, Milano, 1993[a], 125-149.

--: L'immigration africaine en Italie: le cas sénégalais. In: *Etudes internationales* 24(1993[b]), 125-140.

--: Débuts d'une réalité: l'Islam en Italie. In: M. Arkoun, R. Leveau & B. El Jisr (eds.): *L'islam et les musulmans dans le monde Tome I: l'Europe Occidentale.* Beyrouth, Centre Culturel Hariri, 1993[c], vol.I 179-223.

--: *Islam, solidarietà e lavoro. I muridi senegalesi in Italia.* Ed. Fondazione Giovanni Agnelli, Torino, 1994.

--: Les Burkinabè et les Sénégalais dans les contexte de l'immigration ouest-africaine en Italie, *Monde en développement*, Dec. 1995.

Scidà, G: Senegalesi e mauriziani a Catania: due risposte divergenti alla sfida dell'integrazione sociale, *La ricerca sociale* nov. 1993a.

--: Fra carisma e clientelismo: una confraternita musulmana in migrazione, *Studi Emigrazione* 113(1994), 133-156.

Scidà, G. & G. Pollini: *Stranieri in città.* F.Angeli, Milano, 1993b.

Sen, F: Les Turcs dans la communauté européenne. In: B. Falga, C. Wihtol de Wenden & C. Leggewie (eds.): *De l'immigration à l'intégration en France et en Allemagne.* Paris, Le Cerf, 1994.

Shadid, W.A: *Moroccan workers in the Netherlands.* Leiden: Leiden University, 1979 (Ph.D.-dissertation).

Shadid, W.A. & P.S. van Koningsveld: Blaming the system or blaming the victim? Structural barriers facing Muslims in Western Europe. In: W.A. Shadid & P.S. van Koningsveld (eds.): *The integration of Islam and Hinduism in Western Europe.* Kampen, Kok Pharos, 1991, 2-21.

Siddique, M: *Moral Spotlight on Bradford.* Bradford, M.S. Press, 1993.

Smeets, H. M. A. G., E.P. Martens & J. Veenman: *Jaarboek Minderheden '95.* Houten/Zaventem, Bohn Stafleu Van Loghum, 1995.

Soest, R. van & B. Verdonk: *Ethnic Identity. A Study of the Concept and some Theories of Ethnicity.* Rotterdam, Institution for Preventive and Social Psychiatry, Erasmus University, 1984.

Solomos, J. & L. Back: *Race, Politics and Social Change.* London, Routledge, 1995.

Sunier, T: Islam en etniciteit onder jonge leden van Turkse islamitische organisaties in Nederland. *Migrantenstudies* 10(1994)1: 19-32.

Swain, C: *Black Faces Black Interests.* Harvard, 1993.

Sy, C.T: *La confrérie sénégalaise des mourides. Un essai sur l'Islam au Sénégal.* Présence Africaine, Paris, 1969.

--: Ahmadou Bamba et l'islamisation des Wolof. *Bulletin de l'IFAN* 2(1970), 412-433.

Tajfel, H: *Human Groups and Social Categories. Studies in social psychology.* Cambridge, Cambridge University Press, 1981.

Tibi, B: The renewed role of Islam in the political and social development of the Middle East. *The Middle East Journal* 37(1983), 3-13.

Todd, E: *Le destin des immigrés.* Paris, Seuil, 1994.

Travaglini, D., Reyneri, E: *Culture e progetti migratori dei lavoratori africani a Milano.* IRES Lombardia-Provincia di Milano, Milano, 1991.

Trimingham, J.S: *Islam in West Africa*. Oxford, Clarendon Press 1959.

Veen, F., van: Oppositie Marokko pleit voor erkenning islam-partij. *De Volkskrant,* April 14, 1995.

Vertovec, S: Multiculturalism and public incorporation: the model of Leicester Muslims. Paper presented at Workshop on Multiculturalism and Democracy in Urban Europe, Vienna 2-5 December 1993.

--: *Multiculturalism, culturalism and public incorporation*. Forthcoming, 1996.

Wade, A: *La doctrine économique du mouridisme*. L'interafricaine d'Edition, Dakar, 1970.

Wade, M: *Destinée du Mouridisme*. Cote West Informatique, Dakar, 1991.

Weller, P. (ed.): *Religions in the UK A Multi-Faith Directory*. Derby, University of Derby and The Inter Faith Network for the UK, 1993.

Werbner, P: *The Migration Process: Capital, Gifts and Offerings among British Pakistanis*. New York, Berg, 1990.

--: Factionalism and Violence in British Pakistani Politics. In: Donnan, H. & P. Werbner (eds.): *Economy and Culture in Pakistan. Migrants and cities in a Muslim society*. Basingstoke, Macmillan, 1991.

--: Introduction. In: P. Werbner & M. Anwar (eds.): *Black and Ethnic Leaderships in Britain. The cultural dimension of political action*. London, Routledge, 1991[a].

--: The fiction of unity in ethnic politics. In: P. Werbner & M. Anwar (eds.): *Black and Ethnic Leaderships. The cultural dimension of political actions in Britain*. London, Routledge, 1991[b].

--: The fiction of unity in ethnic politics: aspects of representation and the state among British Pakistanis. In: P. Werbner & M. Anwar (eds.): *Black and Ethnic Leaderships in Britain. The cultural dimension of political actions in Britain*. London, Routledge, 1991[c].

--: Diaspora and Millennium: British-Pakistani Global-Local Fabulations of the Gulf War. In: A.S. Ahmed & H. Donnan (eds.): *Islam, Globalization and Postmodernity*. London, Routledge, 1994.

-- & M. Anwar (eds.): *Black and Ethnic Leadership in Britain. The cultural dimensions of political actions*. London, Routledge, 1991.

Wertsch, J.V. & B. Lee: The multiple levels of analysis in a theory of action. *Human Development* 27 (1984), 193-196.

Wiegers, G.A: *Islamic literature in Spanish and Aljamiado. Yça of Segovia (fl. 1450), his antecedents and successors*. Leiden: Brill, 1994.

Wong-Rieger. D. & D. Quintana: Comparative acculturation of South-East Asian and Hispanic immigrants and sojourners. *Journal of Cross-Cultural Psychology* 18 (1987), 345-362.

Yassini, A: Islamic revival and national development in the Arab world. *Journal of Asian and African Studies* 21(1986), 104-121.

Zolo, D: *Democracy and Complexity. A realist approach*. Translated by D. McKie. Cambridge, Polity Press, 1992.